Gifted Children Grown Up

Joan Freeman

David Fulton Publishers
London

David Fulton Publishers Ltd
Ormond House, 26–27 Boswell Street, London WC1N 3JZ

First edition published in Great Britain by David Fulton Publishers 2001

British Library Cataloguing in Publication Data
A catalogue record for this book is available from the British Library

ISBN 1–85346–831–2

The publishers would like to thank John Cox for copyediting and Ray Jarman for proofreading this book.

Typeset by FiSH Books, London
Printed in Great Britain by The Cromwell Press, Trowbridge, Wilts.

Contents

Acknowledgements

Without question, my most sincere gratitude goes to all the people who told me about their experiences, hopes and fears, the young people and their families in this long study. It was a privilege to visit them, and I am immensely grateful for the way everyone made me feel very welcome. Thank you too to the teachers.

Of the many people who enabled this work to get started, I thank the Calouste Gulbenkian Foundation (United Kingdom and Commonwealth Branch), which originally funded the work under the late Peter Brinson who gave me great encouragement. Thanks to the National Association for Gifted Children, guided by Margaret Branch, which gave me free access to their records, and Ivy Brenber at Manchester University who statistically analysed the original data. The organisational skills needed to deal with the largesse of information produced by the naturalistic approach of this study were considerable. My thanks to Penny Wadsworth for typing hundreds of hours of recordings into transcripts. Across the years, two important people not only dealt with the punch-cards, lists and tables, but patiently read and re-read the transcripts as well as taking some part in the interviewing, Gillian Parker (now Professor) and Della Alvarez, thank you. Thanks to David Fulton who set me off on this study for the third time, and to his swift and efficient publishing team.

To my four children, for putting up with our, at times, vastly extended family, and Hugh my husband, who gave me steady encouragement, especially when things looked black, much love.

Joan Freeman
London 2001

About the author

The Author
Professor Joan Freeman is a distinguished psychologist, internationally respected for her work in the area of gifted development. She is Visiting Professor at Middlesex University, London, a Fellow of the British Psychological Society, a chartered psychologist and Founding President of the European Council for High Ability (ECHA).

Preface

I have long been concerned with finding out what it is really like to grow up gifted. My aim has been to open windows on how people's exceptional abilities develop with regard to their social and emotional lives, and how these could affect their achievements in life.

The work described in this book began in 1974 when I was asked to look at the lives of gifted children. I set up a three-way study so these children could be compared both with others of equal ability but unrecognised as gifted, as well as with those of more average ability. Without those careful comparisons it would be difficult to know which aspects of their growing up were pertinent to their gifts and which to their circumstances and personal outlook.

The study was published as *Gifted Children: Their Identification and Development in a Social Context* (Medical Technical Press 1979). Ten years later, the follow-up of the original project was published as *Gifted Children Growing Up* (Cassell, UK and Heinemann Educational USA 1991). That second book integrated what had been learned to date and drew conclusions about the young people's development over the 14 year span in which I was working with them. In this, the third book, the considerably re-written *Gifted Children Grown Up* (David Fulton Publishers 2001) I have been able to look at what has happened to dozens of the people in the study over the 27 years and consider their lives in the light of new international research from my UK government survey (Freeman 1998). (See p. 194.)

The ethical aspects of working with people hold true for any professional – to safeguard confidentiality unless permission is given, and to give unconditional respect to everyone concerned. All those who were interviewed gave their permission for me to record and use what they told me. But there were still times when it did not seem right to disclose intimacies. I have changed everyone's name and tried to disguise any identifying features, so though some may well recognise themselves in this book, I hope it is unlikely that anyone else would.

I have made liberal use of the description 'gifted', simply because it is easier than all the circumlocutions. But I have used 'talented' to refer to high ability in the arts, as is usual. However, these terms are always to be understood as relative among a variety of abilities. In the introductory brief descriptions of the young people, I have sometimes used a shorthand – highly gifted' denoting ability at around the top 1 per cent and 'Gifted' implying the top 5 to 1 per cent. 'Above average' is used for those between the top 20 and 5 per cent, and 'Average' for those within the middle-band of about 20 per cent of the national average. The difficulties of these rough definitions, though, are compounded by overlapping talents and abilities, in areas which are not reliably measurable. Therefore, these terms should only be taken as convenient guides for present use.

The wide variety of views and feelings of the young people, their relationships with parents, teachers, friends and lovers, how they experienced their education, and their reasons for doing what they did, are given at their most illuminative – in their own words. Their valuable psychological insights provide a basis for much needed and clear changes of direction in the care in the education of the gifted. My commentary is intended to be complementary.

CHAPTER 1

Being gifted

Golden lads and girls all must,
As chimney sweepers, come to dust
William Shakespeare, *Cymbeline*.

Sometimes people ask why there should be any particular concern for gifted lads and girls. Is it true, as Shakespeare implied, that these golden ones are in the end just like the others? Yes, in the sense that all potential needs help to reach its fulfilment, but no they are not because the gifted need specific and focused help. They need material help – you can't play a violin without a violin. They need teaching – no one can reach the concert platform without expert tuition, as well as the facilities and encouragement for long hours of practice. Knowledge too is the essential foundation for high-level creative work – Einstein had a sound Swiss education to build his discoveries on. Most children need an example to follow, even though some will go on to discover new ways of doing things. And every human being needs emotional support.

Gifted children are defined here in two ways. Firstly, as those who either demonstrate exceptionally high-level performance, whether across a range of endeavours or in a limited field. Secondly, as those whose potential for excellence has not yet been recognised by either tests or experts. There is a distinction between the recognised gifts of children and those of adolescents and adults. The children's are usually seen in the form of precociousness, in comparison with others of the same age, whilst adults' are seen in performance based on many years of dedication in a chosen area. Unlike gifted adults, however precocious they are, children cannot change the nature of their area of expertise because they lack the time needed to gain sufficient experience.

There are two major reasons for being concerned about helping children to realise their gifted potential:

- Individually – so that each human being may reach personal fulfilment.
- To serve the wider needs of the community. Although gifts are personal, they are also a national resource, and the future course of every society depends on developing the potential of its young. No country can afford to lose it.

Barriers to fulfilling gifted potential

There were many wonderful parents in this study. Without them, both mothers and fathers, many of the young people would not have had the confidence and education to negotiate their ways through the maze of obstacles and opportunities to reach their high levels of achievement and happiness. Now, in 2001 they can pass those benefits on to their own growing families. Their positive effective outlooks were not at all dependent on money, but on dedication to finding the best they could for their children, fired by love.

There is no lack of evidence to show that children's development, outlooks and achievements are influenced by the lifestyle of the families in which they grow up, and that from the beginning, the urge to learn is tempered by opportunity (Freeman 2000a). But unfortunately there is no ideal family for producing giftedness, and no formula to follow.

In this study, how much of the proffered help the children took up varied considerably. Where one might grasp at a small chance and work hard to better themselves, another would let the benefits dribble away. When parents became distressed at seeing their children fail to thrive, they did their best to help. Sometimes they succeeded in righting the downward spiral and sometimes they did not.

Exercising individual choice, though, is different from coming up against social obstacles, which not only put real barriers in the way, but have an effect on children's developing self-concepts and ambitions. There are five major social barriers, which, to a greater or lesser extent, exist everywhere in the world – political and social attitudes, poverty, gender, social disapproval and handicap – and they were all present in this study.

Political and social attitudes

National outlook can be more important in education than the wealth of a nation. Whereas in the USA, for example, millions of dollars are spent annually on programmes for the gifted, in Scandinavian countries it has not been acceptable to distinguish and provide for outstanding potential. In much poorer countries, though, such as China and the ex-Soviet Union, gifted children have for many decades received generous government-sponsored help.

What is more, some gifts are more welcome and so better provided for. Who has ever heard of talented footballers being obliged to keep their kicks at the average level so as not to embarrass the others? Far from it. The clubs' football scouts are always on the lookout for young talent. In schools, talented children are given extra tuition outside school hours, including team clothing, transport and arrangements to play with others like themselves. They are not identified by any test, but instead are encouraged and given practice provision so that those who have the potential to shine may be seen to shine and bring popular honour to the school.

Aesthetic talent is particularly sensitive to cultural encouragement. Fortunately, in most parts of the world there are out-of-school musical activities. Instrument teachers may come into schools to provide lessons and search out talent for local children's orchestras. There are also specialist schools for music and dance, though fewer for drama and fine art. Foreign languages or mathematics may be encouraged in school societies, and there are national and international mathematics contests and get-togethers. But opening up the school laboratory for a Saturday morning practice for keen chemists must be rare, if it happens at all.

The widespread charge of élitism also acts as a barrier to special provision for the gifted. Local education authorities, pressed for more money from many sides, often find pleas for provision for the gifted the easiest to refuse. Compared with slow learners, their needs do not seem to merit an effective portion of the education budget.

The key to altering that negative, old-fashioned élitist view of giftedness is to change the perspective from achievement to potential. Instead of gifted children being considered as different or even superior to others in terms of their examination passes or musical performances, they should be recognised as the carriers of much greater than normal potential. Indeed, thinking of children in terms of future rather than present performances encourages teachers to raise their expectations for all pupils. For the gifted especially, it alerts teachers to look out for those who are just coasting along at average level, to recognise them as capable of better work, and to help them develop their abilities more fully.

Growing up poor

Poor children usually live in less healthy places than rich children. They can lose out in every way – physical health, education and balanced psychological development. The low self-esteem that accompanies poverty is a sort of family tradition. Children learn it in their daily lives. It is like a disease that rots the roots of personal progress, eating away at the confidence to plan ahead and the courage to aim high. It damages children's growing feelings of control over their own lives. On the surface, children living in poverty may appear very 'grown-up'. But that is not real maturity which has been built on the firm foundations of steady trial-and-error learning, which leads to adult competence and creative endeavour. It is more of a bravado, a veneer of the street-smartness needed for survival.

Gender

Ideas of what is suitable for boys and girls can push each into learning areas which may not suit their natural abilities. These have been found to be so similar for each sex that it is in fact possible to compare achievements directly to see the effects of social influences. Spatial abilities, for example, provide a clear example of an area where boys generally do better than girls, so we could expect twice as many male engineering graduates as females – but there are 30 times as many.

There are, however, major changes taking place, at least in the developed world. Girls are now achieving more highly than boys in many subjects: in Britain in *all* subjects at school. (see Chapter 9, section headed 'Gender') This is not true, though, for science and mathematics in the two countries which produce most of the research data on gifted children, the USA and Germany, which shows why it is extremely important to take a cross-cultural look at any evidence. Gender differences are important because of the light they throw on every single aspect of gifted achievement – particularly the effects of expectations and opportunities.

Cultural reasons
It is unfair but true that children who fit-in with their society stand a much better chance of success within it. Being part of a minority culture can be a handicap, though certainly not in all cases: the many great immigrant successes have also shown the power of its impetus. Language provides the first barrier. Children's self-expression may be fluent and creative in their home language but poor at school, and differently cultured and maybe little-educated parents are not always able to help their children at school.

Forms of handicap
Other factors which put the potentially gifted at risk are physical handicap and learning disabilities, such as dyslexia, from which even the most gifted can suffer. Whatever the educational system, there are always some children, however packed with potential, who fail to take advantage of it because something has gone wrong in their lives. This could be as little as a long-running disagreement with an important teacher, or as big as being born in a poor area where obstetric facilities are poor and birth injury brings a lifetime of spasticity to those who will never be recognised for their potential gifts. There were two spastic boys in this research, both of whom has been dismissed by their doctors as of low intelligence. In both cases it was only thanks to their mothers that the boys were able to go on to university and lead full lives.

The development of intelligence

An exceptionally high intelligence is by far the most popular criterion among teachers, parents, pupils and researchers for defining children as gifted. In its broadest sense, everyday intelligence is an individual's power to cope with his or her personal world. This might be the immediate basic objective of getting enough to eat, or a more distant one such as passing exams for a future career. Intelligence is used to assesses the choices available and then work out the most likely effective action in the circumstances.

Everyday intelligence can be improved with practice (like most things in life), in the sense that the more frequently you do something the better you will be at doing it. To a limited extent, measurable intelligence can also be increased by training in the kind of learning that is tapped by intelligence tests, that is by the very act of study, of almost any subject. This idea that learning can of itself improve intelligence, is sometimes given as the reason why the measured intelligence level of Japanese schoolchildren is steadily going up. They stay at school longer than any other nation and work harder while they are there. Certainly, most people's intelligence can be used more efficiently and effectively (see p. 203). No one, though, has yet discovered the answer to increasing the power of people's mental abilities to the extent that would, for example, help slow learners function at even average level.

The differences between people's abilities, including intelligence, are due to the interaction of heredity (the capacity they are born with) and environment (circumstances before and after birth). Give or take ten per cent, the currently accepted figure is that about 70 per cent of the variance between people in intellectual ability is due to inherited differences and the rest to environmental effects. (A few psychologists disagree, saying that we can all reach the highest levels of genius if only we work hard enough!) About 50 per cent of personality is inherited.

But for the intellectually gifted, the situation is somewhat different because input from the environment seems to play a relatively greater role. Though genetic endowment cannot be changed, the environmental proportion of an intelligence test score is relatively greater when a child has extra mental power to absorb and make more effective use of information and ideas (Freeman 1983). It follows, that as brighter children can absorb more, they have a need for high-level educational provision if their potential is to be fully developed.

The development of intelligence

Confusingly, children's intellectual development is not a smooth continuous process. The many interacting aspects neither develop at the same time nor necessarily in the same direction. Theorists such as Howard Gardner (1985) and Robert Sternberg and Davidson (1986) have proposed that instead of one general intelligence there are different kinds of intelligences – which importantly do not overlap. These new theories have encouraged the idea of a kaleidoscope of human abilities which has had a liberating impact on understanding. The template for these modern ideas was formulated in the early part of the twentieth century by Spearman who proposed a general intelligence, 'g', with strengths and weaknesses, a view still accepted and used today by most psychologists.

Whether specific or across the board, gifted-level abilities usually unfold very early (Freeman 1995b). How well little children develop whatever they were born with depends greatly on the environment they live in, and most importantly on that vital mediator of intellectual growth – the language they hear and use (Freeman 2000b). From birth, babies start to learn how to cope with their environments. There is some evidence that demanding babies trigger special family attention and that this extra interaction can stimulate their intellectual development. It is as though potentially gifted babies are thirsty for learning.

But the option is not open to all babies – both they and their parents must be good communicators. Mere stimulation is not the springboard of intellectual growth. In fact, loud clashing noises or screaming at a baby can be confusing or even detrimental, and demanding babies in poorly responding homes are not advantaged. In good homes, a highly intelligent child often demands and gets more stimulation from the family, for instance by initiating conversation. Even by the age of five, a child's measured intelligence is clearly related to the quality of language spoken in the family. In that way, a child can actually contribute to his or her own environment.

The efficient use of intelligence also depends on feelings of self-esteem. These are shaped by emotional security and by protection from stress, since adventures into new ways of thought call for confidence. Intellectual growth therefore thrives best in a setting of steady, balanced, positively responsive relationships, rather than a series of disconnected encounters.

Intelligence tests

An intelligence test can provide a safe harbour in a rough sea of opinion because, unlike people, it doesn't pick up antisocial behaviour or an unfashionable accent. We measure children's abilities to help guide them to an appropriate education, and the tests are extremely helpful in this. A good test can sometimes identify a gifted child who parents and teachers have missed. It can discover, for example, when a child is working above the average at school and yet still be underachieving in terms of measured gifted potential. This could be because emotional distress is getting in the way, or schoolwork seems to have no relevance.

I once measured a whole class with a broad-based test of reasoning in a school in a poor district and discovered that many of the pupils scored in the top five per cent. The class teacher eyeing the results, spotted Jane, one of her dirtier, cheekier and less attractive pupils, among the top few. She obviously didn't think much of Jane's abilities, because she said sharply, 'She must have copied the answers'. 'Impossible,' I replied. But my spirits sank as I left the classroom. It seemed unlikely that Jane would ever be able to show what she was capable of, at least with that teacher. Jane's family had minimal concern for education, she was often absent from school to help out at home, and had obviously been slotted by the teacher into the category of below-average ability. Jane had taken the message to heart. Her schoolwork was way below the level of her measured abilities. The test told the truth, but Jane didn't fit and the teacher wasn't listening.

All over the world, a child's IQ is by far the most widely used measure of giftedness. The IQ – Intelligence Quotient – is a statistical comparison of an individual's test results (on that particular test) with those of the whole population of the same age. Though the IQ is just a number, it is in fact the end result of the orchestration of very many distinct mental activities and learning. If that orchestration can be improved, then so can the performance on the test and the resulting IQ. Such tests are hard to beat as an estimate of how well a child is likely to cope with school learning. But although they are unlikely to overestimate ability, they can underestimate it because of adverse circumstances and illness. Such tests continue to proliferate in number and variety, whether based on the design of the original tests or on new theories of intelligence. IQ tests have to be used knowledgeably.

Morality and intelligence tests

A major problem is that although the tests appear to be unbiased, their makers, not unnaturally, carried and incorporated their own cultural assumptions into them. This is why some children from other cultures can find it difficult to score highly. One of the test makers' assumptions, for instance, is that the child is moral, he or she does their best: lying is neither expected or allowed for in marking. Though a highly intelligent young lawbreaker will not find it difficult to answer one way and act in another, a child from a different culture may not know the rules of the game. Knowing its limitations helps teachers to realise that a holistic view of a child, taking environment into account, is the only one that can provide a just assessment of a child's potential. Some of the questions on morality in the tests are almost explicit. Here are just two examples:

- *What would you do when another child takes your toy?* Instead of grabbing it back or fighting over it, which is a healthy normal reaction, the virtuous child is expected to be cool, rein in any anger, inhibit any reflex to lash out and say politely that he would tell the teacher. How prissy. What a poor lesson for real life. You are unlikely to do well in business with such a procedure. Who would you complain to in the cut-throat market place when someone snitches the deal from under your nose?
- *What would you do if you see a train approaching a broken bridge?* The moral answer is to raise your tiny arm and signal the driver to stop. In the Brazilian jungle, youngsters say that they would run away to protect themselves. This, in Western terms, is selfish behaviour. But then, the children have never seen a train and regard the idea as equivalent to seeing a rocket hurtling to earth. You'd be pretty stupid to stand there and signal it.

Scoring

Some people could get much higher scores than the tests can measure. But an exceptionally high intelligence bumps up against the 'ceiling effect', the upper limit of the test, a place where many children in this sample bumped their heads. A few psychologists have a formula to calculate IQs way above the makers' top scores, but I believe this is scientifically dubious and unreliable. What's more, the difference in real life between calculated scores of 180 and 190 is meaningless. Sometimes IQs are calculated for dead famous people, such as Isaac Newton and Albert Einstein, but no one knows what their real scores might have been because they would have had to be tested in the context of knowledge and understanding of the people of those times. 'The past is another country!'

High IQ scorers can join a variety of social clubs, such as Mensa and the 1% club, to mix with other high scorers. These clubs are all on the Internet. Unfortunately, some of them do not use regular standardised tests for entry; they sometimes even make up their own which do not have much meaning outside the club. And the sterile puzzles the hopeful have to complete for entry are not very useful indications of what they can actually accomplish in life, as many of the members would relate. The highest possible IQ is not enough to predict worldly success, and many people with only average IQs are extremely successful. As always, it depends on how you use what you've got.

How intelligence tests developed

Modern concern for the gifted began when Sir Francis Galton published his book *Hereditary Genius* in Britain in 1869. In his eyes, high-level intelligence was only shown by people from the 'right' social level in the 'right' society, i.e. by people of 'high culture', meaning European culture, notably the best of the 'English race'. In other words, men like him. He considered other races, particularly black ones, to be the bottom of the human pile, although women and Jews were only marginally better. There could be no change in this order; God had given you your engine with its fixed horsepower and there was nothing you could do about it.

Galton's moral thread re-emerged again in 1994, in the controversial book by Murray and Herrnstein, *The Bell Curve* (1994). Like him, the authors were in no doubt as to the relationship between intelligence and virtue, reiterating that old claim: 'high intelligence also provides some protection against lapsing into criminality' (p. 235). Arthur Jensen (1969) was also sure that IQ and crime are associated: he argued that 60 per cent of black Americans have an IQ below 90 and coincidentally a peak crime rate occurs in the IQ range 75–90.

The really big breakthrough in measurement came in 1904 when the brilliant Frenchman, Alfred Binet, set out to measure children's potential for school learning, aiming to help those who were lagging behind. Slowly and carefully, he worked out a set of graded intellectual exercises from which each child's score could be compared with others of the same age. He did not only test what they had learned at school, but did his best to sample what he regarded as intelligent behaviour. He well knew that what he captured on paper was only a part of the children's intelligence, the part concerned with school-type learning. He also knew that just one number could never capture the richness of human mental abilities, a warning to which some later imitators of his test should have paid heed. The French school authorities liked it.

The Americans then took up Binet's idea with enthusiasm and gave the new intelligence wider credibility. The model for intelligence was a mental power, like electricity, which was also becoming widely available at that time. The power of intelligence was beginning to be seen as more adaptable, although geniuses, idiots and criminals were believed to have quite different kinds of it. For the next half century, in spite of Binet's warnings, his numerical IQ score was taken to be absolutely all we needed to know about intelligence, a number to describe the variety of mental life. This rigidity is as strange to us now as attempting to summarise someone's personality by just a number – not very informative – but it has taken many decades to begin to shift the belief that intelligence is fixed for life at the moment the sperm enters the egg.

Most IQ tests today are still based on Binet's idea of children's scores on paper-and-pencil tests compared with others of the same age. The tests are all constantly updated and, like the original, still provide reliable evidence of how well a child will do at school. This age comparison is very helpful for guiding children's education, but comparing a 33-year-old with a 34-year-old makes no sense. Though there are intelligence tests for adults, they are not very good at distinguishing people at the top of the scale.

The practical promotion of intellectual gifts was started in New York in 1900, through Rapid Advancement Classes for high achievers. The characteristics of those turn of the century high achievers in school have provided the image of what people today often recognise as the nature of giftedness in children.

The next big move was Lewis Terman's *Genetic Studies of Genius*, begun in Stanford, California in 1922; this was the first large-scale longitudinal study of the gifted, which is still continuing (Holahan and Sears 1995). However, Professor Terman selected children who conformed to those early ideas of giftedness. He adapted Binet's intelligence test and renamed it the Stanford–Binet Intelligence Test. Using a minimum score of IQ 140, Terman looked for those 'with a degree of brightness that would rate them well within the top one per cent of the school population'. However, in spite of the grandeur of the title of genius with which he endowed his sample of 1,572 children, not one of them has shown signs of it in adulthood

Like Galton, Terman was quite unconcerned about the effects of the sample's home backgrounds. In fact, most of them were the children of white university lecturers, who had enjoyed the best of most things, including good food and education. It is well recognised that IQ (and height) rises as a country's standard of living goes up, but Terman neither took proper account of his sample's exceptional standard of living nor made direct comparisons with any other children. Yet his generalisations that intellectually-gifted children were superior in most things has held sway for more than half a century in America.

Finding the gifted

The first stumbling block to helping the potentially gifted is finding them. And who is chosen as gifted is affected by the reasons for searching as well as the methods used for selection. Children chosen by high school grades, for instance, are likely to be different in outlook from others who have developed their gymnastics to a level of excellence.

Many educators feel that the problems of defining intellectual giftedness, other than by IQ or school marks, are so difficult they stop trying. And if the intellectually gifted are chosen subjectively, well...it all depends on what you mean by giftedness! There are perhaps 100 definitions around, almost all of which refer to children's precocity, either in psychological constructs, such as intelligence and creativity, but more usually in terms of high marks in school subjects (Hany 1993). Yet in formal school education, social or business talents are rarely considered, and physical and artistic prowess is frequently seen as inborn potential which can be developed to excellence by coaching and practice. To some extent, the way a very able child is defined depends on what is being looked for, whether it is academic excellence for formal education, innovation for business or solving paper-and-pencil puzzles for an IQ club.

Not all gifted children possess a wide range of outstanding abilities, and sometimes a single characteristic can indicate a special gift or talent in an otherwise unexceptional child. Though the more ephemeral abilities such as creativity, social awareness, or leadership are included today in definitions of giftedness, there are still so many unanswered questions. Is creativity a part of general high intelligence or independent of it? Is there such a thing as the currently fashionable idea of emotional giftedness, and if so how might it be related to social intelligence, if that exists? What about spiritual giftedness, about to hit the market-place? But the really big one remains – how is it possible to discover unrealised ability?

The word 'gifted'
Part of the problem in finding the gifted lies in this word itself – implying that others are therefore not gifted and so are somehow less worthy. Because of the power of the image behind that word, when a child is labelled gifted, not only does

it have an effect on his or her self-concept, but it alters the attitudes and behaviour of others towards the child. This was seen time and time again in this study. 'Gifted' is a label to be used sparingly and with great care. Indeed, it is often replaced by less provocative, fuzzier descriptions such as 'exceptionally able', 'very able' or 'highly able'. These other terms at least suggest that everyone is able, though to paraphrase George Orwell's pigs in *Animal Farm*, some are more able than others.

In addition, the way the term 'giftedness' is used depends on the context, so that even in the same area of activity, children can be called gifted at different levels of ability and achievement. In a school in a poorly cultured district, for example, pupils may be seen as gifted who would be below average in a highly selective school. If children are identified as gifted only in terms of their precocity, they may appear to have 'burned out' when they lose that advantage, just as a child who is tall at 11-years-old may not be at all outstanding at 16 when the others catch up, though no one calls that burn out. There are always some individuals who will stay at an outstanding ability level, just as some will stay taller than others.

Nevertheless, as the description of gifted is the most common and almost all international researchers use it, it would be verging on the deviant to avoid it. Genius is a description usually saved for adults, referring to the few who have made world-level changes, typically Albert Einstein, Marie Curie or Pablo Picasso, and more recently perhaps, Bill Gates, the builder of Microsoft. It is a rather romantic term, which is hard to apply to people who are still living. In the USA, though, it was applied to small children by Professor Terman, and the popular media often use it for an advanced child.

Who are the gifted?

Identifying the gifted and knowing how they go about their gifted business, is important in deciding how to help them. But the term is flexible and always relative. Some say that children are only gifted if they are in the top one per cent of the population on any measure, others use the top five per cent. It is almost a case of wherever one cares to draw the line; there's no fixed rule. The UK Department for Education and Employment is choosing to take the top five per cent of schoolchildren mostly as judged by their teachers, and considers that ten per cent of these are underachieving. Some American states describe the top 30 per cent as gifted, though in some of the Southern US states minority children are assessed separately, taking into account their sometimes poor diet and local vocabulary. The result is that children who would actually score below average on a standardised national test are selected for special 'gifted' education in their home territory.

If the aim of education is to develop all children's potential, then it must include those with something more than the majority. Finding such exceptionally high ability in children who are not showing it calls for a broad approach. As with any condition, the sooner it can be identified the sooner it can be helped, and to do that, parents and teachers need correct information. However, descriptions often used of the gifted, such as those appearing in checklists for teachers, can be misleading because they are too often based on the list-makers' subjective experiences and can bear little relationship to the evidence.

The results of my long-term study which follow, have thrown considerable light on this tricky area of identification by showing how some children can be mistakenly seen as gifted and so can never satisfy anyone, and yet others with outstanding potential can be missed and fail to develop their gifts.

CHAPTER 2

The study

What a blunt fellow is this grown to be? He was quick mettle when he went to school
William Shakespeare, *Julius Caesar.*

My heart sank as in the spring of 1974 I viewed the piled up dusty grey box-files, bulging with yellowing paper and mostly held together with string. They contained many years of the accumulated, jumbled letters, reports and scribbled notes of the National Association for Gifted Children (NAGC, UK). It took nearly a year to organise what they contained on to punched cards (as we did in those days), before there could be any further investigations. There were about 6,500 sets of correspondence, involving about 4,500 children – letters of enquiry, head teacher's reports, case histories from clinics and many anguished cries from parents. The Association is a registered charity which anyone can join on behalf of a child they think may be gifted. It provides Saturday classes and counselling, and fees are very low. There are branches all over the country, though very few then required any test for the children, which meant that when parents signed up they effectively made a statement of their belief in their child's giftedness.

The association has found the term 'gifted' a mixed blessing, as their Education Officer explained to the high-ability interactive site (high-ability@ngfl.gov.uk (22 February 2000)). This is because it carries attributes of exclusivity, separateness, or worse, a pseudo-medical condition including emotional disturbance. He wrote:

> By far the majority of the parents who make contact with NAGC do so when their child is between 18 months and 4 years old. At this age, testing and assessment is inappropriate, and it is a matter of conjecture as to what the top 5 per cent means. We do, however, broadly support the concept of this percentage, given appropriate measures. Parents are approaching us because of a variety of characteristics which they see in their children but not in their peers: wide vocabulary, early reading (which is not simply memory of familiar books), extended concentration, *socialising with older children and adults and difficulty in peer-relationships* [my italics]. Hence, by the time these children get to their first school a raft of issues are already present for both the child and the parents. For some, the introduction to school can be *traumatic* [my italics].

But is this typical of all gifted children?

The people in the study

From the NAGC collection, I took a sample of 70 children as my Target group, after checking that they were typical of the whole membership. The essential criteria were: parents were members of the NAGC within the last four years, residence in the North West of England and children at school. The children were aged between 5- and 14-years-old.

I had more than a few questions in mind, such as

- Why had the parents joined NAGC?
- Why did they believe their child was gifted?
- What did they expect from a gifted child?
- Were there any differences between the lives of the NAGC children and other children?
- Were these children, seen by their parents and teachers as gifted, actually so?
- Were the families of these children any different from other families?
- What about burn-out?

And so many more . . .

My aim was to compare the NAGC children with two matched groups of children, the first of equal ability whose parents were not members, and the second taken at random. At the start of the research, the Target group's real abilities were untested and unknown. So, acting on the assumption that most were gifted, and so rare in any classroom, I devised a complicated cross-school research design, which proved to be quite unnecessary.

The whole of the Target child's school class was measured for general intelligence on a pattern test, the Raven's Progressive Matrices. This test asks the child to choose one of six possibilities to make up missing parts of a pattern. Although it does require familiarity with the printed page, it is relatively 'culture-free'. It provides a general measure of reasoning ability on which each child can be compared with others of the same age. Sometimes, in order to give useful feedback to the head teacher (and as a sort of thank you for having me), I was asked to test the whole school. Nearly 3,000 children were involved in the initial search.

Using those test results, each Target child was matched up with two comparison children in the same school class – for age, sex, socio-economic status and school class. There was one essential difference between these two. The first, Control–1, was matched for Raven's raw scores whereas Control–2 was taken at random. The ability matching was remarkably accurate; the average Raven's raw score for the Target children was 34.60 and that for the Control–1 children was 34.53 – significantly different from the Control–2's average of 28.75.

This, the first important finding to come from this study – which seemed patently obvious once realised – was that there is a spectrum of ability in every school which reflects the social population it draws on. There is not normally a wide gap between the very brightest in a class and the rest, which means that the gifted are not – as was supposed then – in a position of intellectual isolation among their classmates. I was able to match the Target children for ability perfectly within their own school class. Each trio had identical school education, so home and other influences would stand out more in any comparisons.

At the end of the second year, when all the testing had been done and permissions granted, the sample contained 210 children, 210 sets of parents, 61 head teachers and 61 class teachers.

Getting to know the children and their families

This study involved a greater familiarity with the children and their families than is usual in psychological/educational research. In fact I visited many more than once and for hours at a time, so that I was in fact able to get to know many of them quite well. The children were tested in their homes on a wide variety of measures including a full IQ test, personality, musical ability, and general creativity, and they and their parents were interviewed with open-ended newly designed questionnaires in their homes. The class teachers completed a standardised questionnaire on the children's behaviour in class, and they and the head teachers were interviewed in the schools. I rated the children's environmental circumstances.

Two kinds of intelligence test were given to the children to provide a more rounded picture and also a basis for comparison between the different results. After the Raven's group pattern test, the Stanford–Binet Intelligence Test was given individually, which sometimes took a couple of hours if the child was at the top of the scale. The test demands some previously learned information, including vocabulary, and so to some extent reflects a child's educational environment.

The results of the test (see Table 2.1) are given in terms of an intelligence quota or IQ score (see Chapter 1). This is a calculation of the child's chronological age divided by the mental age (calculated from the raw test score) and multiplied by 100 to round it off. The average IQ is around 100, and about 60 per cent of all children have IQ scores within 17 points either side of that. Only about two per cent have scores above IQ 130, and less than one per cent above 140. Those scoring above IQ 150 are in a very tiny minority – one in a thousand.

Clearly the results did not relate to an average sample of children because of the way they had been selected: the average IQ of the whole sample was very high, in the top two per cent of the population, at IQ 137.36. Two-thirds were boys and one-third was girls – a ratio found in many parts of the world when children are chosen as gifted by parents. The resulting matrix of 210 children and 230 pieces of information about them, was statistically analysed by factor analysis, analysis of variance with orthogonal comparisons, and various non-parametric methods with the smaller subdivisions. The results are overviewed here.

Table 2.1 IQs of the whole sample of 210 children

> - 65 were of about average ability between IQ 97–120
> - 63 were above average at IQ 121–140
> - 82 were in the top one per cent of the population at IQ 141–170, of whom 16 scored 170.

Influences on the children's development

The Raven's pattern test scores were used as a guide to basic general intelligence, and the detailed Stanford–Binet IQs as a measure of the children's intelligence which had taken up learning. In this way the IQ score was regarded in part as an achievement score. The two intelligence test scores were then compared statistically, along with the multitude of other data collected from parents, teachers, and rated observations.

These comparisons showed that children with virtually identical scores on the Raven's pattern test could score very differently on the IQ test. These differences were found to be directly related to their rated home circumstances: the better the provision, the higher the IQ score was likely to be. This study, which had taken home and school settings into account, had demonstrated that a bright child living in a culturally poor environment could score the same IQ as a child of more modest abilities in a really good educational environment (Freeman 1983).

> ### Conclusions concerning gifted IQ scorers
>
> - The assumption of a constant relationship between heredity and environment on the IQ is seen to take different proportions for the gifted, and is particularly dependent on circumstances, more than for other children.
> - The selection of children as gifted – when made solely on the basis of the IQ score – will miss children who have not had the opportunities in that kind of school-type learning. A cut-off point of not more than IQ 130 could be used, and always with the proviso that other measures were considered along with it, which were as culture-free as possible, and with an understanding of the child's circumstances.

- When children are compared in terms of their IQs it is essential to be aware of the input on their scores from their home backgrounds.
- In practical educational terms, because brighter children can take in and use more information and ideas than less bright children, their education has to be both broader and more intense to develop their potential for learning to the full. When the intellectually gifted have poor educational nourishment, they will be relatively more deprived in this respect than less able children, because their potential to make use of it is so much greater. It was clear from this research that the gifted do have special educational needs.

Parental differences

The parents of the three groups of children were found to have distinct and statistically significant differences. For example, although the mothers of each trio had received similar education, far more of the Target group's mothers had reached high-level occupations – and yet they remained much more dissatisfied with their own education. Target mothers often took far more responsibility for their children's education than the fathers. However, both the Target parents said they put greater educational pressure on their children than the parents of either Control groups.

It was useful having the trio in the same school class because it could be seen clearly that the parents of the Target children had made a significantly greater number of complaints (23 per cent) about the school, compared with the equally able Control–1s (16 per cent) and the Control–2s (8 per cent). In addition, on the Stott Social Adjustment Guide the Target children were themselves significantly more frequently described as difficult, both by their parents and their teachers. The parents also reported them as being more troubled by problems of a 'nervous' type, such as poor sleep, poor coordination, asthma, and they were markedly over-active in school. This Target group had a far higher measured level of maladjustment at school than either of the other groups – and far fewer friends.

At this point in the research it did look as though many of the circulating ideas about gifted children were true – their frustration in a normal school, their inability to make friends, their poor sleep and so on. Understandably, the association for gifted children had, and still has, the impression that such problems were common among gifted children. (See p. 13.) But partly intuitively, I felt that it did not ring true. Both Target and Control–1 groups had been accurately matched for general intelligence, and just about everything else, and yet they were neither behaving in the same way, nor did people react to them in the same way.

The next move changed the picture dramatically. I took all the children out of their original categories of Target and the two Controls and statistically compared just their IQ scores with all the other 210 variables in their lives. This showed clearly that IQ alone was not related to the children's emotional problems – but other matters were.

Laying some myths

Emotional development

The evidence that IQ of itself was not directly associated with emotional disturbance was extremely important. Although the labelled Target group had deeper and more frequent emotional problems, this could not have been due to their abilities alone – because those were identical with the first control group's. The identification was not as straightforward as it had seemed.

The mantle of giftedness laid on these young shoulders was seen to have had repercussions. The Target children, described by both parents and teachers as more difficult, also had significantly more unusual home circumstances. For example, their parents may have separated, they had moved home constantly, or they might simply have been a late baby when their siblings had grown up. Sometimes parents tried to live vicariously through them, which was a hard act for the child to live up to every day. For any children, emotional problems could follow from such circumstances, and the gifted are not immune to the effects of parents at war. But for them, their difficulties were often mistaken for the anticipated 'symptoms' of giftedness – though you don't have to be gifted to have temper tantrums.

The idea that the gifted were bound to be 'odd', and unhappy, was rife. Some parents of the Target children appeared to have looked for (and found) early signs of differentness, such as when boys were called 'the little professor' at school. Well-behaved children who simply did well at their lessons, notably girls, were far less likely to be given the label of 'gifted', which possibly explained the high proportion of boys chosen by parents: two for every girl. In fact, it seemed at times that the label was more closely attached to a bright child's somewhat antisocial behaviour than his ability, because always, playing close by, there would be equally able children who were not seen as gifted.

Nor were very high IQ children usually loners: their relationships depended on the context of their lives. They had as many friends at school as other children, but often fewer at home due to the nature of their out-of-school activities, such as music practice, hobbies, and more homework. Even children within the top one per cent of IQ scores did not describe themselves as statistically significantly more bored in school than the other children – though significantly (one per cent) more of the Target group's parents claimed they were (at one per cent significance).

Overall, as the families of the Target group had been more troubled and the parents had shown statistically significantly (at one per cent) different attitudes to their children than those of the control groups, it was very likely that they had been influential in their children's behaviour and outlook – as parents usually are – especially as it was the parents who had labelled them as gifted in the first place. When I asked them why they had joined the National Association for Gifted Children, nearly three-quarters of them replied that it was because of problems they had either experienced or were expecting.

This emotional disturbance seemed to have knocked the edge off the Target group's school achievements, because they had somewhat lower marks than the equally able Control group (statistically significant at five per cent). Yet they had more frequently been grade-skipped, and so felt better recognised for their high ability, even though this move could have lowered their achievements.

Advanced children did, however, meet some emotional problems in schools, such as a teacher's disbelief in a child's capacities, as when a gifted five-year-old, who had been reading fluently at home, was kept at the same reading pace as the rest of the class; a frustrating and upsetting matter for the child.

I could not find any special personality traits among the gifted, other than a tendency to extroversion in the music performers. Even traits such as ambition or curiosity, which are often described as features of high intellect, appear to be related more to culture and upbringing than IQ or achievement at school. It was perhaps the intensity of their curiosity which distinguished the gifted – although at times they appeared to their teachers to be not so much curious as 'know-all'.

Mental development

From their earliest days, the most intelligent children had very often been advanced in the three symbolic skills of talking, reading, and writing. Parents said they noticed their striving for words sometimes within months of birth. As they got older, they became wider and more avid readers than the other children, including the reading of comics. Though they did not make more collections of things, nor play with any different kinds of toys than the other children, as has often been suggested, they did seem to be more intense about what they did. They had a greater variety of interests, and usually enjoyed television though they were more discriminating in their choice of programmes. Most outstandingly, the exceptionally high IQ children had much better abilities to concentrate and memorise, which benefited them greatly.

Physical development

The sample ranged from average to gifted, but there were no discernible differences in physique or pattern of health, except in one aspect – the stereotype of the gifted child being more likely to wear spectacles was found to be true! As with all children, physical coordination was found to be more closely related to general psychological adjustment than IQ. Also as is usual, boys had more difficulty than girls with fine motor control, which was most likely to show up in their poor handwriting, but again it was not associated with IQ.

Outstanding conclusions from the first stage of this research

1. *Emotional development.* Of itself, a high IQ score could not be said to bring about emotional problems: the children of exceptionally high IQ proved to be just as emotionally stable as any others.
2. *Educational influences.* The greatest lift to a child's IQ score and success at school did not come only from the parents' attitudes to education nor even from high expectations. It came from:
   a) The material provision the children had to learn with – books, space, musical instruments, paper, and so on. This tied up with a study in which children who were outstandingly talented in music or fine art were compared with their non-talented classmates, which demonstrated that most of the impetus for the development of those arts had come from the parents (Freeman 2000c). For those arts, although the schools did sometimes initiate interest, they were not usually successful in bringing standards of work up to an outstandingly high level without the parent's cooperation and provision.
   b) Parental involvement with their children. This included the way parents behaved, the example they set, and the cultural milieu they provided. Where the environment was rich and varied in opportunities to learn, then each child could respond according to his or her abilities. The effective parent does not say – 'Do what I tell you. Here is a book about flowers, go out and identify some.' The effective parent says – 'Do what I do. Let's use this book to find out the names of the flowers – together.'

The reaction

The publication of these findings caused anger among people whose experiences in the association for gifted children had convinced them that the gifted were destined for emotionally rough lives. It seemed strange to me that my evidence of the normal emotional development of the gifted was so unwelcome. However, my work did help to shift attitudes towards the gifted away from the focus on their supposed emotional problems to a more balanced and positive concern with the whole child and his or her education, although the myth still clings.

The real differences between the gifted and other children lie in their abilities. To what extent these gifts can unfold naturally and how much they depend on help can only be seen by looking at the way the gifted develop in different circumstances. I was often asked how the children from the study had progressed – what happened next? So, again with very welcome assistance from the Calouste Gulbenkian Foundation (UK), I decided to find this out in the Follow-up study described below.

The Follow-up study

Ten years later, in 1984, I set out to find out what had happened to all the children and their parents since we had last met. I was searching for common threads in their lives as they grew up, any influences to which they might have responded, as well as the impact of chance. Again I aimed for the best of all possible research worlds – in-depth interviewing for the quality of the young people's reactions to what they had experienced, and some statistical analysis to deal with the measurable aspects of their progress, though the Follow-up was much more dependent on verbal reporting than before.

The major value of any longitudinal study is in the long view using descriptions and measurements of events as they are happening, rather than being entirely dependent on people's only too fallible memories. If I had only done a single studies without that continuity, I certainly would have missed vital ongoing information.

However, in psychology, studies which involve talking to people in their homes are rare, because they are heavy on time and therefore very expensive. But as life is not normally lived either in a clinic or a laboratory, I was determined to reach a closer understanding of the fabric of the young people's lives, not least by talking with them where they spent their time. This worthy intent, however, proved to be no small feat to carry out. Although they had all lived in the North West of England ten years earlier, they had spread across Britain, from Inverness to Jersey, and from Exeter to Harwich. And worse, from the interview point of view, the young people did not always live with their parents any more, so that in about half the cases it meant two journeys per family to talk to both the parents and their children wherever they were. It was physically hard going at times, but always tremendously interesting and worthwhile.

Finding the Follow-up sample

As there had been no contact for ten years, it took nearly six months to find the, by now, young people. This involved a variety of devious methods and dogged, foot-in-the-door persistence. All long-term studies are subject to human vicissitudes – particularly to losing contact with some of the subjects – although compared with most, the loss in this one was very small. Some families had vanished without trace. Just a few of the original children refused – one because of illness, two because their parents told me that their sons had become drug addicts and were not capable of responding intelligently, two youths were too depressed, which they put down to their unemployment, and one because he said he was working and 'there's nothing in it for me': the level of financial inducement I could offer had no effect. If any one of the original comparison trios was missing, I dropped the other two so that I would have a Follow-up sample which truly reflected the original. This was rather painful sometimes, when finding the other two had taken a great deal of time and energy.

In the end, 81 per cent of the original sample of both children and parents agreed to take part, in proportions which were indeed representative of all the original groupings. (See Table 2.2.)

Table 2.2 The make up of samples

The make up of the 1974 and 1984 samples (per cent)		
	1974	*1984*
Boys	64.3	64.5
Girls	35.7	35.5
Target	33.3	32.0
Control–1	33.3	34.9
Control–2	33.3	33.1
High IQ (140+)	39	42
Moderate IQ (–140)	61	58
Follow-up sample		
	Spread	*Mean*
Age	14 to 22	18
IQ	97–170	135.4
Raven's percentile	50–99	90
Gender	Boys 109	Girls 60
Total in sample	169	

The research outlook

To try to understand children without concern for their worlds is rather like a zoologist examining fish behaviour without considering water. So often in research, such as experimental classroom work, the subject's own words are presented as merely interesting, if they are considered at all. But in fact what an individual thinks and feels is vital to understanding why they behave as they do. There is no escape from the importance of the environment in all aspects of development: it is not something 'out there', but is almost as much a part of anyone as the working out of their genes.

The first stage of this study used standardised tests as well as newly-made questionnaires for the children, parents and teachers. But by 1984, as most of the young people had left school, and tests on older people are not always reliable, the study was based on self-reports within structured interviews of the young people and their parents only. Descriptions of their experiences and individual reactions to them were intended to throw some light on the often subtle influences underlying the exceptionality of giftedness.

Self-reports

People vary in their ability to be introspective – or at least some produce better-seeming reports of themselves than others. Possibly introspective ability is developmental, a form of learning to perceive in another mode, so one could be particularly gifted at it. There is the added risk, though, that by the very act of looking in – introspection – the description can become distorted. Yet how else is it possible to identify some of the most exciting aspects of mental life, like why people perceive the world as they do, their hopes and concerns, and the way they deal with their experiences?

Self-reports yield a gloriously richer quality of information than ticking a box on a questionnaire (especially by post). Not only do the individual's own descriptions tell a story, but so do tone of voice and facial expression – of both subject and interviewer. The sense of involvement in the interviews maintains the flow of the interaction, which also helps to keep everyone involved, especially important in keeping up the high level of participants across time. It was extraordinary to me how different the style and content of each interview was, as was my interaction with each subject; clues were picked up on the spur of the moment and relationships interpreted as they flowed. One can never know exactly what will happen, so the process can never be as objective as a laboratory experiment or a test score.

And there are always unknown influences operating. For example, although I made conscious efforts not to influence the young people I was researching, two of them told me that they were inspired by our interactions to go on to study psychology at university. And who can say what other repercussions there might have been?

Not only is it important to work sensitively in discovering the emotional meaning of other people's lives, but also in unravelling the very intricate web of data when there is no set method of analysis and few standardised measures. The thread has to be extracted by both reasoning and feeling. For me, working on the fringes of what is measurable and reaching out to what looks like impressions, is a dangerous game for a respectable psychologist. As with any scientist, I am expected to be able to distinguish what I see in my world from the worlds of the people I am trying to understand. It would have been far easier (and very much quicker) to hide in jargon and statistics, in the way I'd been trained, and present a picture of objectivity, than to run the risk of appearing to be both unscientific and unsophisticated. Oscar Wilde put the danger succinctly in *Lady Windermere's Fan* – 'To be intelligible is to be found out.'

The Follow-up in action

The nation-wide visits for the Follow-up study began in an exceptionally long, icy winter, succeeded by extravagant spring blossom and the converging emerald stripes of new shoots in the lines of the plough across English fields; then bright summer sun on flowers. Soft, misty evenings in the country were balanced by an industrial compound's flashing fairy lights against the black night sky, and long clean rows of terraced houses in northern towns stretching to the horizon.

I spent many black, wet nights in strange cities jarring through rush-hour traffic, lights glancing on wet roads, searching narrowing suburban streets with increasing desperation as they became more intricate and without signs. At last the right road, the right house, and on a strange doorstep, battered by rain and wind, questionnaires and tape recorder warm in my bag, I pressed the doorbell. The door would open on a smiling face and soon a hot cup of tea would be thrust in my hands; I was a guest in a family and the privilege was real.

The interviews were conducted in places as different as the governor's office in a women's open prison, a brewery laboratory, often sitting on beds in student accommodation, a corner of a kitchen, a cafe in a department store, the back of a taxi, and a very kind head master once vacated his own office for me. The homes I visited varied between a Georgian mansion in a National Park, a freezing slum, rich mansions in acres of grounds, an old farmhouse high on a bleak hill and a seventeenth-century cottage in a vale of glorious spring daffodils. Most, though, were in the typical British dwelling – a three bedroom, semi-detached house in a city suburb.

I had piloted and made a prepared questionnaire as a base (see Appendix 2) for the interviews, but they were really more like conversations or even at times like counselling. These bright young people were often very articulate and keen to discourse – often into the small hours – an excellent time for good communication. At times the same story, when seen through the eyes of children and parents, took on quite a different slant. Even the effects of grandparents on their grandchildren was clear to see.

Interpreting the interviews
There is an infinite variety and quality of experience in everyday life which impinges on an individual, of which my interviews could taste just a tiny morsel. Yet the quality of my conclusions depended on how that morsel was taken and how

it was interpreted. To escape many of my own preconceptions and fallible memory, I recorded every word of the about 500 interviews on audiotape, which proved to be a valuable safeguard against mistakes.

Although my major advantage in this study was my qualification in counselling, highly gifted people may use concepts and ideas which confound the non-gifted – myself included. More than one gifted mathematician among these young people found it hard to understand the difficulties we normal people face in what they saw as simple. I had the impression that Sarah Mortimer (Highly gifted, aged 20, studying computer science at university), rather enjoyed the difference:

> 'In class, I might suddenly say, "Oh, this is wrong", re-write the programme, churn it through and find it works. Someone will ask, "Why did you do that?" and I reply, "Well, it's obvious. We didn't do this, that and the other", and sometimes they can't follow, because I jump too many steps at once. In the time they've taken to think what they're going to do, I've written down the whole formula, and then the next line.'

A total of 338 filled-in questionnaires, as well as over 500 interview and report transcripts, were rated and statistically analysed. They were also read and re-read by a small team searching for ideas that I had not thought of beforehand. The personal experiences of the young people – during the most important, formative parts of their lives – were teased out from those many hundreds of hours of recorded conversations. Though I have edited and woven them into a whole here, it was their own words which provided the information and the vitality, offering a true picture of what the gifted and non-gifted teenager's world looked and felt like in Britain in the mid 1980s.

So, 27 years on

The Follow-up study integrated what had been learned from the 1974 work with the details of what had happened to the young people over ten more years. In this, the 2001 'up-date', I have reconsidered 27 years in the lives of the sample in the light of new international research from my UK government survey (Freeman 1998). Catching up with dozens of people, including the parents, and their children now in their mid-thirties and often with partners and children of their own, has provided further confirmation that gifts can emerge in many different ways and at different times. While for some, their precocity developed into adult gifts, it did not for others; some chose to ignore their gifts, and it was clear that high-level school achievement was not a passport to adult success. Above all, fate can have the final say.

CHAPTER 3

Some problems in being gifted

No man is an Island, entire of itself
John Donne, *Devotions*

Gifts do not come with problems attached. The special problems associated with giftedness seem to be largely of other people's making, as was seen in this study and that of many others (overview in Freeman 1987). For example, some parents try to live through them, or a child may be gifted in a limited area but expected to be gifted all round, while less secure children may grasp at the role of being 'gifted' to gain attention and self-esteem.

High achievers may have to cope with the 'tall poppy' syndrome, when people feel resentment to others for doing well and try to cut them down. In an investigation into the experiences of 18 Australian athletes who won Olympic gold medals between 1984 and 1992, Susan Jackson and her colleagues (1998) found that it had created long lasting changes to most of their lives. There were many negatives, including burn-out, feelings of lack of support, personal life problems and lack of recognition. The athletes said that people either wanted to pull them down – the tall poppy syndrome - or the reverse, making them live on a pedestal. One athlete said: 'When you don't win you are a nobody'.

The problem of being stereotyped
The gifted are unusual, and so in a sense an affront to order and conformity. Maybe that is why so many strange ideas and stereotypes circulate about them. Those biased views can affect their feelings about themselves, as well as acting as brakes to their identification and development. The label of gifted places a child into a special category of exceptionality, so that he or she might be expected to have particular characteristics and problems. Popular stereotypes of the gifted child vary considerably from place to place, such as on either side of the Atlantic, where they are often in opposition.

The North American popular stereotype is of a super-child: he (for it is always he) is a brilliant sportsman, a natural leader, and a straight-A scholar. He is expected to be physically well-formed and probably good to look at – a hero. But the British stereotype is of a weedy lad: he (for he is still male) is bespectacled, lonely, and much given to solitary reading. He may also play the violin. The British stereotype is a juvenile intellectual, at times referred to by his schoolmates and maybe his teachers as 'the little professor'. He will look old-fashioned, move awkwardly, be difficult to bring up, and will find it hard if not impossible to make friends. He is certainly not a leader, for in Britain talent in leadership and sport are assumed to be the province of non-intellectuals.

Such expected characteristics bring problems to the gifted in other people's expectations of them. For example, if gifted American children do not conform to that super-boy stereotype, if they are undersized, or shy, or only shine in one area, they can be missed by teachers. Added to that is the burden of living up to the perfect image, so that when an A-grade student drops to an occasional B it is seen as failure. In this study, a significant number of the Target children were described by their parents as 'typically' gifted, of course in the British mould. In fact, the major concern in the collected correspondence from the National Association for Gifted Children was the child's 'symptoms', which were seen as making difficulties in the family's life – such as over-activity, making excessive demands, needing little sleep and not fitting-in at school.

'Career giftedness'

The very long view over the 27 years of this study showed some of the deeper aspects of being a designated gifted child. I do not believe that this information could have been discovered by questionnaire or by superficial interviewing, most surely not in the short term.

I have called the youngsters whose sense of self-worth appeared to be dependent on being seen as brilliant – whether they were or not – Career Gifteds. A notable feature of such people (children and adults) is that they often 'dine out on it', informing the world both of how difficult it is for them as gifted people, and how tiresome they find it having to cope with normal (mediocre) people. Parents may play along with this image. Career Gifteds normally work very hard, achieve superbly and accept their laurels with a smile, but some insist that were it not for . . . insert excuse . . . they could show their true and brilliant colours.

Behind the facade and the bravado of the Career Gifteds, whether achieving or not, lies fear. It is fear of being a nobody, of being undeserving of attention, of appearing unworthy to oneself and others and of being exposed as fraudulently gifted. Such fear has inhibiting spin-offs, both to academic study and to creative expression. Career Gifteds, as in this study, chose to present themselves in that way because of the combination of high ability, emotional make-up and encouragement from others.

Update 2001: Jeremy Kramer at 36 threw a very different light on what had appeared to be his supremely successful life as a gifted child with an IQ bumping the top of the scale and extremely advanced music performance. At 21 he had appeared to be in entire control of this own life, (see p. 148). I was as taken-in by his appearance and air of self-confidence as everyone else. Only now did Jeremy have the courage to explain:

'Being labelled gifted has distorted my life. From the age of seven, my all-consuming thoughts were – "Why am I so unhappy?" My gifts are associated with negative emotions. Alongside them were awful deficiencies in other areas which were exacerbated by my being seen as gifted. On the one hand I took pleasure in the applause and admiration that gave me a false confidence, but my personality problems ran alongside and were never noticed. I clung on to that positive feedback of being admired, but I never felt gifted as a person, and I certainly don't now. I became emotionally detached and it's become worse as I grew up. There were two parts to me, one was a calculator. But a calculator can't appreciate a work of art; he can only get good results at school. I'm still trying to make up for lost opportunities – but I can't go back to school again.

How do you learn to be creative? I could do almost any task that someone else set for me, but creativity was and still is a blank. I never achieved anything except where the parameters were totally set. You can go on like that in all education until someone asks for originality. I was pleased to make other people feel I was gifted, but I was terrified in case I was asked to do anything original. It is true for all the music I have ever played; it wasn't from me, just something I'd learned, a regurgitation, something that someone else had created. I never played a piece that I hadn't been told to learn by my teacher. In all my life I have never once bought a record to listen to and in all my youth I never read a book for pleasure. But I am trying very hard to read now. I have read perhaps 20 books in all my life.

I was emotionally scarred by being made to perform. All the time it was "Look what Jeremy can do". I used to feel like a performing penguin. But I feared that one day there would come a time when I would be being "found out". I could do almost anything on demand, but I was only using 40 per cent of myself, the other 60 per cent was underused. The 40 per cent grew to compensate for something that was missing, something that I could creatively enjoy. It was a defence mechanism to hide from that fear of being found out as being less than average. It had a compulsive element. It's only in this last four years that I'm beginning to see things more truthfully.'

Some of the other less happy young people, also in the Target group, had tried very hard to live up to the characteristics of the image they were given. Like

Jeremy, the problem had usually begun early in their lives, and they had learned (as do all children) to adapt to their circumstances. But adaptation which is appropriate at one time of life can be harmful and inappropriate later. For instance, a child who is outstandingly brilliant at primary school may be showered with approval and praise from adults, classmates too looking on in admiration. What an attractive, satisfying role in life it seems to be – being gifted. But then the child moves on, perhaps to a selective school, and discovers with shock that he is no longer the best at everything. What sometimes follows is a lowering of self-respect. If you had been labelled 'gifted" and staked your all on that image, but now find you are no better than all the others, where does that leave you? Who are you? That was a question that Jeremy would probably ask himself for the rest of his life.

If a child decides (usually unconsciously) to cling to that first outstanding role of being the most brilliant, there are two major ways to avoid the risk of slipping off the pinnacle. If you have the ability you can work extremely hard to stay at the top. Alternatively, you can avoid testing situations as much as possible so you don't run the risk of failing and showing your true ungifted colours. This involves keeping a set of excuses to hand to explain poor performance in tests which are unavoidable. The most common excuse I heard for not doing well was to make a show of disdain for the work required – 'Of course I didn't do well because I chose not to work' – implying that it was beneath them. Unfortunately, that ploy often has the side-effect of stunting the very ability to study, and in addition, the downward spiral of excuses and general failure produces a state of dissatisfaction if not depression in pupils who know in their hearts that they are not fulfilling their potential. So they can end up in the worst possible position – second best – further alienated by nagging from confused parents and teachers, who do not understand what is happening. It is not negative nagging the children need, but morale boosting, a restoration of their sense of worth of feeling valued for themselves, whatever their performance.

Gail Pattison was a Career Gifted. Within minutes of our meeting and talking without a break (for several hours), she had told me how nobody could understand the depth of her philosophy, and how uncomfortable she felt with her life among students with lesser brain-power. Her barrage of words struck me as the combination of a hook to hold my attention and a defence against hurt. She seemed desperate to be different.

As a very small child in an uncomplicated loving family, Gail had enthusiastically adopted the image of 'the gifted child who finds it difficult to live in a mediocre world'. At the time, it seemed to suit everyone; her parents were very proud of her. Then, to protect herself from losing this glory, she had carefully avoided any real test of her abilities by demonstrating contempt for the educational system. It was beneath her, she said, to revise for school exams and had therefore done badly. As an unqualified school-leaver, she then found herself doing unskilled work where the hours were long and hard for very little reward. It did not fit in with her self-image. So, she had put in some effort at study and scraped together enough qualifications to take a teacher training course at a small not too demanding college. She was a student there when she told me: 'When this college said I could have a place, I didn't bother about it very much, occasionally remembered I was taking the exams, got them and came here.' It might have been emotionally too difficult for her to spar with her intellectual equals at a university. As part of her daily performance as a brilliant philosopher, Gail produced what she described as her 'deep unanswerable questions', with which she taunted her teachers. But I found that trying to follow her non-stop, undisciplined flow of words was rather like chasing a zig-zagging rabbit which was trying to throw me, the pursuer, off the scent.

Gail Pattison (Highly gifted, aged 21, at college):

> 'It's difficult for people like me with a very high intelligence, because we think we know so much and are influenced by bigger things. I say a lot of things that other people would never say, and do things that other people wouldn't do. I live how other people wouldn't live. I've got a lot of thoughts that other people can't possible begin to understand because they've probably never thought that hard before. It's unfortunate, but they just don't know what I'm going on about. Last week, I thought about truth – nothing's real because what you see one day may be seen the next day as totally different. So reality is always real, but it changes and it's a different reality. When I say things like that, they say, "Yes ... I think I'll go and have a cup of coffee".'

> I can't help myself crying if I'm depressed. It's a natural reaction. But I can't stop it. I can cry and cry and really get myself into a state, and then I stop and sort it out; then the depression will just go. I'm never going to be happy until I've got what I want, which is a very small farmhouse with a farmer. That's all I want, with a four-poster bed to make love in. I want to make my four-poster bed and carve it and make my patchwork quilt, and build the house too, stone by stone.'

Update 2001: Gail graduated from college with a good but not first-class degree. But 27 years later, she was still playing her habitual role: 'I didn't do any work for it. I could have got a first but I didn't realise how easy it was until I'd done it.' She had tried for a year to find a teaching job, but somehow didn't make it past the interview for a number of reasons which she explained, such as not knowing how to interview, couldn't drive, it was an inside appointment. She had married straight out of college and found herself supporting them both as well as doing the housework in the evenings. Now, she adores her two daughters aged three and five, one of whom is like her, 'different' and a potential genius. They give her, she said, 'freedom' to think and be herself. She works as a waitress in a small restaurant, but hopes to take up counselling for which she has acquired a diploma. 'If only', she said 'I could live to my full potential for just one day.'

There seemed to be far more reason for Stephen Kaye to become a Career Gifted. Life had already put many rocks in the path of this sad teenager, who had reacted by withdrawing into his own world – at some cost to his happiness. He attributed his emotional problems and constant tiredness entirely to his undoubted giftedness. His mother was keen on the conventional stereotype and apparently unaware of the possible reasons for her son's distress:

> 'It's probably what you find a lot with gifted children isn't it? They just don't mix. Stephen's too academic, a bit like an absent-minded professor; just so oblivious of human beings all around him.'

Stephen presented a brave face. His mother had gone to live with another man; his father was given to listening to classical music in his own room for hours, often even eating alone there. Stephen never once spoke of him spontaneously, and though they shared the same house, the father hardly seemed to exist. Added to that, his younger brother seemed to have reacted in a very different way to his parent's problems as an apparently carefree extrovert who filled the house with many noisy friends, although there seemed to be some desperation about that too as it was way above the level of most teenagers' interactions.

Measured as one of the brightest boys in the whole study, way over the top of any scale, Stephen's greatest gift was mathematics. Although his junior school had accelerated him just for that subject, which he had found a great relief, his present comprehensive school sometimes sent him for lessons with older boys, but he stayed with his own age-group. He was not in a happy position, with little support from home, school or companions. He needed the emotional security and steady reassurance that he was valued for himself.

Stephen Kaye (Highly gifted, aged 14, at school):

> 'However bad I think I am, I'm one of the top scorers in most tests in every subject. The teachers don't tell me I'm doing well because it's obvious, and the others only get jealous. It used to hurt me, but it doesn't any more because I've developed a hard skin, and now it's just annoying. I wouldn't lower my marks on purpose to please them; it would be silly. My study habits are not studying. I normally remember things as they're coming through in the lesson, but my memory's not as good as it used to be. Lessons have to hold my attention more and I can't really remember what I felt like a few years ago, though I remember things that have happened to me in the past very well. I don't read around because, in general I won't be tested on it, so what's the point?

Probably because I'm an introvert, I don't like going out. I've never read a newspaper, and I'm quite happy to do nothing without being bored. When I'm with other people I immediately find things that I don't like about them. I know I'm very sensitive; I get annoyed quite easily and irritated and upset. I often feel with other people when people get at them, sort of cringe in sympathy. I just don't trust anyone any more because of the number of times people have tricked me just as a practical joke, and it depresses me. The way people react to me is very stupid; they don't understand me and think I'm weird or mental: sometimes it's on purpose, even if I say something really simple, because that's what they're expecting to do with somebody more intelligent than them. All my viewpoints seem to be different from everybody else in my year. I seem to be the only person who isn't a racist, or bopping along to the latest pop album.

I've realised that I don't have to try to stand in with the crowd because it doesn't really matter. I never seem to get the time to rest: I don't know why, because it's what I'd like to do most.'

Update 2001: Stephen took 4 A-levels at 17 and achieved two As and two Bs. He went on to study physics and got a first, then did nothing for a year except 'socialising', followed by a computer training course. He is now Senior Analyst Programmer with a large firm. He suffers, he told me three times, from inertia; doesn't see any need to change his occupation and has no particular ambition. He lived at home until the age of 30, paying his way, until his father suggested firmly that he get his own home. Now he's renting a small house and, he says, is likely to stay because of that inertia. He's had a girlfriend, another programmer, for five years but hasn't got round to getting married or having kids. (Perhaps they both suffer from inertia.) Like his dad, he's keen on music, but makes his own alone on a multi-tape deck. At 32, he is pleased with his progress and likes what he does. He is happy, goes out for a drink with friends, though he feels he was 'a late-starter on the social skills front'.

Career gifted families

There were several whole families in the sample who could also be described as Career Gifted. Charles Hadley's mother warned me that she was 'loquacious': I was in that house for five hours – fixed like a fly by a couple of spiders. Both she and her son provided exhaustively detailed considerations in response to the simplest of questions, using words as complicated as they could muster. Charles was noticeably dependent on being recognised as gifted for his sense of self and dignity, and was finding some difficulties with friendships at university where he had met many who were his intellectual match. His mother used the classic stereotype of gifted in describing how difficult it was for him: 'Before he went to university, he very frequently used to say how he felt different from other people and that they were mainly stupid. He is always on about PBs – personal bests – so he tries to beat himself – runs himself into the ground.'

Update 2001: Charles' world, at 36, had settled and his ambition was severely dampened. He was working for a big airline as a system analyst, having graduated from Cambridge with a modest degree. He said wistfully: 'When you are younger you think you can conquer the world.' Instead, he had opted for a steady secure job where he had been for 15 years. He could have earned a lot more elsewhere, he said, but enjoyed what he was doing. He had been living with his girlfriend for 11 years and they hadn't thought about marriage: 'Maybe she has but we haven't talked about it.' His earlier almost desperate need to impress had been replaced by warm friendliness. But he still saw his extremely high intelligence as a problem: 'Too high an intelligence', he suggested, 'is no good for career progress. People with middling to high intelligence do best.'

It was hard for highly gifted Richard Neville when he went to school and found that the other children there did not give him the same devoted attention as his parents, which was, as his mother pointed out, 'regardless of anybody else'. She did recognise, though, that his behaviour could appear to be selfish:

'He had always been encouraged to talk to grown-ups and ask questions, and he will go on and on and on till he's got to the bottom of it. I could see why teachers might want to let off steam about that arrogant kid who thought that he could run the lesson, and that this wasn't going to be good for personal relationships all round. But if a child is top amongst fairly competitive children then he's going to provoke jealousy, which is why the junior school class ganged up on him. So that he wouldn't always be top, we then sent him to a high-powered school for the extra stimulation. But even when he was 16 his chemistry teacher said, "God, he drives me mad sometimes!"'

Sometimes the child was able to reject the gifted role which parents had placed on them. Though she had little education herself, Mrs Jacobs had been a powerful force behind her gentle son, Vincent, guiding, cajoling and verbally battering his teachers:

'I made an appointment to see the junior head master, who I couldn't stand at all, to get him to put Vincent up a year. When we'd finished, he said "I've never had a parent speak to me like you've spoken before!" I said "Well, I don't frankly care." He put Vincent up.'

She had devoted her life to her only son. Every photograph in the house was of him, and since he'd been a toddler he'd been allocated two rooms, one as a study and one as a bedroom. Even at the age of four, he was having four outside-school lessons a week, and when I first met him at aged six, it had increased to seven subjects – chess, swimming, elocution, French, Hebrew, etc. – one every day. The stereotype of the problem gifted child dominated his mother's thinking, even to the extent that she wouldn't have any more children, as this one was so demanding – 'All my friends, they were very amazed!' Even ten years later she was still complaining about his poor sleep and his insatiable curiosity.

Vincent, however, seemed to me not only decidedly uncurious, but I had heard more interesting views on life from much less able youngsters. He had taken a very 'laid back', sanguine approach to his mother's view of him, seeing it as her opinion rather than his obligation. He had a fine sense of self which was clearly not dependent on his capacity for learning, so that, unlike other young people under the similar pressure, he neither felt the need to make excuses for avoiding testing situations nor to strive frantically for success. He was working steadily at his own very high level, with plenty of friends and a good social life. He did appreciate, though, his mother's faith in him and they understood and loved each other well.

Update 2001: Vincent at 31 is making steady progress up the career ladder aiming at being a hospital consultant in paediatrics, and currently holding a teaching fellowship.

Lopsided gifts

All children can have problems if their abilities develop unevenly. But when it happens to the gifted the results for both child and parents can be much more extreme and difficult to cope with. There are two ways this unbalanced development happens to the gifted. Firstly, their intellectual ability can sometimes far outstrip their emotional or physical development. The resulting and disturbing lack of harmony can cause a child to retreat into babyishness, more than others of the same age, especially at bedtimes. Normal emotional distress, such as from normal childhood anxieties, is not easily dismissed by reason (in either children or adults), so that however powerful the child's intellect it is not useful as a means of coping. It is like simply telling a child there is no bogeyman hiding in the darkness; he knows in his heart that there is. Additionally, a small highly perceptive child may pick up information which other children might miss, and which he or she is not yet mature enough to deal with. This causes stress which needs help to be resolved.

The second reason for imbalance is that the child is not gifted all-round but in a specifically limited way. This is how it was for Laura Grunberger (Gifted, aged 16, at school) who had an outstanding facility for languages. Her mother told me that Laura had a vocabulary of 200 words by the age of 12 months. This gift, though, had to be shelved for the time being, to allow her life to be balanced, happy and normal, except for her voracious reading – a book a day. Her mother is the best person to explain why.

'You remember that when you first saw Laura when she was seven, she was speaking fluent Hebrew, so you suggested Greek lessons. Well, I rang the Greek Orthodox Church, and they recommended someone who teaches the children of mixed marriages, and she used to teach Laura with her own children. Laura was doing fantastically at Greek, she was adoring it and the teacher was most impressed. Then the children at school found out that she was learning Greek and they teased her so unmercifully she wouldn't go any more, and she stopped. It was such a shame.

In the junior school, she was completely shutting off. What she used to do, was to go off in a corner on her own and read, because she really was quite bored with the whole system. She read her way through the whole library of her own classroom and three other classrooms as well. She'd still read and read to the exclusion of all else if we'd let her. Now, she'll take a shopping bag to the library for 12 or 14 books at a time. If there wasn't a library, we couldn't keep her in books; her room is filled with them, and she reads almost anything that she can get hold of.'

There were several youths in this sample who were unquestionably brilliant in their field of science, but otherwise socially immature, uncultured, unthinking and inarticulate. Their lopsided development had resulted in less happy outcomes than Laura's. The following two provide excellent examples.

For Michael Grayling (Gifted, aged 20, studying science at university) it was only science that he was capable of taking to gifted level. He was a slight, extremely shy fellow, who looked about 14. His mother said – 'He hasn't brought one person to this house since we moved here 14 months ago. He stays alone in his room.' Although he had scraped through the necessary school English lessons, his ability to string sentences together was decidedly limited and I found it hard going to elicit a response to my questions. Nor did his solitude appear to have been spent thinking about things. Very often, when I asked him what he thought about this and that, where most young people had decided opinions Michael said that he'd never given the matter any consideration before. In the first study, his intelligence scores had been wildly different on the two kinds of tests. The non-verbal pattern test of logical thinking had identified him as well within the top one per cent of the population, but the IQ test which includes the use of language had found him just above average. The intervening ten years had demonstrated the accuracy of those earlier measurements.

In John Whitcombe's case, it was neither him nor his whole family, but his father who had taken on the role of Career Gifted, and was strongly into the image for himself and, through him, his son. He provided me with a great variety of excuses as to why he had not done well at school himself and why he was working as a shop manager; and was living somewhat vicariously through his son's singular brilliance. The headmaster of John's primary school told me how he had been regularly button-holed by this extremely verbal man, whose great love was poetry, he said, though he had a strangely stilted manner of speech. By a quirk of fate, though, his son did not share his father's verbosity; his strength was entirely numerical, to the extent that he knew his great difficulty in expressing himself in words.

John Whitcombe's father:

> 'There are brilliant members of the family on both sides. I was gifted myself. John was like blotting paper as a child. I was alerted to his potential giftedness when he told me one day at four years old, 'I don't sleep, I dream', and he possibly slept only four hours a night. So I had him tested. With the confirmation, I fed him books and taught him `body language'. When he was little, he'd told me that his mother didn't talk to him, and I was furious. He was accepted for Millfield (an expensive private school), with a scholarship, but I wouldn't let him go, as his accent and the divorce would have handicapped him. I've remarried you see, but I kept the kids, as John needed my brain.

> He was sent to the comprehensive school a year early. But things were bad then . . . the divorce, it wasn't good for him and he had to settle back with his age group. He lives and breathes maths; saved up and bought himself a computer, and used to crack the codes of the computer games for fun. When he got on to advanced levels at school, that's when he really woke up and got all A grades. His handwriting is atrocious – looks like a child's. But he's left handed. Spelling is damn good – he'd be cross with himself if it wasn't perfect.

> He's gifted, but I told him not to boast, just to get on with it. Now that he's at Cambridge, he is able to stand on his own feet amongst his peers, a crowd of bright students. He has made friends and loves his work. His tutor thinks he'll get a first. He may have to go to America when he qualifies.'

John Whitcombe (Gifted, aged 19, at university studying mathematics):

> 'At school, I used to be very shy but very conceited. I thought I was better than everyone else – at everything really – but I was actually only top in maths. I think the problem of getting on with people was due to my ability, because I was more intelligent than them. They didn't trust me. I felt they were all suspicious of me. It wasn't my whole problem, but it made me feel isolated. Now I've got to know people better, started actually caring about people more, I usually go round to visit someone else every day after I've stopped working. But I could quite happily work all hours God sends, and still not have enough time to work all I wanted to.'

The effects of disadvantage

Whereas some children may be pushed into the role of gifted child, others, because of individual or social disadvantage, may not show signs of their very high potential, and so are easily overlooked as gifted. Of the many kinds of disadvantage which can hamper children, even within my relatively small sample I found physical, emotional, cultural and economical problems which had clearly inhibited the growth of some of the children's exceptional potential. There is a difference between those who do not show their gifts because of psychological reasons, such as lack of motivation or social pressures, and those who cannot because of poor nervous functioning. Obviously, it is important to know the cause if the child is to be helped appropriately.

Individual handicaps can be, for example, poor verbal ability due to mild deafness, or developmental delay in fine motor skills which affects handwriting and many school activities. Emotionally, children who are crippled with shyness, so that they never answer questions in class or strive towards the goals the teacher sets, are also handicapped in their learning. The disability may be social, such as for children of non-majority cultures, who have to adapt both to home life and school, and whose self-expression may be considerably better in the home language than in English. This also applies to inner city children, who may have limited school English but excellent 'street language', or are maybe part of a culture which is dead-set against school and all it stands for. It is not unreasonable for parents or teachers to see a child who has difficulty in following simple directions, controlling the impulse to talk, concentrating on work, or completing tasks on time as being far from gifted. The problem for teachers is too often a basic lack of information, and the answer is in getting to know the child completely as a person, especially being in close communication with parents.

Physical disadvantage

Gifted minds trapped in bodies which will not obey instructions from the brain make children appear to be stupid. Neurological damage can be genetic, or can happen during a difficult birth, leaving babies with spastic handicaps, perhaps even without speech. Until recently, children with severe physical disability were often treated as though they were also mentally retarded. But with advances in technology, such as word processors workable by feet or head movements, it has become possible to see that physical damage does not imply intellectual damage. Separating the two has meant that children imprisoned by their handicapped bodies are gradually being released from a lifetime of torment.

A less dramatic problem coming more and more to notice, is a child with difficulties in learning to read and write, as in dyslexia. Naturally it confuses and sometimes irritates teachers when they can see that a child is very bright, though not producing the expected level of work. Both Thomas Edison and Leonardo da Vinci had literacy difficulties which today would be called dyslexia.

It was noticeable the first time I saw Scott Kendall at six years old, that he had a problem with pronouncing words clearly, and that was still true ten years later. His reading standard was also well below where it should have been, and he was sent to the remedial class. His parents had accepted the school's authority that nothing more need be done, and not taken action themselves, even though they felt uneasy. In the Follow-up, Scott at nearly 16 was about to visit a psychologist for the first time for help on this matter. The effects of his problems with words, and the extremely long delay in treating his problem properly, had been educationally disastrous for this very bright boy.

Scott Kendall (Gifted, aged 15, at school):

> 'Sometimes I can spell a word right then the next time I'll spell it wrong, but it looks right to me. Sometimes I can write essays and not get any spelling mistakes, and then sometimes I write one and nearly every word will be a spelling mistake. It comes and goes. Sometimes when I'm reading, one letter out of a word will make me stop: just that one letter will stand out, and I don't know what's wrong. I can see the word, but I just can't say it.'

Update 2001: Scott's reading at 32 is much the same, though his speech is almost normal. His A-level results were poor; no allowance was made for him. He reads words from the middle outwards, then gets stuck on certain letter shapes. But his high IQ is useful. At secondary school, for example, when he was set a play to read he would memorise the whole thing so he wouldn't get found out, until one awful day he was asked to read something that he hadn't memorised. His dyslexia has caused him to lose confidence in simple actions which others could do easily. He firmly believes his vocabulary to be large and he understands everything. When he reads he has to do it three times, once to get the words, again to get the understanding and a third time to get the full feeling. This does not make him inclined to curl up with a book. But he doesn't feel it has affected him in his daily life. Scott has held a responsible engineering job for ten years, with 20 people under him. He is engaged with two children and they will be married in a couple of years. He is wonderfully happy.

No-one in this sample suffered from severe nerve damage, but even among these apparently normal individuals, some had difficult physical handicaps to overcome. The families' medical practitioners were often not only less than helpful, but several mothers told me they had been called 'neurotic' because of their concern, resulting in delays of a year or more before vitally important remedial action was taken. Only the determined mothers really won through to get help, and there must be many more whose bright children were simply treated as of poor potential when they were in fact gifted. One mother was sharp – 'He was ill at six months, so we took him to the hospital, and they said it was allergy because he was very intelligent – to which I replied that intelligence is not an illness.'

Philip Bessant had been tall for his age when I first met him at nine-years-old. But he had real problems of muscle control. At 19 he was still tall, with a delicate little-boy face. His movements were obviously clumsy and he had a constant tremor which caused him problems in making us coffee. Interestingly, he was studying chemistry, a subject needing fine motor control. Listening to him was not easy, because he had difficulty controlling his mouth sufficiently for clear speech. He told me that he talked too fast for people to follow, though I suspected that they become impatient waiting for the end of the sentence. He also had problems with social relationships, but it was difficult to distinguish how much was due to his own personality and how much to the hardships he had endured with his muscle clumsiness. Fortunately, he had a mother who had not waited for medical authority to find help for him.

Philip Bessant's mother:

'Our doctor had seen Philip going upstairs at about the age of three, first one foot then together, like a younger child, and I hadn't realised that was unusual. Without any concern, the doctor turned to me and said – "You know you've got an ESN (educationally subnormal) child there". I said "He may be anything but he's not ESN", because I could remember all sorts of things he'd done. Once, when he was under two, he and his grandmother weren't speaking because he said a certain car was a Minor and she said it was a Mini! He's probably ten years ahead of what he would have been if I hadn't seen to it all.

They really didn't know what to make of Philip when they assessed him at the Children's Hospital. Coordination-wise he was way down, clumsy, but he'd got great concentration, and was intellectually gifted. I found a remedial teacher without qualifications, who did a lot for him, and I taught him how to write myself. His worst difficulty was with reading, because he couldn't coordinate his eyes along the line, so he was reading encyclopaedias with short lines for the information, but he couldn't manage stories. The school was very kind, but they couldn't understand it.

We chose a private, more disciplined, traditional sort of education, because we felt that with his problems, he would flounder in a free-expression kind of school. He needed to know where he was. At first the less able boys teased him, but when he was put with boys of similar ability, he seemed to cope pretty well. His writing was appalling, so the teachers didn't upset him. Most of them used to just tick it, and say, "Yes, that was fine". The English master gave him real confidence when he said, "I don't care how you write; I love your ideas." He did so well with him.

He's helped himself enormously, because he's got determination and discipline; if he has to do something, he gets it done. If he had an assignment in the holidays, he'd do it the first two or three days. Of course he can't be sporty, but he doesn't seem to mind that at all. He can hold his own in company, but when the time comes for him to look at jobs, I worry that he's not had enough practice in dealing with people.'

Philip Bessant (Highly gifted, aged 20, at university studying science):

'I do care that people think well of me, but there are certain things that I wouldn't be prepared to change. The reason why I disregard people is that I've had to build up some sort of shield for myself over the years, and it's made me very much more of an individual. I do worry, which I suppose could be partly anger, and I tend to find my hands perspiring a lot. I'm also a slightly withdrawn person: I don't enjoy parties, or pubs or restaurants nearly as much as most people in my age group. On that count, principally, I consider myself to be different. But no matter how unlucky I am – I am very lucky compared to lots and lots of other people.'

Update 2001: It is horrific to think of what might have happened to Philip if the doctor's diagnosis had been acted on: possibly the sort of school that Charles Hadley's brother went to (immediately below) – and the appropriate self-concept and aims along with it. In fact, after his PhD in chemistry, Philip is working at an extremely high level, researching new automatic catalysis and better computer chips to deal with it. At 35, he lives alone in the house he is paying for himself.

Several mothers told me similar stories of being ridiculed by their GP over their concern for their children. Mrs Hadley was the mother of both gifted Charles and another son with learning difficulties. She'd taken him time and time again to her GP, who told her she was creating a fuss about nothing. A year had gone by, and nothing had been done for the boy. Eventually, desperate, she told me:

'I went to the hospital without any appointment, sat down in the waiting room and said "I'm not going to go until somebody looks at this child, because I know something's wrong". The staff were rolling their eyes a little bit, thinking "Stupid woman. That child, she should just take him home." He was on phenobarbs; they'd put him on phenobarbs.

I was lucky. The consultant saw him and ran every test in the book on him. He found an epileptic problem, and his fits were soon under control. He couldn't speak, and they sent him to a school for very handicapped children, you know the locked doors and the special bus variety. But there was always a twinkle in his eye, and his comprehension was very great indeed, it was just that he wouldn't respond. You know when you're talking to someone, you know they understand in their eyes.

Nothing was working, so I resorted to bribery. Smarties at that point were the passport to everything for him, and we decided to do one final testing simply to please me, when he was about six. Before we went I'd bought a very big tube of Smarties – bought about a dozen, tipped them all into a washing-up bowl, and said "Do test" because he refused to do anything, you see, "and then when you come home you can have those". So he did the test.

With the result he was transferred into ordinary school, into the annexe. Having not been able to read and write, and just to speak – within oh, a six-month period he was reading and he was writing. He's now just left school, he's on a work opportunity thing, can make anything with his hands, can read and write as well as anybody else, is obsessed with maps, cartography. Of all my children, if I was going to put them on a scale of worry, that one would be at the bottom of it, because he is a very self-contained person, he loves music and it doesn't matter what he ends up doing, he'll be all right – he's comfortable with himself, is what I mean.'

Cultural disadvantage

Not all the gifted young people in the Follow-up had developed steadily over the years. Some who had been well advanced and full of promise ten years ago were working at only average level. Could this have been the 'early ripe – early rot', the 'burn-out' syndrome? But there was no evidence of that, rather that for some children progress had been impeded by the circumstances of their lives. There was never an instance of parents who did not love their children or want to help them, but there were parents who were simply not able to provide what their gifted children needed. It was at that point that the school could and should have stepped in, but even when it offered help the family culture was not always open to it and so the child missed out.

Poorly cultured families are often intellectually deprived, most noticeably in the lack of breadth and flexibility in their use of language. A broad language base is vital for building knowledge, yet for some families it seems almost a time-wasting luxury to 'play' with it. For them, communication is more practical, sufficient for everyday needs and feelings, but not enough for problem-solving and creativity. Where intellectual stimulation of the young child has a low priority, his or her curiosity is less likely to be appreciated, and spending time reading books and thinking can be unacceptable behaviour.

It was in this context of being pulled between the two cultures of home and school that nature had played a mean trick on Ann Youngman (Gifted, aged 17, at school). She had been born to parents who loved her, but were so different in ability and temperament from her that she was like a gifted changeling left in the crib of a poor peasant couple. As communication had became more difficult, she developed some resentment towards them, simply because they could not give her the support and direction she so desperately needed. She knew it, and did not like herself for those feelings, but she was slowly beginning to give in to her home culture. Her grammar school teachers had tried to help this obviously highly able girl, but failed. She told me bluntly:

> 'I don't like school, so I don't always bother turning up. I used to disrupt the classes and I was banned from most of them in the end, but I've stayed on because I knew there would be no job otherwise. I've never revised for exams, I don't know how to, so everything I know is from what I remember during class. I just go and do them, and I always do well. I've never had any problems with them.'

His home culture had also moulded Duncan Sutherland's low opinion of academic work, though on his intelligence test score he was clearly gifted. His sailor father's accent was so Liverpool-thick that I had to ask him to repeat almost everything he said several times. To cover up his gentler side, Duncan had adopted a tough macho image, and was aiming to serve in the Navy and hoped to fight a war. But as he came to trust me, he told me more about himself.

Duncan Sutherland (Gifted, aged 18, leaving school):

> 'A lot of the teachers had the sense of humour of a rat; they hated me. Simple as that. If someone comes at me, then there would be absolutely no backing down, I wouldn't give one inch. I like going shooting with air rifles. Anything that moves. The television's on most of the day, and I spent most of my time being bored. But if it's something that really needs thinking out, I'll spend about 90 per cent of my time thinking about it. Could be about a week – 90 per cent of a week just thinking! When I was little, I used to remember a story by putting it into a poem or a rhyme. Even though I'll say it with scorn, poetry is the most powerful way of saying something. The last few generations of poets have been really good. You can get more from some of the short poems than you can from a book.'

Update 2001: Although he continued with martial arts for many years, Duncan settled for the civil service, and has worked devotedly for the Inland Revenue for 16 years. He failed most of his exams because he didn't care enough. But at 34, married with two sons, he believes that the work he enjoys and the security it offers will last.

Liverpool toughness had also touched Nicholas Fawcett, though he was well aware that his great physical and mental gifts were under-used and that at 21, with already more than 15 dead-end jobs behind him, he was in desperate need of help. His disturbed home life had also affected his siblings. Poor self-confidence and lack of sophistication had kept his ambitions very low. His reading was minimal, his television watching desultory, and his only activities were running hard and girlfriends.

Nicholas Fawcett (Highly gifted, aged 21, out of work):

'I always felt that I was one of the school's better pupils, because I was usually in the top set without trying. I never studied, but I knew I could do better than most of them. It might have been the old ego thing, you know. If I turned into a studier and a boffin, all my friends might look at me and think ... maybe it was just a pride thing. It wasn't that I hated school, I just couldn't be bothered. I'd come home and try to revise, but after half an hour I was bored. I'd be sat there looking through a book, and I'd prefer to be outside, physically active. Even so, I still was one of the best in the class, but I thought ... well sod it ... s o I left school.

I know I'm intelligent and capable of doing anything really, with the right guidance. People recognise I'm intelligent. If I'm interested I can concentrate for hours, like when I go training at the gym, I give it all I've got. I didn't leave all those jobs because I didn't like them, I left, because of the person who's above me – I felt that I could have done a better job than what he was doing. It just didn't seem right. I want to be somewhere at the top. I'm starting to realise that the next job that I get, I'll make a career of it.'

Update in 2001: Nicholas continued going from job to job, and mostly remained bored. I heard that he joined the Foreign Legion, but cannot find him to ask.

Poverty

Even in a modern industrial society there are pockets of poverty, and where wealth enables, poverty disables. In a cold damp home, where the quality of food is poor, illness and low spirits are frequent visitors. All children in those situations suffer, but it is an added detriment to a child of high potential that intellectual stimulation is often inadequate too.

For Dennis Foster, it was the physical aspects of his poverty that were pulling him down. He seemed to have glazed over his exceptional gifts and was working at just above average level. Poignantly, his goal at eight-years-old had been the most ambitious of all the sample – to be a tycoon.

The Foster's house was part of a poor terrace by the railway shunting yard – on the wrong side of the tracks. All the windows were permanently covered with grey rags, admitting just a little daylight. Inside, the floors were bare of any covering, as were most of the walls. Loose strips of wallpaper hung down, and the few ceiling tiles that remained up hung at angles by their corners. Old pink rayon curtains were pinned on the walls here and there, maybe to cover damp patches, and a few family photographs decorated a shelf. Everything was clean, but furniture and possessions were torn and decrepit, and the old display cabinet was quite empty. The room was extremely damp and cold, though they had done their best to warm it, and even during the few hours I was there, I began to feel drawn and listless. In fact, after the visit, I repaired to a warm department store in the city to drink several cups of hot coffee and thaw out. Dennis suffered constantly from bronchitis, sinusitis and every other kind of respiratory problem. At 19, he was thin, pale and a little stooped, with a particularly sweet face.

His parents were courteous and articulate; disregarding their very poor surroundings, they made me feel very welcome. Mr Foster was too ill to work, but assured me with pride that he was 'not a scrounger' living off the state, and so was refusing most of the social benefits to which he was entitled. They did what they could for their son with what they had, encouraging him, loving him, and were concerned for his future, but felt they had little support from his school, which had clearly not recognised his great potential. His father said: 'They didn't seem to be bothered about his continuous absences, or his level of work. They seemed to think that because he was keeping up it was alright.' Dennis was a highly intelligent boy, who was doing so well at school that his teachers saw no cause for concern, and yet he was decidely underachieving in terms of his own potential. He could have done so much better.

Dennis Foster (Highly gifted, aged 17, at college):

> 'I was always terribly ill. All winter I'd get constant streaming colds and flu, and I'm still not a healthy boy so I missed a lot of school. And I sleep a lot. At school, I used to turn in the odd decent piece of work to prove that I could, but there was nothing else they could have done with me; it wasn't their fault. School and life were completely separate things to me, though I think my parents feel they've failed me too. I can't remember actually having revised. The exams I did well in were those you can get by on a very small amount of information, things I'd heard in class when I was there. Still, I did get average marks for the class.

> I write poems in spurts. Every few months, I write about twenty or so, then come back six months later, rip half of them up and write a few more. I never show them to anybody except a few of my friends; certainly not school. I did send some to Faber and Faber (poetry publishers) and they sent a letter back saying they might publish some in an anthology, but I haven't heard from them for over a year, so I've given up hope on that. I can't think of anything I want to do, so mostly I lie in bed and think. Then I get really angry because I'm bored.

> I hardly ever express anger as I'm terrified of violence of any kind, and generally there's nothing worth getting angry about at a personal level. But I'm depressed a

lot of the time, about once a week, and sometimes lonely as well. But I only get really badly depressed about three or four times a year, when I get to an almost suicidal "end it all" hopeless state. I don't want sympathy off anyone. Deep down, I've still got the feeling that it's going to pass, but it's still not very pleasant. Sometimes I get sucked away in my depression and think, "Is there no end to it and no hope for the future?" Not on this planet at any rate.

I'd much rather have been a middle-class kid, Edwardian or 1950s. I've got a stereotyped idea from old black and white films of lots of rosy-cheeked postwar boom kids running round brand new schools and housing projects, all well fed when rationing was over, and it was always sunny and really nice and cosy and middle class.'

Update 2001: Alas, Dennis' study at the College of Art only lasted a term when he realised that 'I would never be good enough to cut it in the commercial art world'. The next few years were spent 'attending free festivals, hitchhiking around the country and taking part rather half-heartedly in various animal rights demonstrations and related activities. During this period I became acquainted with alcohol and the recreational use of "soft" drugs. Tried writing poetry with no success and formed a short-lived band which only played three gigs.' Since then he has held several government administrative clerical posts until starting a business studies course, which again did not last. But then he began to study again part-time, and spurred by success, gave up his Civil Service career (again) and spent three happy years obtaining a degree in English Literature and Linguistic Science, though he felt that his 2:1 was less than his capacity. He was accepted by a university to study for a higher degree, but couldn't secure any funding. So he has gone back to being an administrator for a government department and is active in his trade union. However, he has suffered from anxiety/stress for several years and is now on sick leave.

Dennis married a library manager in September 1989 and they live in a quiet suburb with their two dogs. He reads a lot of history and biography, cooks, drinks nice wine and smokes more than he should. 'I still write the odd bit of prose, but no more poetry. I think Paul McCartney's latest foray into the literary world is enough of a lesson, should anyone need it, that poetry is damn hard to do well, no matter how much of a way with words you might have in other areas of life.'

Mistaken identity

The labelling of children as gifted may be mistaken. Yet it is bound to happen at times, for example when a child is so heavily tutored that he appears to be advanced for his age, or because of his parents' hopes. Such a mistake means that a child is put into the terrible situation of trying to follow a prescribed but impossible role. The awful choices he then faces are about the best way to fail expectations while keeping up a modicum of self-respect. There are two major options. He can either fail after striving ferociously to succeed or fail after presenting his excuses. Several young people in this sample had indeed become worker ants, each one's energy pitted against heavy odds for modest results. In one girl's case it had begun to interfere with her health, so that her worried parents had placed an upper limit to her voluntary study of four post-homework hours a night.

Of the original Target group, those whose parents had joined the National Association for Gifted Children, a few (5.4 per cent) were not found to be measurable as gifted in any way, nor did there seem to be any mitigating reasons for their average-level performances on either the tests or at school. The conclusion could not be avoided that in spite of their labels they were not in fact gifted. Their parents had joined the Association for a variety of reasons. Mostly, because they thought it would do something for their child, but also because the child was difficult to live with and seemed bright, so they had assumed (hoped) the cause of the behaviour problems would be giftedness. After all, it did fit in with the stereotype.

Bernard Harrison was certainly of above average ability (aged 20, at a Technical College), but he had accepted his mother's belief that he was more intelligent than almost everybody else he knew. She referred to him quite simply as a 'genius'. Bernard did his best to comply. But what his mother called his 'incredible promise' was dealt a blow when he had failed the entrance examination for the selective secondary school. His mother told me:

> 'At the junior school, the teachers treated him as though he was backward. A private education was the only way out. I started going out to work to pay the fees and continued for nine years. I just couldn't stop thanking them because he was so happy there.'

Bernard's modest school-leaving results were well below what he could have got in terms of his measured ability, and far short of gifted achievement. He knew in his heart that it was the best he could do. His mother was very proud of him, claiming that the reason for his non-gifted performance was that he had never revised, though she did not say why. Although superficially his self-esteem appeared to have benefited from being put on a pedestal, he said he had never had many friends because he was an 'intellectual snob'. He had a very subdued emotional life, living at home, was rather overweight and at 20 years old often fell asleep while watching television.

Update 2001: Everything worked out well in the end. Bernard took a year between the two years of his 'sandwich' computer course to work for a big electronics company, and returned to them on qualification. Then into a bank to help set up their branch network, rising to their website design team, eventually to become team leader. Now he is a web systems architect. He is 34, very happily married with two little girls aged four and two. Interestingly, the older one has difficulties with word and number recognition. He said he had the same problem but it was not given credence, whereas she is receiving help before it is too late. He said that he had worked hard for his examinations but had not done well because he 'hasn't got a good memory for facts'. Maybe with some early help his life would have been much less stressful.

Anne Charlton's was a very different story. At the age of six, when I'd measured her IQ, she was well above average but not in the gifted range. Even this was possibly a high estimation, because she came from a very bookish and verbal family, which helped to increase her score. There were no excuses about her poor examination performance from Anne herself, however – her mother provided them all. She could not accept that her belief in her daughter's giftedness could possibly have been a mistake, which had put Anne on the receiving end of constant conflicting messages from home and school. At home she was seen as brilliant yet failing her mother, but at school she was seen as of average ability with a troublesome mother. Her resulting confusion about her sense of self possibly had a negative influence on her growing up, for it was far from smooth.

Mrs Charlton had joined the National Association for Gifted Children believing her daughter to be in a state of considerable intellectual frustration at the junior school. Her failure to get into the selective secondary school, her mother believed, was due to the poor teaching and attitude of the junior school, as well as to Anne's flu the week before. If they had had enough money to send Anne to the small private school nearby, it might well have been better for her, but as it was she had opted out of all educational endeavour. Her only thoughts were of boys, clothes, pop music, and the disco every night of the week. It took a lot of persuasion for Anne to talk to me, and she soon lost interest in considering her answers, though she didn't quit. She seemed to me to be physically lively but academically asleep. Since her mother was hardworking and competent, it was becoming very difficult for them both to live together.

Anne Charlton's mother:

> 'Sometimes, if it weren't for the fact that Anne looks like me, I'd thing somebody had swapped babies at the hospital.
>
> As a small child, she always followed me about with her books. She wanted to know all the time. She was one of these children that wouldn't rest. It didn't matter if you were in the middle of washing up, or something, she had to know immediately. Or she'd be reading and she couldn't manage one word, so you had to stop everything. She drove me mad.

She's got in with a rough lot, but you can't pick their friends. She'd have been better off at a single sex school, because there's no distraction from the boys. Oh, she's quite an attractive girl you see. It's a case of, "It's my life and I'll do what I want with it". At 16 you can't expect much else. She wants a wage packet. She wants the money. I've told her, "I'll keep you as long as you want to study, even if you're 22 like the other one was. But if you're going to throw it all up, then you'll have to fend for yourself." Obviously I'm not going to throw her out. I don't know what she'll do.'

Update 2001: Anne is 32; she left home soon after I'd last seen her which eased the pressure considerably. She worked in a nursing home as a care assistant and paid her own way, which she said had made her grow up. She had two children with her lover while taking in 'boring' factory outwork, gluing shoes by day and working at the nursing home in the evenings. Her lover's mental problems finally drove her to leave him. She has been with her present fiancé for eight years, living happily in separate homes, because as she said, 'Once bitten twice shy'. They run a motor repair service. Anne does all the paperwork including the accounts and he does the mechanics. She gets on beautifully with her parents who live nearby. Her mother is immensely proud of Anne's gifted daughter.

CHAPTER 4

Growing up gifted

Of Queen Elizabeth I at 16, her tutor said: 'Her mind has no womanly weakness, her perseverance is equal to that of a man and her memory keeps what it quickly picks up . . . at first sight (she) understands everything ... in a way to strike you with astonishment'.
Alison Fairturn, *Lady Jane Grey and the House of Suffolk.*

All young people are likely to face challenges in growing up, but it is somewhat different for the gifted simply because they are exceptional. Although those in this sample were neither seen to be more or less stable nor morally different, at times they did have to find subtle personal skills to see them through some specific and delicate situations – such as always coming top. The great majority delighted in their high-level abilities of all kinds, but some (like their parents) blamed their gifts for emotional problems, particularly those which had resulted in poor relationships. In 2001, Alison at the age of 37, told me that being labelled gifted had been 'the bane of her life' and she wished she'd never been given that tag. Growing up, she felt she could never live up to the expectations it brought, so she had always felt a failure. Now, she said that her greatest successes were her children: they did not know about the label and loved her for herself.

At ease with others

Learning to be at ease with others starts with the first touches and cooing between mother and baby, then develops with increasing contact with the world outside the family. On the whole, human beings stay true to themselves over great lengths of time, continuing the individual habits and style they began in infancy. At first, children copy the behaviour and attitudes of adults, but as they move into the teenage years they also blend in the outlooks of their contemporaries. Adolescence, though, is a time of sharpening and defining personal ways of dealing with such matters as work commitment, sexual life and above all the need for a sense of self in one's family and in society. The greater the feeling each individual gains of being in control of his or her own life at that time, then the more effective he or she will be as an adult. For those with no close friends to learn with and from, the gap in development can be hard to close later.

Every family has a style of operating in which each member learns to negotiate for themselves. But the normal constraints may be strained to breaking during the turbulence of adolescence. The reasons are not so much because the young person's moods are either different from before, or from an adult's, but because they have greater intensity and can alter rapidly, swinging to greater extremes of dejection or exhilaration. Adolescents may experience a wider range of short-lived states, more like flashes of emotion, and unlike the adults they will become, they are less protected from the effects of these strong experiences by memories of past ones. In the words of one teenager in this study, 'One time, when we went up in the hills walking, the air was fresh, and I just suddenly felt that it was a really beautiful place. That's all.'

For most of the young people in this Follow-up study, their growing up was smooth. I asked all of them about it, and their general opinion was that the old *sturm und drang* idea of adolescence was highly overrated. Typically, I would be told: 'It's been a lot easier than I was led to expect. At the age of 12 or 13, I thought I'd feel ... this puberty and all the rest of it ... what's it going to be like? But I've never even noticed that I was growing up.'

Ten years on, many earlier problems associated with giftedness, such as the parents' complaints of poor sleep, had vanished, probably because they were really the problems of childhood and had simply been grown out of. The intellectually gifted were not found to sleep less or more fitfully than other children, unless they were emotionally distressed, and parents had been questioned very carefully on this matter. The length of a child's sleep was directly related to age – younger children slept more.

As time went by, the Target children's parents had eased off their earlier pressure. At the beginning, a significant number of them (37 per cent) had expressed much keener ambitions for their children than the other two groups (Control–1 23 per cent, Control–2 6 per cent), and told me that they had put some pressure on their children to fulfil those ambitions (Target 30 per cent, Control–1 13 per cent, Control–2 6 per cent). Most now said they simply wanted their children to be happy whatever they did.

By 2001, when most of the sample were in their thirties, it was encouraging to hear that very few, neither parents nor children, still seemed to hold the view that being gifted was a handicap to being at ease with other people.

Relationships

Almost all the problems between the gifted young people and their parents were due to the normal reasons of growing up and breaking away. Though a higher proportion of the labelled gifted group continued to have less good relationships than the other two groups. But then, as in so many things, the gifted do tend to head for the extremes, and it was not always easy or possible for parents to provide the attention demanded of them. Their children's urgent ideas, which must be discussed the instant they burst, did not always come at convenient times. Also, when the highly intelligent get their teeth into an argument, especially with parents who are just as lively, there can be a particularly stimulating intellectual confrontation!

Sharp highly articulate words sparked, for example, between Justine Williams, a mature gifted 17-year-old, and her mother. To Justine, life was a vivid palette of deep issues of morality, justice and beliefs, which she desperately wanted to talk about at home, especially since her teachers showed little interest in listening to her. The girls' grammar school she attended was more concerned with getting pupils high marks in examinations. Stalemate; neither Justine nor her equally outspoken mother felt able to communicate. It was fortunate that I interviewed each one separately. Each understood the other and the situation, her mother saying, 'I appreciate Justine – I don't know whether she does likewise – but I think she finds me very difficult.' On her part, Justine asked me to funnel some of what she wanted to say to her mother because – 'She can't accept that I'm growing up'. I suggested they talk it over directly. Justine's words encapsulate the everyday frictions of growing up gifted; she is wise, understanding, curious, eager to learn, and frustrated.

Justine Williams (Gifted, aged 17, at school):

'As I get older, I get on less and less with my mum. I want her to be perfect and she's not because she's a human being. But as she runs my life to a certain extent, it's important to me what she thinks and does. She doesn't know how I think; she's been too busy. She comes home from work and reads the paper, and I resent that she doesn't ask me what I've been doing. If I say something thoughtful, she's so sarcastic – "Stop trying to be profound". If I tell her that she's been bad about bringing me up in some ways, then she calls me arrogant. I don't know where I'm up to really.'

Update 2001: Through Justine, now 33, and her mother live nearby, they still prefer to keep at a distance via the telephone. Her mother is extremely hard-working and high-powered as governor of a male prison, yet Justine as deputy manager of an electrical shop, considers they are very alike, each happy as 'big fish in a small pond'. Justine remembered that she had 'loathed school', and because she 'didn't do a stitch of work' her achievements fell far below her potential. She had no intention of going on to higher education. Yet she is learning all the time, and very happy, explaining that there was a life for a gifted person outside university:

'Some of my family seemed to think that my life was over when I didn't go to university. I've always been stretched in my work, almost to breaking point. I've had a colourful and varied existence. Its really been quite hard work.'

Feeling different

Throughout this study, those in the top one per cent of the IQ range had said they felt different at a high level of statistical significance. For most, the gifts which made them different were a source of pride and pleasure, just like any other blessings of nature. One boy said – 'To be quite honest, I'm quite proud of the fact that I'm brighter than most others. If you've got good looks you might as well enhance them, so if you've got intelligence you might as well let everybody know it.'

Parents said these feelings of difference had started very early in their children's lives and often felt that the bad aspects of these feelings were due to other people, typically – 'Alison was always top at school, so some parents counted their child's order in the class as though she wasn't there. She used to keep her hand down in the class, things like that, so she wouldn't stand out.' But those less happy aspects attributed to feeling different usually diminished with growing up and the increased freedom to choose companions more like themselves. One happy student said – 'When I was about 15 or 16, it was the academic side that made me different, but now I'm a student with other students. OK, there are some of us who are at polytechnics and some at universities, but we're all going for degrees so I don't come into contact with many people that make me feel noticeably different any more.'

For just a few of the gifted young people, though, life had compounded those early feelings by adding some extra problems, and the combination became even harder to cope with. The way they handled their problems seemed to be not so much dependent on reasoning power, but on the actual circumstances, such as how early in their lives the trouble had started and how long it had taken to erupt.

Andy Spurgeon handled his many differences with skill and sophistication. He was an intriguing youth of 17, with pale grey eyes, long dark lashes and a mouth which curled easily into direct friendly smiles. After both my long visits to his home he treated me to wonderful performances of classical music on the piano. He was dark skinned and thickset like his African father, though his brother and sisters were slender, pale and white blond. Andy and his mother were good for each other, and she had given Andy enormous emotional and intellectual support, as well as an exceptionally long rein of freedom, to be himself. The family had come up in the world: three generations out of the workhouse, through the grammar school, to his mother's Master's degree. And now there was Andy, brilliant in everything he touched.

Andy Spurgeon's mother:

'From about the age of three he was very difficult, tremendously aggressive; it was dreadful if he was crossed. The child psychologist said he was just very frustrated. But he was living in a household that was offering him books, music, theatre visits, stately homes, swimming, tennis, people who talk and are lively. I think that when our marriage was going downhill I'd been trying to keep him quiet, avoiding the issues which were more between his father and him really than with me. He certainly got better once we were divorced.

Now he's just argumentative, mostly about what he considers to be my very untidy and illogical mind. He has no false modesty at all about his. I end up shouting at him that he's overbearing, arrogant etc, etc. But I don't think it's as much to do with adolescence as to do with him and me. He said that he was living in a nest full of feminists and he would report us to the social services for maltreating him – not valuing his male personality!

It's not only the supreme self-confidence and his brightness that makes him different; it's also the fact that he's black, half-caste as it were. And also in the past year, he's decided that he's gay – and his is a very macho, male school. When he first told me, my reaction was "Don't be so silly, of course you're not". But it's OK now; it isn't a problem to me any more, though I am anxious about the AIDS thing and the exploitation of young people. You'd think it would be quite a load, with his colour and his sexual preference, but in fact, he hasn't presented me with that problem at all. He's perfectly happy.'

Andrew Spurgeon (Highly gifted, aged 17, at school):

'I'm not very black, so sometimes people don't notice, and their reaction is a surprise because I'm coloured when everyone else in my family is white: it is a bit weird. It's not a nice position to be in, half-caste; I get the whole range of insults that go with it. But I'm difficult to hurt emotionally. Going through life as somebody who's very good at things but coloured, I've had to build up defences. When I get to school, I've learned to isolate myself mentally from anything that might hurt me; I just sort of close the door. My music is a useful emotional outlet, and it's also something that I gain emotion from, so it's an input as well. I can please myself quite easily playing the piano, and if I'm angry it'll help me to control myself and bring myself round. But my home is free. If I bring somebody back to this house, a friend or a lover, they always say, "Isn't your house amazing, there's so few restrictions?" Even at a younger age where there are often more restrictions, my mother was very loose and let us do what we thought was best. We are all fairly bright and intelligent and trustworthy, and she trusts us. There's a really nice atmosphere here.

What gives me pleasure? You ready for this? Have you got any more tape? Playing the piano, playing the recorder, playing the clarinet, talking to people, reading books, learning new things, experiencing new things, playing tennis, playing badminton, playing squash, playing rugby when I get the chance, playing table tennis. Going to new places in my personal and everyday life, seeing new sides to people that you didn't know were there before. Everything, everything's something new, there's nothing that I dislike. Watching the leaves on the trees shake about, watching a fly trying to get to the bottom of a flower – just literally anything, because everything has it's own relevance, so it's always interesting. Even if I was to go to jail for doing something that I didn't do, that wouldn't be bad, because it would be another experience, another new thing to be interested in, new people around you, and such things.

I used to find it very frustrating that there wasn't anyone at school that I could really sit down and talk to, but now I accept it. I refuse to conform, and I don't like to get drawn into conversations where the limit is sex. Homosexual people are just ordinary people in my experience. Being good at a lot of things seems to be disturbing to other people, and though I might play down "me" in the introduction into a new group, making myself less obtrusive than I really am, really I'm strongly independent. I'm the type of person that's going to do something, somewhere along the line. Hopefully quite a few things. Yeah, I think I will.'

Update 2001: Now 34, Andy is extremely ill with AIDS, but was able to marry the man he loves under Dutch law. (see p. 154.)

Like Sleeping Beauty, Caroline Hardman must have had two fairy godmothers in attendance at her birth. The good one had given her an intelligence over the top of any scale and great beauty – a girl with potential to do almost anything in the world – but the bad fairy had given her a heavy burden. In her sensitive early years her sense of worth had been dealt a terrible blow when she was effectively orphaned for years by her mother's constant hospitalisation, and was cared for by whoever was to hand while her father worked.

Being intellectually gifted, she had been advanced a year at her highly academic school, but the one thing the good fairy had forgotten to give her was the advanced maturity to cope. In addition, travelling to and from school was exhausting – out before eight, and sometimes not home until nearly six in the evening. At the first stirrings of adolescence, her latent distress had erupted to shatter the family's peace. She left school at 16, having acquired 9 good O-levels, for a briefly free but disastrous life.

Update 2001: Now 36, Caroline has followed a zigzag path to a stable and very happy life. She has three healthy children, though one died at six-days-old, and a loving partner. Both are teachers in the special needs area. She is still angry about her schooldays. Of her acceleration she said: 'It was a waste of time'. A particular problem was that she was tiny, and in a class of girls at least a year older it seemed to diminish her even further. And, she never should have gone to an all girls' school, she said. It was petty and boring. She would have been much better off at a comprehensive school. What is more, it made the boys too special. If they had been there in the class all the time, she said, she would have felt less attracted to them! She demanded to leave.

Caroline became aware that her mother (who is no longer communicating with the family) was an alcoholic, which was possibly the reason for her frequent and long absences. She realised that she had become accustomed to stepping over her mother's comatose body in the kitchen and had taken it as normal. It was only as she grew up that she realised that other people's mothers didn't behave in that way.

Her first employment was as a laboratory technician in a building chemicals firm. After a year, she was instructed to train the new boys. They were then sent on courses, which were not offered to the girls, after which they were promoted while she seethed at the bottom of the pile. She left. She pulled herself together and started a BEd degree at a teacher training college. For the first time she greatly enjoyed learning. But she never studied alone, always in the company of friends. Although she well knew that they were much below her own level of ability, she seemed frightened by the latent power of her mind, and they helped her to rein it in. Were she to release that power, she told me, she feared losing their friendship, and perhaps worse, having to face up to it herself. But she had learned much from her wild life, and the signs were promising – 'I know I'm on my last chance', she said, 'if I blow it this time, then that's it.'

After qualification she had several teaching posts, and now in charge of mathematics at a secondary school for special needs children. Maybe when the youngest starts nursery school she will take a master's degree: 'Hopefully', she said, 'before I'm forty'.

Parental break up
Ten years from the start of the study, several of the young people had lost contact with one of their parents through divorce, the boys appearing to take it more to heart than the girls. Two highly gifted boys had been suddenly deserted by their fathers at educationally crucial times. In both cases, the boys' exceptional abilities appeared to have played an important role in that breakup, certainly in the timing and possibly in their happening at all. Although intellectually both had survived that deep blow, it had seriously affected their potential for relationships with girls.

Richard Neville's father was a college lecturer who had struggled hard to reach his position, and who must have been keenly aware of the importance of examination hurdles. Yet he chose to walk out of the house when his gifted son, Richard, was 15 – just two weeks before his son's first vital set of examinations. Indeed, Richard's mother suggested – 'One of the chief reasons for him leaving was perhaps having a son who's bigger, stronger, cleverer and generally more socially effective.'

It was all true. Richard was over six foot tall, handsome, thoroughly charming, and over the top of the intelligence scale. He burned to do better and better, always working to his limits. In spite of being two years advanced at school, and with the handicap of almost three hours travel a day, he had achieved all A grades in his leaving exams. Although this did not allow him enough time for friends, it seemed not to bother him. He had even found a girlfriend at Cambridge University was very like him, even to the extent of cutting down the Christmas vacation break to a few days so that they could put more work in. He seemed to have the ability, not only to adapt to his environment, but also to get other people to adapt to him.

Richard Neville (Highly gifted, aged 19, at university):

> 'I hadn't known he was going to go. He just said, "It's like this, son, I'm going away". It wasn't particularly good timing, but he wasn't going to ruin my chances – they were more important. I retreated into my room, into my revision, and it probably made me do more work, which kept my mind off it. But it was quite difficult for me. All of a sudden I had to do a lot of things myself, and I'd been presented with all the responsibility of my Mum. It was his job and he ought to have done it. For a very long time I was quite angry. But it's a bit like water under the bridge now, but my sister still rather misses her Dad. It had a knock-on effect of personal relationships for a while afterwards, particularly with girls. I became rather sceptical and cynical about the whole idea of marriage and relationships, thinking, "What's the point, they don't work anyway." But I've grown out of that now.'

Tom Dewhurst chose a different approach of using his powerful mind when his father walked out. He thought up a strongly rationalised psychological defence system. His mother described father and son as alike, 'determined and strong-willed', and explained:

> 'Tom had been really close with his father, and he was only 12. My ex-husband phoned and said he wasn't coming home, and we've never seen him since. I don't suppose I'll ever quite know what really happened.'

At 21, Tom was studying medicine and I could see him as a rather gruff practitioner well loved by his patients, but who wouldn't allow himself much overt sympathy for their worries – a 'pull-yourself-together' man. He said:

'When my father disappeared, I became a bit detached and couldn't concentrate properly at school, but I got used to it. The family, me, my Mum and sister, we became closer and that helped. I suppose I'm a bit of an insensitive person, things don't normally hurt me, though I have to admit it really did at the beginning. Now, when I look at my life, I don't suppose it's made that much of a difference to me. Just that I feel that I ought to be really sure before I marry someone.'

The effect of Adrian Lambert's parents' stormy marriage and eventual break up had been to severely cripple his high-level creative and intellectual potential. He was a big cheery fellow who now joked about his ignorance and inability to study. He lived in a tiny terraced house with his fiancée, who had also dropped out of higher education. According to his father, Adrian's disturbed behaviour was the culmination of three generations of unhappiness. However, it seemed to me to be more immediate, for in the first part of the study his mother had blamed her attempted suicides entirely on him, her only child, and told me that she had 'detested him' when he was little. Adrian had managed to exert some control over his three addictions of gambling, drink, and cigarettes. He had been through the worst, was neither flippant nor depressed, but working and aiming to improve himself. What he needed, and what he had organised for himself, was a healing mental peace in his own home.

Adrian Lambert's father was a quiet, sad man, who thought that because his son was intellectually gifted this also implied a magnanimity beyond a gifted emotional intelligence, rather more like sainthood:

'I'd rather expected Adrian's intelligence to help him understand his mother and her problems, and he did try until he went bitter and he still can't forgive. To an outsider, the life my wife led was pretty unforgivable; I have the most enormous amount of tolerance which bordered on stupidity. The basic cause was that there were so many men in her life, mainly because, poor girl, she was too damn good-looking. Adrian couldn't take it. It was he who eventually said "You can't stay here and have that fellow; it's got to be Dad or him." "Well, you can't tell me what to do," she said, and off she went. He has been desperately unhappy. I know that fathers and sons don't often get to talk to each other very deeply, but I have managed to talk to him on a couple of occasions.

He used to have so much imagination as a child, I gloried his humour and his wit. When he was very young he had read and written a lot, but in his first weeks at the secondary school a most dreadful English teacher made him look a fool in front of the class, and he never wrote another thing; stopped absolutely, even reading for pleasure. I was appalled, because his imagination still shone through.'

Adrian Lambert (Highly gifted, aged 22, a milkman) was indeed bitter. His unhappy home life had affected his life progress badly, though not, fortunately, his relations with the opposite sex:

'My dad cherished the way that I dealt with English; he loved the stories I wrote. I still love writing, though, and I do when I can get round to it. The teachers at my comprehensive were very supportive and encouraging. It was much more than I deserved. They tried everything, even ringing me up at home. I really let them down and I still feel guilty. I was amazed to pass my A-levels, because I hadn't turned up for weeks, so I decided to take them again to improve my marks. I went to see the head master, but he treated it as a joke. I didn't blame him. That knocked me back, so that's how I ended up on the dole for the best part of a year. It was terrible and I reckoned that anything was going to be better than that.

Then I enrolled at the Polytechnic, and left after a year by mutual consent. I'd picked the wrong course, History of Art, Design and Film, and I couldn't draw a stick man, or name ten painters or one designer – I'd never even heard of Turner then. The only thing I knew was ten films that John Wayne had starred in, and what Captain Kirk did in Star Trek. I met my fiancée, there, so it did do something for me, but not education-wise. Then I decided to earn some money. I was very very lucky to get this job as a milkman. I'd go into the Job Centre and they say, "You've had no experience", and also I was competing with cheap 16-year-olds. Fortunately, I knew someone who recommended me – and it's not temporary. I've enjoyed the job a lot. It's a physical release. I can run everywhere, and the faster I go, the faster I'm done. I've got the afternoons free to myself, though I'm zonked out by eight – I'm up at half-three in the morning. I must have a good memory, because this is only my sixth week and I can remember most of the people in over 400 houses.

My mother had left on several occasions when I was a child. I suppose I stored it inside, which is what gave me all the trouble and guilt later on. I used to get very intense bouts of anger. It ended up once in my taking a few tablets, tranquillisers and booze, or I'd zoom off on my motorbike as fast as it could go. I'd used to get a terrible feeling of desperation. I always thought of myself as very mature at school and yet I acted very immaturely, but I have eventually developed through the trauma, learned through experience. It's a pretty weird situation: I'm driving a milk-float round and worrying about what time I'm going to get finished today. How can that be so structured and so definite on this planet, and yet on all the other millions of planets, you've got a simple little amoeba floating around in space?' It's such an imbalance. I get so wound up with all the thoughts and theories. It's very much easier to get back to today, driving the milk-float around, and trying to get finished by 12 o'clock. So I concentrate on that.'

Academic ostriches

Only eight gifted young people said their giftedness was a terrible barrier to making friends, and all but one were male. For them, their loneliness could be grim, and by the time of the Follow-up the outlook for its ultimate relief seemed bleak. Like ostriches some had buried their heads in their studies, thinking that the rest of the world could no longer see them.

Sigmund Freud was the first to describe the workings of psychological defences. These protective emotional strategies are formed when people are up against an anxiety-provoking situation and unconsciously avoid seeing it. Some may simply 'repress' the cause of the anxiety, appearing to be quite unaware of any criticism. The politician's thick skin, for example, is well known. Very commonly, others 'project' the problem on to someone or something else, as in – 'It's not my fault I was late, the traffic was very heavy'. Some bend over backwards to deny any difficulty, like the girl with the limp who wears red stockings, or in Shakespeare's words from Macbeth, 'Methinks the lady doth protest too much.' Although defences are cover-ups for insecurity, they can be decidedly aggressive in the sense of 'I'll hit you before you hit me'. This aggressive defensiveness of course often provokes an angry return which can send the spiral of relationships spinning downward. The attacked person's sharp reaction simply convincing the self-defender of the need to keep the barriers up.

The favoured psychological defence of the labelled intellectually gifted child is to hide behind a facade of scholarship, so opting out of the normal cut and thrust of learning how to make relationships. Some experts and parents even encourage this attitude when it fits in with their idea of the emotional problems of a gifted child. Yet the gifted need relationships as much as any one else. Nor do these carefully devised defences serve to put an end to unhappiness, because the defender is retreating further into isolation even more disabled by the presented psychological wall itself from reaching out for reassurance, and maybe angrily preventing anyone from offering it. Children in hiding from the threatening world, mingling less and less with others, develop poor feelings towards themselves and others.

For some of the highly gifted young people in the sample, the psychological defence systems they had built against anxiety had started in early childhood. Over the years, their withdrawal behind those barriers had gone to extremes, cutting them off from emotional contact with others. Six young men had gone so far as to almost sever any intimacy with other people – a process which they all blamed on being gifted.

Ian Nicholson's mother said, 'You'll find him interesting', and indeed I did, and also gentle, thoughtful and sincere. At 20, Ian was a slim, tall, slightly stooping young man in an old-fashioned dark suit with a plain tie, studying classics at Oxford. He had started to set up his strong psychological barriers against the rest of the world as a very small child. His difficulties in communication, he explained, were because he was so intellectual, but he also was aware that he chose to hide behind long words and concepts which his listener might not be able to understand. His brilliance, he thought, was a barrier to any friendship, and although he claimed not to care much that he did not have a single friend in the world, to me he seemed distressed while he was talking about it. To protect his sensitivity, his life had become all work and no play. He had started early and the habit of hiding had become deeply ingrained; he didn't know what else to do. He sought succour and support for his ego in his religious beliefs, though primarily the excellence of his academic work was his way to feel worthwhile, and he knew it.

Ian Nicholson's mother:

> 'He's never had a friend, and can go for days without speaking to another soul. His teachers used to say he was a loner. He never even told them when his father died – nobody in the class knew. I've known other boys make friendly advances to him, but he doesn't respond. He's had parents who've loved him, who've been interested in him, and been prepared to spend as much time with him as he wanted. Now he's staying on to do his D.Phil. Another three years at Oxford's just putting off the evil day of coming into the world and having to fight for a living. If he can get a job as a don, I believe that he'll stay in those quarters for the rest of his life.'

Ian Nicholson (Highly gifted, aged 21, studying for a D.Phil.):

> 'The only school activity I was involved in was the Christian Union. I also worked in the school library for six months as an assistant. I had a really good time then.
>
> Even at Oxford I'm conscious that I'm brighter than most people. I also work harder than most, and I tend to keep to myself more than most people. But I work incredibly slowly. At times, it's taken me three hours to read an article, and I wonder where all the time's gone. Having Christian beliefs, where the majority of people do not, and because those matter to me very much, I'm in a radically different set-up from most of the people about me. I was very disappointed that I was not accepted to become a clergyman. My bishop said that although there was the positive factor that I can relate to people and be sensitive to their feelings, the negative factor was that I am very independent and tend to work on my own, and wasn't in a position to cope with a group of people. Obviously, though, I had thought that I could. I suppose that having taken on an enormous workload has meant that I've not had much time to see people. The trouble is that the things which I value seem to be in decline – classics, the Church, railways, the countryside. But then, perhaps I've always had work as a let-out.'

The nasty crop of acne which Martin Glaskin was enduring cannot have helped him in his unkind world. He said he did have a friend once. His intense reserve was off-putting to anyone who would have liked to get to know him, and he lacked some basic social graces – such as offering me coffee during the three hours of the freezing morning we were together in his university room. Like him, his father was an academic scientist, and of firm views, especially about the roles of males and females. His mother was a housewife, who always waited for her husband to speak first.

Sadly, each of Martin's academic successes, such as his first-class degree, turned to dust in his hands, so that he needed to aim higher and higher. At 21 and in the first year of his PhD, he was worried that he wouldn't be able to keep up the pace. He found it impossible to envisage the future and could not even muster some youthful optimism about anything. Even at school he had worked very comprehensively, reading around the subject, writing notes to summarise it over and over again until he understood the concept behind it – 'I never wanted to know my teachers, I just wanted the instruction'. Now, he had moved even further into isolated study, cutting down on his feelings towards other people and sliding closer and closer towards the stereotype of the backroom scientist; he pored down microscopes by day and returned alone to his room at night. Yet he never took any steps to alleviate the pain of his sorrow; I felt he was almost wallowing in it, sinking himself deeper and deeper into the mire.

Martin Glaskin (Highly gifted, aged 21, studying for a PhD):

'I feel alienated; maybe I'm too sensitive. If people like me I don't understand why, though I don't usually notice other people's reactions, and anyway, nobody's ever told me anything about myself. I give up very easily in social life, probably because I never concentrate on what people say. I just watch them talking. I know I'm selfish and negative, and a bit of a snob as well. I may be 21, but I don't think I've grown up yet. Getting depressed holds you back. I spend my time on my own really. It's getting worse, and I don't always know that I'm going to come out of it. It's especially bad because I'm not in an environment where I'm forced into contact with people, so I have to go out to find them. If I'm thrown together with somebody I get on with them alright – like I might go out to the pub, unless of course I'm feeling depressed. It's quite a while since I felt angry. I feel disillusioned, and I've given up wondering why I'm here, because it just depresses me.'

Just good friends

In direct contrast to those sad youths, the majority of the gifted young people enjoyed perfectly normal relationships with friends of both sexes. Few, however were as gifted as Jeremy Kramer, who seemed to have perfect control over his emotional relationships, as indeed he had over his study habits (see p. 87 'Competition and IQ'). He was tall, very attractive, and it was neither for lack of opportunity nor know-how that he had made the decision that until his studies were more advanced, he would avoid emotional ties with girls.

Jeremy Kramer (Highly gifted, aged 20, studying medicine):

> 'I made a conscious decision to give up girlfriends – I suppose I've never met one who is quite irresistible. I get all I need in life from my friends of both sexes – apart from physical pleasure of course. But it's almost as if the only extra thing that a girlfriend could give me is sex. My best friend is a girl, and if I'm worried about something I'll go to her and we'll sort it out – she knows me down to a tee. Any real girlfriend's going to get pissed off about the time I spend with her; and it only creates problems. If I do mess around with girls, I make it plain where I stand, and it's worked well for me.'

No matter how splendid their gifts, good relationships seemed to be more a matter of outlook; as Danny Smith put it, 'I've got some life in me, always something to talk about, and being a lively sort of person, I get along with a lot of people'. What did make a significant difference to relationships was respect for others. This made it difficult for those who had accepted that their giftedness made them somehow superior. One highly gifted youth studying physics at Cambridge, spoke for many like himself who had friends of many kinds and abilities, providing an excellent guideline for all of us in our relationships: 'I give my full attention to people, and take them seriously most of the time. But I've got academic integrity, not putting up with second best. I want friends who will stand up to me in conversation, pick me up when I'm being stupid, not put up with idiocy; friends that are stimulating.'

However, some of the gifted did find it irritating that they could not always keep to the high standard of discourse they would have preferred – 'Small talk is very boring, and sometimes I don't make the effort'. It could become tiresome, for example, in a mixed-ability school, where being friendly and open to one's classmates was intellectually not satisfying enough, at least not all the time, and so some tried to find older friends. Even at her selective girls' grammar school, mature and lively Justine Williams complained – 'I definitely don't like the company of people younger than myself, not even if it's by just a year, because they're going through something that I've already done – been there, done that. At school, in all the corners, everybody, morning after morning, tells you about what they did the night before and sometimes it gets so boring. It's hard to look interested. Hopefully, university might be different.'

Love hit the gifted just as it hits other young people, when powerful intellect and well-honed reasoning seems to simply fly out of the window. As one bright teenage girl said – 'I thought I'd never fall in love because I couldn't imagine anybody ever liking me, and if they did they'd have bad taste, so I wouldn't like them. But I've overcome that. Also I just think he's gorgeous. I'm not sure. I think I love him. This is the best yet.'

Exceptional sensitivity

It is not easy to live with exceptional sensitivity. As with a heightened sense of smell, although the scent of the peach may be more exquisite, so too are the feet of the diner at the next table in the restaurant. Many gifted children seem to have a high level of sensitivity so not only do they take modest criticism terribly to heart, but they can also react to a wider range of subtleties. This sensitivity can be encouraged and used creatively or it can be blunted by ridicule. For some less robust personalities, like Ian Nicholson (above) it can turn them inwards from a world which they find too painful to bear. Yet paradoxically, it may be exactly that high level of innate sensitivity which enables giftedness to develop.

In the first part of the study, even for the youngest children the higher their IQs the more they said they could see life through another's eyes, to empathise. For children, then, a high IQ suggested a high sensitivity to others. In the Follow-up, though, the results still held but were less distinct. Yet, however high their IQ, that empathy was not available to everyone. Many had not developed enough maturity and self-awareness to feel at ease with other people and still remain themselves, so they changed with the prevailing wind. It is also a feature of being a teenager, which most of the Follow-up sample were at that time. Their sensitivity was, for some, a difficult part of themselves to cope with, as one 17-year-old explained: 'Sometimes I will play the part people expect. I don't really know the real me, I'm not sure.'

Being highly sensitive and passionate, even at 17 David Baker needed to give vent to his emotions. His parents told me he would 'rant' for over two hours – in his articulate way – and cry openly when things upset him, such as a play on television. His prickly, uncomfortable relationship with his fellows in his mixed-ability school was not eased by his 'arty' style of dressing, for which he was sneered at with some derogative terms for homosexual – and the barbs stung sharply.

David Baker (Gifted, aged 17, at school) was keen to tell me how it was for him. Unlike those boys who had repressed their feelings and denied any anger, David was very explicit. We talked till nearly two in the morning:

> 'I think more deeply than a lot of people, and I feel more than they do. It's as though I had a depth of feeling that has to be used up, though I wish it wasn't like that, because I feel too strongly over people and things. Sometimes I cry or feel incredibly happy over just one thing.
>
> I'm far too sensitive because it results in depression which is generally self-pity and a waste of time. Loneliness brings on really deep depression almost immediately, even though there might be people all around me, and even while I'm talking to somebody. Half the time when I'm sad I'm enjoying it. It's genuine, though. I lose the will to do things, but I don't get depressed out of laziness, it's

just that it doesn't seem to matter any longer. Perhaps it's a desperate need for a rest, because when I'm ready, somebody can say something that pulls me right out of it and makes me very, very happy, and very active and animated quickly.

Anger is easier; it generally comes out. At home I can shout and scream, and cry and cry, and really just get it out. Then I'm tired. But life carries on, and I've not changed anything. I just say, "Sorry" and I'm annoyed with myself for getting angry.

Sometimes I can feel with people, even without speaking to them, thinking how they think. But I feel very, very different to the people who sit in the school common-room. I'll come in after I've had so much fun looking at things, sketching and talking, and they'll say, "Oh, he must be drunk". Well, that's partly our school, and it's because I'm so much happier than them, and they don't seem to be able to visualise happiness through thinking and friendship very much. While people grow up it's essential that sexes are mixed. Essential. It's so sickening listening to the attitudes of boys who are in an all-boys environment. They're so narrow-minded. A lot of my friends are girls, and I find that a bit worrying. You question your identity as a male if you fit in with females. One of my teachers calls me 'A decadent namby-pamby boy'.

I usually laugh it off as a joke, being labelled 'queer', but it's also an insult, and because I've not fitted in sexually sometimes. I'm not prepared to get-off with girls just because it's the done thing. You should be what you are, and I do find some gay men incredibly attractive; not that I'm wildly mad about them sexually. I think they're so sweet and loving and they've got so much, though some of them are degenerate. Gay women are butch and absolutely great. But sometimes two men making love turns my stomach up and I realise it's not natural. It's not something that appeals to me. It's always a good thing if you can find love and it doesn't matter about male or female.'

The measurement of social giftedness, in the sense of being able to take another's perspective, is not easy. But in a well devised experiment it was measured with children between the ages of three and six. They were asked to think up what someone else would like as a birthday present, and given a range of toys to choose from. The intellectually gifted did in fact make the most correct choices, confirmed by the other child, which as in this study showed a high level of empathy associated with IQ. However, other studies of little gifted children have shown that although they score higher than average on the theoretical understanding of moral reasoning, as measured by tests, their playground behaviour is not necessarily in tune.

Those in this sample who said they used empathy consciously and frequently in their daily lives were most often the intellectually gifted. Suzanne Murphy (Highly gifted, aged 16, at school) was beautiful, with a pale, clear complexion and a gentle but firm demeanour. She was working to full capacity and radiated happiness, which she distributed generously to all who needed it. She used her empathy in her studying (though only for the arts subjects), as she explained in her sing-song Welsh way:

'In English, I'm very empathetic, so that when I read a really good novel I experience it as though I were there. So whatever I've read about, I've experienced. I care very much about almost everyone I meet, even people on a bus. It's very strange. I've always thought that was why I could comfort people. At school, girls came to me with their problems. Maybe it was because I had a very happy outlook, because I had a basically happy life.

In history, I'm pretty good at empathising too. You have to do that to exist in harmony with people around you. To understand someone, you've got to see things from their point of view. That's why I'm so good at history; I empathise with times past and also with the people from them. And you've got to do it then with a restricted amount of information, because you're never going to have as much information as you do about a person who's standing there.'

Like many, Suzanne also used her sensitivity and empathy to help others, telling me – 'When I'm helping someone, the quality I have is in not saying – "Well, if I were you I'd do this", its because I am them, so I'm thinking exactly the same way that they think. It's different for every person, so I'd give different advice in the same situation. That's why it always seems to work.'

This positive use of her exceptional sensitivity in the form of empathy, had also provided her with a way to make relationships and keep her serenity in a mixed-ability school.

'Everybody comes to me with their problems and I help them sort them out; in fact, I'm a bit like an agony aunt at school. I'm a believing Christian, so I try to put other people first. I try to understand things from their point of view to be able to comfort them, and if I'm truly patient I always can. Often, I can identify so closely with people who are in trouble that it really upsets me, even moves me to tears sometimes.

I work hard for things I feel strongly about. For example, a lot of my friends smoke and I won't tolerate that. I've managed to persuade my choir master to cut down from 20 to two or three a day. And if people start smoking, I'll just walk away and they know why. I do get angry at times, but then I try to look at myself and ask why I'm feeling so angry, and what can I do about it. Am I just being impatient or silly? It calms me down. When I was younger, all I could see was what was happening to me, and I used to feel – poor little me; but now I can look at how other people feel, and try to take that into consideration. If people really tried, they could get on.'

Boredom

Boredom drains energy, detracting from the ability to cope and the will to strive. Most children experience boredom at school, as most people do in everyday life. It means that for some they are just filling in time – 'In lessons, I draw, write a bit, think, and day-dream a bit'. Being bored, is though, partly a state of mind, an approach to the world which one can suffer in an experience which is exciting to another. But it can become developed in early childhood to the extent that the habit of expecting boredom stays though life and lowers achievement.

Yet the intellectually gifted can have special problems of boredom because of the speed of their learning, that is in coping with the problem of a teacher's repetition (see 'The Three Times Problem' p. 127). But this study has shown that boredom is unlikely to be a major problem, unless the youngsters have other problems, such as being unhappy because of home circumstances, or the school is too rigid to accept them for what they are. In the first survey, only six parents from the 210 families said their children were constantly bored at school, and those children spanned the ability range. Not one of the children complained of it specifically. In fact, as they were growing up the parents dropped the complaint about boredom at school, while the young people complained far more about boredom at home. One said poignantly – 'I'm often left in the house bored stiff with only my Mum and Dad for company'.

It seemed to be one of those problems of childhood which eases off with growing up, as most of the sample found – 'The further back I remember school the more boredom I remember, because I was enjoying fewer subjects then'. Though some expressed longing for their earlier simpler lives – 'When I was younger I used to be very happy sitting down with a book. Now, I haven't time to do that, so there's more potential for being bored.' But the boredom they described was well within the normal range, as many parents will attest, even for those who had it badly – 'I get bored at school, I get bored at home, and I get bored in the holidays because since we moved to the country there's nothing to do.'

In general, it was difficult to conclude that these gifted young people were more or less bored than others of their age. But far more high achievers reported the well-known feeling of 'let-down' which can come to everyone at the completion of hard work with the release of tension and the sudden vacuum of time – also well recognised as an aspect of stress in the business world. It came to many in the sample who had worked hard for a project or examinations, and it was sometimes seen in terms of boredom. One boy put it clearly: 'The harder I work, the more bored I get when I stop, if you know what I mean. Like after exams, I've worked like mad and I'll go straight down to the pub, put down a couple, and think what the hell am I going to do now? I can't seem to strike a balance between working too much, then not having enough to do and getting bored.'

That sudden vacuum which masqueraded as boredom could also come in a more extended way to those at university, particularly those who devoted so much of their young lives to getting there. Rachel Wallace explained the effects of the heavy tutoring and study which had brought her a scholarship: 'At school I was occupied, then I had my homework to do, so I didn't get a chance to be bored. Now, when I can't think of anything I want to do, I walk around Oxford for hours feeling bored. It also happens to me frequently during the holidays. That's when I tend to be lazy. But if I was forced to do something, told to "Go and do that, now!", the feeling might leave me again.'

Leadership and morality

There are two moral aspects to giftedness. Firstly, there is the morality of the society which influences which gifts are acceptable and encouraged. For example, we in the wider Western society do not support talented young thieves or encourage the kind of violence seen in boy soldiers active in some parts of the world. In the Far East, children may be honoured for communicating with the gods (or by being a god), but here we generally see this as a case for psychological treatment! Where we approve of their gifts we reward children well, particularly those who learn their lessons, do their homework, pass their examinations with high marks – and do not cause trouble by questioning too deeply.

Secondly, there are opposing and strongly held views of the personal morality of the gifted themselves. Some see them as having exceptional moral strength, along with the frightening assumption that children of exceptionally high intelligence are somehow morally superior and therefore better suited to directing others. This forms a basis of the selection of high-IQ children for leadership courses, where they are tutored in how to manage the lives of others. From earliest childhood, the gifted leader is supposed to show enthusiasm, easy communication, problem-solving skills, humour, self-control and conscientiousness, as well as very high intelligence. These courses are almost entirely in North America, as Europeans, several times bitten, are shy of the idea that selected children should be trained to lead.

Alternatively, the intellectually gifted are seen as morally more fragile than other children. I've been told a number of times and even heard people lecture on how the prisons are packed with frustrated men who were once gifted children. Yet prisoners are, of course, those who have been caught!

We certainly need morally sound leaders. We are familiar with the names of a few famous people, such as Nelson Mandela with his infinite capacity for forgiveness and Mahatma Ghandi who promoted non-violent action for reform. But there are millions of unknown wonderful people in the world who lead by example, organising medical help and famine relief, caring for people in need, working for low pay and low status for the good of others.

When I asked the whole Follow-up sample about their religious beliefs, two thirds told me that they prayed in private but often explained that their idea of God was more of a general life spirit than a 'sentient being' who listened in. Many said they did it as a good-luck device, which could do no harm. Although expressed strength in religious beliefs in these young people was not related to intelligence, whether believers or atheists, the gifted were often more intense. Those of nearer average intellectual ability were far more likely to push such questions aside as beyond them and accept, at least overtly, what they were expected to believe.

However, the ability to think and act independently of the crowd is an aspect of leadership which several of the intellectually gifted in my sample were aiming for quite purposefully. Those young people spent time in deep and critical consideration of the ideas they had been given, and they worked independently and honestly towards living by their own principles, to a greater extent than the non-gifted. In doing so, the clarity of thought they felt they had sometimes distanced them from others who did not see as they did – a problem often shared with other teenagers, though the gifted felt it was special to them.

Andrew Spurgeon (Highly gifted, aged 17, at school):

> 'The outlook of really bright people is never going to be the general view. Just by virtue of being brighter, they're operating on a different level, more interested in what's going on around them. I'm different because I think more than other boys my age, who tend to take things at face value, views which are strengthened by the establishment, and school in particular. It's important to me to be honest, and if asked, I'll always say what I think or what I feel – and quite often when not asked! But more importantly, I'm honest to myself, I know what I can do, what my limitations and my abilities are, and what I feel within myself. And if I were to suppress what I am in order to be part of the group, I wouldn't feel happy with myself.'

It is said that you can't put an old head on young shoulders, but someone must have done it for Quentine Cooke (Highly gifted, aged 14, at school). He was a round, beaming teenager, with the manner of a bank manager who knew what was best for you. However, it did not seem to me to be his advanced moral thinking which had denied him friends, but rather his general lack of tolerance. He certainly stuck to his guns, whether from moral and physical courage, or from a defensive inflexibility born of fear. Quentine explained:

> 'I often feel that I have a more mature outlook from most people my age. It's sounds a terribly high-minded attitude to take, and some people pretend not to understand me, because if they did, then I'd explode all their myths about their petty little values. Sometimes it seems that the only way that everybody agrees is when they all disagree with me.'

His mother described what would happen, and one can imagine the feelings of the other boys to whom he was moralising in his priggish manner:

'He was always morally two years ahead of any of his peers. Where they were still hitting each other for fun, Quentine had worked out that this was silly. He used to try and reason with them, but they didn't know what he was talking about. So while they were hitting him, he was busily pointing out the reasons why they shouldn't.'

Danny Smith, who was every bit as gifted, had a very different personality, lively and laughing a good deal. But though less dogmatic, he had also encountered social problems because of his principled moral outlook. As he spoke, he seemed to be trying out ideas with me, not only to see how I reacted, but how it sounded to his own ears.

Danny Smith (Gifted, aged 17, at school):

'I don't think I'm any better or any worse than other people and I don't like to blow my own trumpet, but – you're lowering my barriers of modesty here – I'm a devout humanist, and I don't think many other people are. If people would be nicer to each other, the world would be a much happier place. People have got a lot within them, but they just won't show it. I try and bring it out, you see, and that lays me open because boys like to make out that they're big, hard and tough. If you're more gentle in your feelings, you're more vulnerable. I'm quite willing to accept it, because I'm trying to show them there's a better way – you don't need to be horrible to people. But I have very few friends at school, and at times no friends at all. I'm trying to be honest with myself. That's a big thing of mine. Everybody's unique and personal, though sometimes it's very hard to see where they're coming from.'

Update 2001: Danny studied psychology at university. He said he got the idea from me.

It is impossible to say that morality and IQ are directly related. What, then, about the unarguably high positive correlation between scores on IQ tests and morality tests, such as the well known Kohlberg's Test of Moral Development? But there are many cultural assumptions built into the test. Look at this item:

A married couple are extremely poor. The wife is dying and the husband can't afford the drugs needed to save her. The underlying assumption is that because he hasn't enough money he can't get the drugs and his beloved wife will die. The child is asked whether the man should break into a pharmacy and steal what she needs.

What sort of society obliges a man to consider such drastic immoral action to save his beloved? Most Western countries have adequate social benefits providing free essential medicines and treatment. What moral convolutions do children have to perform when they live in a caring society which provides medicines as of need and they want to score a point on this test? It looks as though children with extremely high IQs know how they should answer – they know how to play the game – but, of course, they may or may not choose to abide by the rules in real life.

Indeed, neither extremely high scores on a paper-and-pencil test of morality nor a high IQ score will serve to keep an individual on the straight and narrow, although all children become somewhat better at aligning their moral reasoning and social behaviour as they grow up. In spite of my closeness with these young people, I would not be prepared to hazard a guess at which of them, of any ability, were on the way to leadership. The lessons of history show that it is something which results from the interplay of circumstances, personal experience and constitution. Poignantly, there were no differences in outlook across the sample when asked whether they thought they could help in any way to change the world. Most of these young people felt helpless.

CHAPTER 5

Inside gifted minds

The highest intellects, like the tops of mountains, are the first to catch and to reflect the dawn.
Thomas Macaulay

The major difference between the very highly intelligent and others is in the way they deal with information, usually from an early age. They are better able to take an overview of the best way for them to work – metacognition – and so can marshal their intellectual forces with greater flexibility and speed to be at their most effective. This is equally advantageous both for flying though exams at school and for business projects in adult life. But when a child's learning environment is inadequate for its development and exercise, smooth metacognition is impeded. So, children of high potential living in culturally poor circumstances which detract from their energy and positive attitudes to learning, need assistance to function at their best.

To think at one's best requires the confidence to take an overview of both the subject under consideration and of one's own mental approach. In this research, I found that those who were intellectually gifted often had an advanced degree of such awareness, so they could function nearer to their best for longer than the others in the sample. These techniques cannot be unique to the gifted; all children can become more aware of their thought processes and learning strategies to widen their thinking repertoire and know when to select and apply different procedures. Neither development nor performance can be looked at separately from the context in which they function – good performance in one context may be poor in another. – yet adaptable thinkers can operate appropriately in a wide variety of contexts.

The roots of thinking skills

Once a baby is in the world, every sense is active, though with a bias towards vision and hearing. Even in the first days of life, infants are curious and look around for what interests them, staring at some objects and events more than others. The refinement of their earliest perceptions is very rapid, and what they are learning then provides a very important foundation for their future thinking.

Even in babies, intellectual development can be thought of in terms of problem-solving skills. By a few weeks old, they begin to use their own experiences for simple problem-solving, and so must have begun to store them in memory – however fragile and unreliable. It may be that gifted infants, whose super-sensitivity intensifies their awareness, have to manage an exceptional amount of incoming information. They would then need an appropriately more complex or advanced system of mental organisation than their baby-age peers in order to reach the highest levels of thought and performance of which they are capable.

The human brain is never passive; we always try to make sense of our experiences by transforming them into simplified, coded, versions. Adults have many thousands of these short cut codes in memory, such as judging distance by using perspective cues learned from experience. The earliest coding starts with coordinating sensory impressions, such as the way a ball feels round and watching it roll. But good perceptual skills do not just happen. Improved performance requires practice, and so the best children's toys are those which provide physical characteristics to be explored, problems to be solved and the possibility of classifying things. Culturally disadvantaged children, though, find it more difficult to practice and increase the complexity of their early perceptual learning. Children from unstimulating homes where play material is scarce, have been measured as falling significantly behind others by the time they reach five years of age (Mascie-Taylor 1989).

In many if not most societies, mothers provide a baby's introduction to the prevailing culture by mediating or filtering experiences of the world. The mother's own emotions play a role in this mediation, which can significantly affect the intellectual growth of the baby. Even infants of ten weeks can recognise the difference between happiness, sadness, or anger in the mother (Collins and Gunnar 1990). Her happiness encourages the infant to explore, her sadness producing sadness or anger, whereas her distress causes the infant to withdraw.

Any condition that causes stress to infants increases their need for security, and decreases their urge to explore, and the ill-effects of anxiety-arousing experiences are cumulative. Consequently, children raised in a stable happy home are more likely to be curious and to persist with their own explorations, especially when the tasks become more complex. In a comparison study, three-and-a-half-year-olds, who had been classified as securely attached when they were babies, thought of more new ideas and participated more in nursery activities, and they also attracted more friends than the less secure children. Their teachers rated them as more curious, eager to learn, self-directed, and effective (Waters *et al.* 1979).

The strongest early indicator of a future lively mind is the ability to communicate, which is traceable from the age of three months, (Bryant 1992; Freeman 1995b). Vygotsky, the great Russian psychologist, believed that while children are learning words they are also taking in 'ready made' parcels of culture to use in thinking (Vygotsky 1990). In addition, almost all words carry emotional meanings from the situation in which they were learned. Language also influences thought by firming-up perceptions, and children with poor verbal ability can also have poor perceptual and other intellectual abilities.

Things that parents do together with their child have a far-reaching effect on the child's understanding and thinking. Games, conversation, stories, walks in the park, even arguments, positively foster the child's intellectual growth. The problem for research is how to establish which factors result in what characteristics, because the interaction works both ways. For example, a highly verbal and demanding child can affect parents' behaviour by stimulating them to offer more conversation and read more stories. On the other hand, those parents who do talk to children a lot were probably verbal people before they had a family.

Thinking style

The effects of children's experiences and the way they approach new ones can be seen in the development of their personal way of thinking – their 'cognitive style'. This can partly be seen in terms of how much they use either side of the brain, or more usefully how much 'divergent' and 'convergent' thinking they do. A convergent thinker goes by the rules, will probably reach conclusions quite logically and generally does well in scientific or mathematical activities. Divergent thinkers are more creative, coming up with new ideas and approaches, and often prefer more artistic activities. At school, convergent-minded pupils do better with straightforward question-and-answer-type tests, whereas divergent pupils prefer essays, where they can use their imaginations. Traditional teaching in schools usually overemphasises the convergent style.

But there is a danger in knowing your own style. Once mental strategies have been found useful, such as in examinations, people often find it quicker and less energy consuming to stick to well entrenched pathways of thinking. The learning habits which exams produce encourage the accumulation of information rather than thinking things through, which inhibits creative thinking. In order to accept and deal with new information and ideas, learning has to remain flexible and open. Sometimes when one familiar idea is put unexpectedly against another a moment of creative insight can occur. An everyday example is when we use tired stock responses in conversation, instead of really considering what has been said. Many people find this useful at times, because they can follow their own trains of thought while responding politely. The intellectually gifted, who are much better at following more than one idea at the same time, may be tempted to use it too much, getting into bad conversational habits which distance them from other people – possibly the root of the absent-minded professor syndrome.

The mature thinkers in this sample had a good knowledge of how to work at their best. One gifted mathematics student at university told me:

> 'The secret of my learning is that I've got to understand what I'm doing. For me, there are two approaches to work. If it's a subject that bores me, or a problem I find difficult to understand, I know I have to plough through it, referring to notes and back, just learning by heart. But if it's something I enjoy, like maths, I just sit back, look for the important points, and I can do it.'

Competent planning for learning involves choosing from different possible strategies, and perhaps even rehearsing them mentally to see how these feel for a particular task. Indeed, the highest level of planning starts out in a broad and generalised way, but has a variety of sub-plans available to be tried out. The most frequent strategy used by the successful young people in this study was to look for the principles in their work first, and then fill in the details appropriately. To do that calls for the confidence to take an authoritative overview of both the subject under consideration and of one's own mental approach. A gifted flexible learner, studying medicine, told me – 'I'm a great believer in trying to find a rule that makes things work. I can very often remember the principles first time through. I certainly avoid learning things by rote.'

Lack of discipline

Samantha Goldman (Highly gifted, aged 21, studying science at university) had found her wonderful memory a great blessing. It provided her with a stunning six A grades at A-level. But her poor metacognition, that is her lack of awareness of how best to use her powerful mind, showed up when she had to survive on her own at university. Samantha described her problems in thinking when she was out of the structured school learning situation:

> 'People say I'm weird because I will think of something which will remind me of something else, then my mind will go racing along the new train of thought. I'll arrive at an observation which has got no relevance to anything that anyone else can see. It's a handicap when I'm trying to learn, because, say I'm looking something up in an index, I'll be triggered into finding something else to look up, but then I won't get back to the original thing for hours. I still have to rely on my memory.
>
> Until I got to university I'd never actually had to work – I did my homework on the bus or while eating my tea, even at A-level stage. It was never difficult. When I started my degree course, I tried to do the same with the first maths problem sheet we were given. I soon realised that this was "hard"! And most of the others on the course had been used to finding this stuff hard, and settled down to work at it. I'd never had to learn how to work – and being away from home at the first

time, at the age of 17, is not the best time to have to do that! So I never really put in the necessary effort, right from the start. It was much easier to spend lots of time doing Music Society stuff, so that's what I did. And that's why I failed.'

Update 2001: That problem of her darting mind continued to beset Samantha. Although she eventually acquired a vast array of knowledge and skills, she did not focus sufficiently on any one area to make real headway in it, to become an expert. As a teacher in a secondary school for 12 years she taught mathematics and physics, as well as flutes, oboes, bassoons, conducted choirs, woodwind ensembles and the wind band. But only this year in her mid thirties is she taking her A-level music exam. Having been a star of her music school until the age of 18, she was allowed to teach music– but could not take it further.

Learning as a slog
To different degrees, about a dozen gifted youngsters had allowed their study habits to become really rigid, and relied heavily on their exceptional memories in a relatively superficial and unthinking way. Rote-learning, memorising pages of information, is still common in schools, especially in developing counties. It is not only inefficient in the long term but very boring. Its attraction is that it appears to require less effort from the teacher. It also offers the learner an immature, spurious emotional security, in that he or she does not have to make their own learning decisions, but only reproduces what an authority such as a teacher or textbook writer has said. In the panic before big exams, even the most sophisticated thinkers in this study sometimes abandoned their valuable, higher-level strategies for a frenzied, indiscriminate search through their notes.

Even at the age of 10, I had observed that Raymond Grey (Highly gifted, aged 20, at university) had an anxious personality and natural reserve, which appeared to have been reinforced by unrelieved academic pressure at his school. He was aware that he used the false security of rigid, learning strategies as a shield to hide from his emotional self. No one had ever helped him develop a feeling of competence in his own thinking so that he could use his extremely high potential in a flexible and productive way. As a science specialist, his school had obliged him to drop all the arts subjects, and he had developed little insight into or love of the more creative aspects of life. His responses to my wider questions about how he saw life were simple and immature, though commenting on his experience of being advanced two years at school he said, 'Its not a good idea … no.' Even at university, Raymond was becoming desperate about what he felt was missing from his life, so much so that he was considering dropping-out before his finals. Nor had his study methods improved, his poor (but examination effective) learning habits had become ingrained. He looked at the ground despondently when told me:

'I don't read textbooks: I'm not very good with them. My notes are so vast, fifty pages of dense writing. I go through them again and again, just writing down occasional sentences. I learn all those, and then go through problem sheets and exam papers.'

Overdoing it

Alternately, the intellectually gifted are sometimes faced with the temptation of frenetic mental activity, which may not appear to be to any productive purpose. It seems to happen when the emotional part of a person becomes either disregarded or actually crippled, as though it were irrelevant to the individual's thinking and creativity, almost as though someone has become just a brain physically supported by the rest of the body. Such a person can enter a maze of ideas, developing theories and sub-theories which have no useful function other than intellectual exercise. William Sidis, the American genius who supposedly had one of the highest IQs ever measured, found himself trapped by such mental convolutions. His upbringing had led him to believe that he was only valued for his intellect, compounded by the devastation of his peace of mind though his media fame for being brilliant. His relatively little productive work has not withstood the test of time (Wallace 1986).

Some youngsters in this study devised exquisite intellectual manoeuvres, especially on computers, to avoid threat. Stephen Kaye, a supremely gifted 14-year-old, was the child of warring divorced parents, somewhat emotionally neglected and lonely. He told me:

'I learned to program when I was eight. Now, I'm working out a formula to translate into computer language. It's quite a simple program, finding elements in Pascal's triangle. But the thing that made it a lot more complicated was that I wanted to do it for very large numbers, so it required a different method of storage from the ones the computer actually provides for you. At the moment, I'm working on a version of Manic Minor, a computer game on a large scale with fifty different screens. I invented a card game once called Seven Card Wiggle and typed the rules for that, which I don't think I'll ever finish because there are about seven thousand.'

This emotional insecurity can be seen in many high school-achievers as they go through life. Rather than daring to create ideas, they seem almost desperate to show how much they know by answering other people's questions correctly and being informative, as though life was one long educational grilling on which they were to be judged. This situation was described in a follow-up of 1964-1968 Presidential Scholars in America (Kaufman 1992). She found that although the ex-scholars continued to do well, they knew they often relied on school-type learning, not only to provide them with an identity but also a feeling of worth. But at any age, being a 'know-all' is not perhaps the best way of attracting friends.

The 'Figaro gift'

In Rossini's opera *The Barber of Seville*, Figaro the barber made great efforts to attend to the demands of his many customers at once – obviously a gifted man – although at times he found it difficult. He was working at the intuitive end of the thinking spectrum, of which the opposite end is analytical thinking. At each extreme, information is processed differently. Most intellectual activity and all creative work uses an amalgam of both kinds, sometimes one kind dominates and sometimes the other (Schofield and Ashman 1987).

- Analytical thinking (successive processing) uses information in a time sequence. One thought must follow another, each link in the chain of reasoning being dependent on the last. It is slow, because although it uses only a limited amount of information the thinker has to keep it all in mind at the same time while working with it. It can also produce large errors, because a contradicting detail or a missing link can break the thread of an argument. An example might be working out a bus route with perfect connections without considering any alternative such as the train which is direct.
- Intuitive thinking (simultaneous processing) is when all the parts and relationships between the elements are worked with together – such as the city's whole transport system, as well as alternative possibilities. This includes planning and decision-making and implies the ability to overview one's own thinking – metacognition. Intuitive thinking works like perception, in the sense that 'A picture is worth a thousand words'. It is fast and impressionistic without the person being conscious of all the details, so there is no limit to the data that can be called upon. Indeed, it demands a bird's-eye view of all the ideas on the subject that could be relevant, including one's own feelings about it.

In the first phase of this research, when they were children, I'd asked them all whether they could follow and cope with two or more things at once – that is, whether they could process them simultaneously. Of those with an IQ of more than 141, 43 per cent said they could – almost twice the proportion claimed by those with IQs of between 97 and 140 (24 per cent). Ten years later, when they were asked the same question, the results were much the same. The higher the IQ of the young people, the more likely they were to say that they were able, not only to give attention to more than one thing at a time, but to process them together. However, they sometimes found this frustrating when listening to several people as they couldn't answer them all at the same time.

Almost all the young people of average ability had found it extremely difficult to take a metacognitive overview of their learning processes, and none had been given any help from their teachers in attempting it. Many of the more average ability young people described it like this unskilled learner:

'I used to read a book, close it, then try to write the stuff down. Then I'd open it up to see if I was right, and invariably find I was wrong. On the odd occasion, I spoke into a tape but I found it did me no good at all. I'd go off by myself, working up in my bedroom shut off from the television, but I still wasn't very good at revising, so I used to walk out of the room and forget it.'

Not only did the youngsters of very high IQ appear to be distinctly better at simultaneous processing than the others, but in the whole sample significantly more of the girls (86 per cent) claimed this Figaro gift than the boys (66 per cent). Although this ability of females to do many things at once has been recognised in many studies (and life in general), it may be partly learned. Among these young people, for example, the education of the brightest boys was often in more academic, single-sex schools, which usually have a more funnelled achievement-orientated approach to learning. The education which the bright girls received was much less specialised, enabling them to range more broadly. The ability to be focused has its advantages in that often greater progress can be made in the desired direction. But working in several areas at once is also useful in both intellectual and practical ways. Sarah Mortimer (Highly gifted, aged 20, at university studying Computer Systems Engineering) explained:

'I often do two things at once. Right now I'm building a synthesiser, so I've got piles of components and bits of things to stick to this piece of board. Unfortunately, as I haven't got them all, it's a bit difficult trying to imagine where they're going. I've brought it home to do, so I do it while I watch television. I like to have something on in the background, because it's a boring job; the first component in is much like the eightieth component in.'

The efficiency of how one uses available mental resources shows up best in a novel situation. That is where the gifted are most likely to shine in their capacity to combine a speedy overview, go on to form an effective strategy, as well as monitoring their own performance. Indeed, the American psychologist Robert Sternberg (Sternberg and Davidson 1986) suggested that the main difference between the intellectually gifted and other children is in the way each gets hold of and carries out a new task. The adult-like planning competencies of the gifted are often noticed by teachers and parents, and are probably the major reason for their greater speed in problem-solving. But this exceptional facility may not work for all kinds of planning. It is important for adults to understand how an individual learns and thinks, so that in an educational situation, each learner can work in a style which best suits them. It is not that a teacher has to adapt to each pupil's personal style, which would be impossible in a classroom, but that each pupil should have enough freedom to learn to some extent in their own way.

Speed of thinking

Some psychologists have said that the level of intelligence can be measured by its speed, either by electro-encephalographic traces of brain action, or from how quickly people can discriminate between similar test signals, but this measure is not reliable (although it is indeed true that a high proportion of these gifted young people could think very rapidly).

Sarah Mortimer, the gifted girl who could process many ideas at once (above), had also taken full advantage of her ability to think at speed. She learned efficiently, knew her learning style and the subject area in which she worked best, was fortunate in finding herself in all the right places at the right times, and made the most of every opportunity. She lived in an intellectual English home; one where dogs were welcome. It overflowed with books and some choice antiques, along with some plain well-loved and used furniture, a comforting rug was slung across the back of the couch. Musical instruments, audiotapes and records lay around untidily. Her parents listed their hobbies as walking and reading. Whereas in the average home I would be welcomed with a heart-warming 'Make yourself comfortable' and 'Would you like a cup of tea?', in Sarah's home I was something of a source of intellectual curiosity. After I'd found somewhere to put my coat and a place to sit, I sipped my dry sherry and enjoyed a hail of questions and suggestions about the research.

As well as having highly intelligent, supportive parents, Sarah went to a school where her brilliance and hard work were recognised and handsomely provided for. At university, she was the youngest as well as one of the most outstanding students, enjoying many happy relationships. She was excited there with the fresh rush of ideas and insights, coping with them smoothly, brilliantly and swiftly. There was a powerful brain at work behind the big specs and under the carroty hair.

Sarah Mortimer (Highly gifted, aged 20 studying Computer Systems Engineering):

> 'At school, because I was the only one doing Further Maths, it meant that I went at my own speed, so I would say to my teacher, "I think I know this well enough now", and we would move on. We were streamed for the other subjects, but at university it's mixed ability, everybody in one class. There are twenty-five of us on our course, and we're spread out across the whole ability range. Those who want to work quickly can get on and then take more free time than others. But I'd really prefer to be in a group where everybody wants to work quickly.
>
> I like working quickly. You don't sit next to Sarah unless you want the answer before you've started the problem! I sit there, and the question will be written on the board, and before the lecturer's finished the question, I've started writing. And while everybody else is writing down the first formula, still wondering what to do, I'll say, "Finished!" But that speed only works for logic and maths because it's

numbers and figures and symbols. Something I could do symbolically in a couple of minutes might take me upwards of half an hour to explain to somebody else. Anything where I've got to express my own ideas and explain why something happens, or write an essay, takes a lot longer, because you've really got to stop and think.

There's a work gear and there's a social gear, and I'm almost two different people. It's not difficult to switch, though, because it's very rare to be working hard and then suddenly socialise, so there's always a gap between the two. But if I've been working intensely, like during an exam, when I'm really hyped-up, it's quite hard coming down and getting back to everybody else's speed. My thoughts tend to come in big chunks rather than little bits, which means there's a danger of skipping steps – I might have a mistake glaring at me, and not notice it because I've been just too quick. But I find it very hard to stop to think in the middle of a flow. I'd much rather get it down, then go back and check through every step. In an exam, I'll whiz through the paper, spending about two-thirds of the time writing, and the other third going through, checking my answers and often changing things. It's a case of, does it feel right and does it make sense?'

The intellectually speedy mind not only showed itself in studying, but in all other aspects of everyday life; as one bright boy said – 'The kids at my school, you knew what they're going to say. So you could get far ahead of them, and just think about anything while you were waiting.'

Andy Spurgeon (Highly gifted, aged 17, at school) provided more details of the everyday problem:

'Oh yes, gosh yes! I not only have to wait whilst other people understand what I explain to them, but I also have to wait whilst people explain to me what I've already understood. In an argument or a discussion I'm very fast, and people find that a bit jarring sometimes, so I try to slow myself down occasionally, just to make it a bit easier for them. I always hone my ideas down to a very precise form, and I do get impatient if other people don't get that precision. And it's not for lack of words, I've got a fairly wide vocabulary. The worst thing is when people start saying something, and you understand what they want to say immediately, but they persist because they've got to get that bit out, and you have to come back again when they've finished.

I'm very pleased with my mental abilities really. I'm glad that I can do things. I like being able to sit back and ignore lectures and then do the work. I know now that I do understand things faster than other people. I can grasp things faster, and as a result, I'm usually idling when they're working hard. But it's got that I idle more and they work harder, so eventually they will begin to find the work easier than I do.'

Those who were in beautiful command of their faculties enjoyed using them, and in doing so seemed to be spurred on to even greater mental agility. Not one of the speedy thinkers found it such a handicap in their dealings with other people that it got in the way of good relationships. However, conversing with the mentally quickest of these young people, I found it better to use crisp, short questions rather than lose the last few words in their enthusiastic responses who could not wait for the question mark. It was exhilarating and kept me on my mental toes.

How the high achievers studied

When psychologists and educational researchers investigate learning and thinking, they normally do it in an experimental way. For example, they might set up one kind of teaching process and find out how different categories of pupil learn through it, or set up different teaching processes and see how similar children get on with them. Such experimental designs are intended to keep the measurement as focused as possible, to avoid as much as possible the influence of the child's personality and social environment. Because they are experimental, they try to set up an exceptionally ordered learning world that follows clear rules, unlike real life, whether in the classroom or the home. It is also easier to carry out experiments which are largely controllable, than to study the endless complexity of natural interactions between people.

Mental skills, however, are part of the whole child in his or her life circumstances. They are demonstrated in each one's cognitive style – the way each person approaches experiences, whether emotional or intellectual, practical or academic – one's personal manner of learning. Cognitive style includes personal preferences for the learning set-up, such as working alone or with others, learning by hearing or by reading, choice of subject area, persistence, and the rhythm and length of concentration.

Cognitive style can be explained in terms of the relative use of the two sides of the brain, each of which has different ways of operating. The left hemisphere (opposite the right hand) is considered to work in a careful, ordered way, tackling problems analytically (successive processing), while the right hemisphere takes an all-over, more picture-like view (simultaneous processing). Given enough time, students have been found to reach equally deep levels of learning via many different styles, though the more creative aspects of putting that learning into action call for both sides of the brain to be used.

The high achievers in this sample often had a good grasp of metacognition – knowing how they learned, and with the ability to use it in ways which suited them. They were often able to describe their own cognitive style explicitly, and say how it could affect their results. In that way they were often able to harness the mental power they were born with in hard work that was well aimed and coordinated, although very few had been taught how to do it. They were also much more keenly aware of different possible approaches to the work than the relatively less successful students, who had to use more energy to cope in a more rigid way with less success in their learning. It was succinctly explained by Sarah Moritmer:

> 'Everyone knows which is the best way for themselves to work. Children have got to choose their own way, otherwise they're not going to do their best, and it may be difficult for them to express themselves in a way which doesn't fit their style. I would have liked the teachers to know what we thought. It would have been nice for us to have been able to say, "Look, I don't like the way it's done. Is there nothing we can do to change it?"'

Using the IQ scores

It was clear from this study (as well as those of countless others) that the young people's IQ scores (measured in 1974) had provided a reliable and regular indicator of their future educational achievements. Therefore, after investigations with other methods – and in full recognition of all the problems associated with it – the IQ score was chosen as the statistically reliable measure of intellectual ability. The whole sample was sorted into three groups for comparison – High-IQ (170–140), Above-average IQ (139–120), and Average-IQ (119–97), as seen in Table 4.1.

Table 5.1 The IQ groups

IQ group	IQ Range	Percentage of sample
High	140–170	44
Above average	120–139	31
Average	92–119	25

Although each one of the young people had answered the questions about their mental processes alone with me in their homes and without any contact with others in the sample, many of their responses were very closely associated with their IQ group. Statistical analysis showed some associations to be highly significant (1 per cent), so that this relationship was extremely unlikely to have arisen by chance. In line with their IQs, the young people described very different styles of approach to their study.

Concentration, emotion and IQ

Concentration is greatly affected by emotion. All children experience potentially stressful events, such as the arrival of a new step-parent, family rows, going to hospital or moving house. Sometimes those moments of heightened emotion, though they need be no more than people expressing differing points of view, can remain vivid throughout life. But each individually reacts differently, depending on temperament and circumstances. Although intellectual growth has even been found to peak in certain situations of mental discord, unhappiness is far more usually detrimental. The energy required for a child to keep 'afloat', when disturbed and unhappy, makes it particularly difficult to focus on learning – to concentrate. If this happens early in life, it can put a brake on the formation of good study habits, and a child who had failed to learn them is then handicapped in learning. This is an important reason why nearly all children from emotionally disturbed backgrounds, so often fail to develop their full potential. Instead, a child may exercise his talents by becoming streetwise instead of school-wise.

Sometimes the High-IQ young people in my study had indeed been ground down by their circumstances, and in their distress they were learning in a much less efficient and productive way than they could have been. The 12 young people who had had a very high measured level of emotional maladjustment in the first survey, had all achieved at a much lower level in school than would have been expected from their IQ scores This was pinpointed in both their lowered abilities to concentrate and also to take an overview of the subject matter to be learned. That is, they relied on successive mental processing rather than exercise their simultaneous processing abilities. Of the well adjusted, 33 per cent said they would usually try to see the whole picture as they studied, compared with only 9 per cent of the least well adjusted.

It was difficult for Helen Sergeant, who I had noted as nervous even when she had been ten-years-old. Now, although she had a new father (whose name she had not taken), her family was not happy and she had tried to distance herself from them emotionally. In addition, her home was so cold and dank that it chilled even on the warm, summer day. There were packages and parcels all over the house, smelling strongly of damp paper, the bare boards on the bathroom floor were stained and the badly cracked lavatory had no seat. Because her circumstances were psychologically very painful, she had had to use energy to keep herself mentally steady. She had also partly cut herself off from that pain by escaping into day-dreams, but this route had become so tempting and frequent that it was threatening her progress. As a further defence against anxiety, and without the necessary free energy to think around her subjects of study, she had become excessively self-controlled, relying on highly structured successive processing. She was probably the most assiduous worker in the whole sample, though sadly not the most efficient.

Helen Sergeant (Gifted, aged 17, at school):

'I can't just do it in my head. I always feel sleepy the minute I've got to do some work, so I drift off, and realise that I've wasted ten or fifteen minutes. Sometimes

I slip into bed for a while where it's warm. I find myself day-dreaming, and it gets to be a habit, even during exams where there's terrific pressure, and it can't do my marks any good. When I study I make brief notes on cards, with dates and facts in different coloured pens to emphasise different points. I also record on tape – I read my notes into it, and then listen to it. I read through my notes several times, and the textbooks, to see how they differ. I can't be bothered to think it through, so I try to memorise as much as possible. I write down what I can remember, maybe two or three times, basically learning it off by heart. I then write myself a short point-test on it, and then maybe I do a timed essay. The only thing that gets me through is determination I suppose.'

It was a different picture, though, for most of the high academic achievers. They seemed to recognise and use their own optimum rhythm of concentration and relaxation as an integrated part of their study methods. In her crisp way, Sarah Mortimer (Highly gifted, aged 20) knew her personal best style of working quite specifically, which contrasted sharply with Helen Sergeant's:

'I like to work half an hour hard, then take quarter of an hour break – in fits and starts, because that's how I think. When the natural flow stops, I take a break and then come back, and it starts to go again. Probably I don't get through any more work than other people in the same physical time; they may even take less time, because I have to stop quite often. It causes chaos if I'm trying to work on a group project.'

The higher the IQ of the young person, the better able they seemed to be at controlling their mental focusing, to use it to prime advantage. While some said their normal concentration span was only a few minutes with constant breaks, others claimed many hours of unbroken concentration. Others described how they could adapt to whatever the circumstances called for, altering the length and depth of concentration appropriately. A gifted boy said:

'I usually take breaks about every ten minutes. Once though, I worked from four o'clock when I got home, till half-past one in the morning, and then had my break for tea. I concentrated totally. It was just something that had to be done.'

For most of the young people of all abilities, their longest concentration span came at times of deep involvement in what they were doing, such as in exams – 'motivated by fear, enveloped in it!'. The potential for deep concentration was present in most of these young people and could be pulled out for specific purposes and left unused at other times. The successful students seemed better able to call upon it – 'In music, when you're practising, you simply have to learn to concentrate intensely'. Again Sarah Mortimer had the words to describe that involvement:

'I love what I'm doing; I could do College work till it came out of my ears. I've really enjoyed computer programming and never notice the time when I'm tapping it in, running it, finding a bug, changing something, running it again. I'm just staring at this little screen and watching things run by, and I tend to work all the way through, until I suddenly think – "Gosh, it feels as though I've been here a while". Sometimes it's twice as long as I thought it was. I sometimes talk like that too – once I get going, you can't turn me off!'

But whatever the rhythm of or the reason for concentrating, overall, the higher the young person's IQ, the longer the span they were able to manage. The relationship between IQ and length of time concentrating is very close indeed, as can be seen in Table 5.2.

Table 5.2 Question: What's the longest you have ever concentrated?

Mean IQ	Concentration
144	Four or more hours
138	Three hours
131	Two hours
124	One hour

Many had their longest spells of concentration in the activities they chose to do outside school while doing what they were really interested in. At 16, Derek Girling (Highly gifted, aged 23) longed for a car, but his parents had said no, there was no money for it. One day, though, his mother coming home from work found a battered wreck in front of the house – with Stephen underneath it poring over an instruction manual. His mechanical skills had come entirely from such reading since there was no one who could tell him what to do. He took nearly a year to put that car right, then sold it at a handsome profit and went on to other cars. He loved it – 'I've spent spells under the car of four or five hours at a time without coming up for air.'

Andy Spurgeon (Highly gifted, aged 17, at school) found that his exceptional ability to concentrate had unexpected effects:

'My concentration span it at its longest when I play music, like the length of Mozart's Piano Concerto Number 21, because then I can completely lose myself. I'm sure I could go longer, but it's difficult to say how long your concentration lasts, and how much you're actually just playing by memory without having to concentrate too much on it. I used to stay on after school to play the piano. Once, I got so carried away, that by the time I'd reached the front door there were enough alarm bells going to wake the dead. I was in a quandary then whether to stay and wait for the caretakers to come and shout at me for not leaving – although really they should have cleared me out – but in the end, I climbed out a window and ran away.'

Most of the highly able had taken their lifelong facility to concentrate at will for granted, though the assumption that it was always available when they wanted it caused some problems when extra mental discipline was needed for higher level study.

Gina Emerson (Highly gifted, aged 20, and studying English):

'This last term at Cambridge, I've found concentration incredibly difficult. It's very irritating, because I'm not used to it. I sit in the library for three hours and I think I'm working, but I know that I'm not. I read the things we're told to read, but I don't get inspired and write impassioned essays, which everybody else seems to be doing. It gets vaguer and vaguer and less and less controlled as I go on, and I find I have to discipline myself more than I used to. I feel much less intelligent than I was about ten years ago. Even in concerts now I don't concentrate for a second together on the music, because I'm thinking about other things, like what I'm going to say to the person next to me when it finishes. I have too many things in my mind at once. I'm always thinking a bit about what I'm going to do tomorrow and why I didn't do the washing-up tonight. But reading novels, I do really get carried away and then I'm shocked that it's two in the morning.'

Redundancy control

The ability to concentrate is influenced both by the amount of distraction around and by how much one can resist its intrusion – redundancy control. Background noises like traffic or soft music can be used to absorb emotional responses, leaving the mind free, though they have to be carefully controlled: too much, and they compete with what one is trying to do. The most successful achievers appeared to be better able to adjust their learning environments for prime effectiveness, using the type of redundancy control which suited them. The academically less successful, though, appeared to be less aware both of the variety of options and of what would best suit them.

Many successful students chose music to blanket intruding, unexpected noises – 'It blocks out all other sound, and I start associating music with work; certain pieces even with particular exams'. Others went for silence. Sometimes, paradoxically, exam anxiety itself can take up energy and so impede study, but the highest achievers had their own ways of controlling that form of redundancy too.

Richard Neville (Highly gifted, aged 21, at university) purposely transferred the skills he had sharpened in chess to checkmate his anxiety:

'Chess has helped me practice concentrating and not getting flustered. If your opponent hits you with a good move, there's no good falling apart. It's the same with a question that you can't do. In exams, I'll go out for five minutes if necessary – shut my eyes, count to ten, take deep breaths. The next day, there's another three-hour exam, and my friends around me get very exhausted, very tired, and very strung-up about it, but I don't.'

The Three-times Problem described in p. 127 was not an uncommon feature of the gifted learner, involving very sophisticated skills for controlling redundant repetition from the teacher.

Competition and IQ

Competition is a way of finding out and defining one's own capabilities, but the comparison must be meaningful or it is a waste of time and effort. Self-validation, or assessing one's own progress, is not the same as seeking the approval of authority. It involves commitment to the experience, and can promote independence of action and a sense of competence, of power in oneself. That is different from neurotic competitiveness, where the thrill of winning is all but the experience itself means little. Very young mathematicians seem particularly keen on competition with themselves. They may spend more time than other gifted children on their own, practising calculations and thinking about their mathematical interest (Radford 1990).

From early childhood, many of the potentially high achievers in this sample had been described by their parents as competitive, comparing themselves with both their own previous performances and those of others. In the first interviews with me they had far more frequently chosen a high status occupation for themselves in the future than the others (72 per cent compared with 40 per cent). Nor did they leave it to chance. They often went to great lengths to do their best, taking time and effort over the learning and practice needed to get a skill right in their own eyes, yet often expressing less than total satisfaction with the results. The High-IQ group had the highest aims of all, sometimes accompanied by an urge to perfection. Their combination of high ability, motivation to succeed, and a capacity for hard work, proved to be an excellent recipe for success in reaching their goals.

Jeremy Kramer's mother said he was such a keen learner that he had even demanded more teaching in nursery school! As he grew up, he knew he had control of his learning. He knew the best way for him using his mastery of his metacognitive processes. He had consciously devised a self-challenging style of approach to his work along with an excellent repertoire of learning strategies which suited his personality.

Jeremy Kramer (IQ 170 aged 20, studying medicine):

'When I was younger, I thrived on competition with friends, but now I do it for myself. I always set myself an aim, and have to achieve it. Even during the day, I'll find my own little challenges. Like, I can just go down for a game of snooker, not because it's nice and relaxing, but sometimes, it's "Right, I'm going to beat this guy, and I'm going to really go for it, get the best score I've ever done."

I've got exams in three or four weeks, and I'm being quite honest when I say that I haven't opened a book all year. I like to feel the pressure, to build up some anxiety, so I know that if I don't start now, I'm definitely going to fail. It's the challenge of doing that. I'm fully dedicated to working at this point, and only at this point. For my first year exams, I only started revising two days before. My method is to cram for a couple of weeks, doing 24 hours a day, and not sleep for a few nights. I'm a totally different person when it gets to that stage. Everything seems to go in at that point, so I must be able to absorb the stuff.

I can do this last minute stuff because I understand the principles, so I understand the subject before I even start working for it. If I were totally lost, then I'd really start worrying. A lot of students sit in their room with a book and slog away at details, but if you test them on the principles, like something that they're supposed to deduce, then they fall down. That's something that I can get right and they won't. I'm only learning the details at the last minute, and I find that a lot of them stay with me. Even now, I remember a lot of last year's work, which I'd only learnt in a few days, where other people I know have forgotten it.

It's important for me to spend a very large period of time each day on my own thinking and sorting out what I've been doing. I need that thinking time to be productive. Even if it's three o'clock in the morning when I get to bed, although I might be very tired, I'll probably stay up another two hours just thinking.'

Update 2001: By the age of 36 Jeremy's view of his earlier thinking and learning processes gave quite a different slant. He told me that he was still suffering from his early identification as a gifted child, and explained the background to the above description of his learning and thinking at 20.

'The only mental tools I knew how to use was for something abstract, to manipulate my thoughts. I was good at sequences, at testing, and I am still good at them. But as to knowledge of the world, that was always missing. To make up, I used to read encyclopaedias and the Guinness Book of Records. My thinking processes were circular. I had a style of argument which was that when someone said something to me I'd turn it on its head. Mostly I can't follow someone else's train of thought, which makes me socially anxious, so I use that technique to get them on to my agenda. But it causes social problems.

I overused my memory and overcompensated. The way I used to work, that last minute swotting, is maladaptive behaviour. It was because I didn't want to do it and only fear of definite failure made me do it in the end. How I got those great results was to do a detailed survey of which questions were likely to turn up. Then I'd put all my energy into them. So I could make a brilliant response to, say, three questions on embryology but know nothing much else about embryology, whereas others would know more about embryology and get lower marks than me.

I'm highly responsive to the way people see me. I'd hate to be called a swot. I can only work in fear: I have adapted to it.'

Memory and IQ

Anyone who has studied for exams knows that the most valuable mental asset is a good memory. Indeed, for the highly achieving young people in this study, it seemed to be the most powerful weapon in their academic armoury because unfortunately so much school-level examination success is based on the ability to reproduce material in the few hours allowed, rather than to think it through. The close positive correlation between memory and IQ had been seen in the first survey when the parents of the High-IQ children described them as having exceptionally good memories nearly three times as often (35 per cent) as the parents of all the other children (13 per cent). And that picture still held in the Follow-up; the correlation between IQ, memory and examination success was statistically highly significant. The higher the young person's IQ score, the more likely they were to claim an excellent memory – and the better their examination results.

For a high proportion of those in the top one per cent of the IQ range the facility of memory came very easily, and at that level of intelligence it showed in both the arts and the sciences, as described by two highly gifted girls at Cambridge University. Rachel, who was studying English said:

'I never worked as hard as other people because I never had to. It's terribly easy for me to remember things short-term, like revising for my O-levels the night before. If I read things through, shut my eyes and repeated my notes to myself, it would be there for the exam the next day.'

Anne, a scientist, said:

'I remember pretty well from class, so for my A-levels I didn't open my school notes once. But the morning of my Physics A-level, I got up at five o'clock, and revised the whole syllabus. It took me two and a bit hours. But it was only a multiple-choice question paper, so you don't have to know anything very well if you know the principles.'

This relationship between memory and IQ was especially close for those who said they remembered facts best, although the High-IQ group did not all have identical types of memory. The types of memory, whether for facts, people or generally good are listed in Table 5.3.

Table 5.3 Type of memory

IQ Group	Good %	Facts %	People %	General %
High	84	46	8	45
Above-average	66	23	15	62
Average	57	17	14	69
Mean IQ	–	143	131	132

Girls particularly, made much use of their visual memory and a few even said they had a true photographic memory, such as the gifted 16-year-old who said of her revision:

'I'm able to picture it wherever it was. Things like poems and diagrams, I can remember where the bits stick out: once I've drawn a diagram a couple of times, then that's enough, I picture it in my mind. I never put a bookmark in; I always remember what page I'm on. I can sometimes remember enough from the page to take it with me into the exam and read it off; it comes back to me which side the page is on, what colour the ink's in. But I remember better the things I want to remember than those I have to. I'm always forgetting things I have to do and things I should have done.'

Others had auditory memories:

'I never write when I'm revising, I recite, like for learning muscles and muscle attachments. I'll read it through, then cover it up, and say it over out loud. If it's a subject I find easy, it will go in with a couple of reading throughs. Almost all my A-level revision was just a matter of reading through my notes two or three times, though every now and again, I would need to write down things like a Physics derivation.'

Anna, a brilliant pianist remembered by touch:

'I'm a very tactile person – certainly when I'm memorising music; I can't memorise away from the keyboard. I've got to physically feel and hear what I'm doing, whereas there are some people who can sit on a train from Edinburgh to

London and have a piece learned and go away and play it. It's all visual memory; they actually see the music then – actually see the page as they're playing it. I always hear it and feel it.'

Most of the young people had only vague (if any) memories of my visit to them ten or more years ago. Four boys though, remembered it in uncanny detail – and each one had left school with all A grades. Richard Neville (Highly gifted, aged 19, studying physics) was one. 'Oh, I remember', he said, 'it was March 1975'. How did he remember? 'Oh, I just remembered, because I remember things'. On checking, he was absolutely correct. He continued:

'I can remember when you gave me your last interview when I was eleven, and I can tell you virtually everything that went on then, like some of the tests you gave me. One of them, the only one I got wrong, was the string of beads. You got me to do a bearing test, and I stood up with my hands like this, and worked it out East, West, South, and a few other questions. That's just the way I learn academically, with things that have happened to me, rather than from a book. I can remember vivid things in my childhood, and the words that were spoken to me then. I do it by making relationships, almost like a rhyme, but in pictures. But I haven't got a real photographic memory of books, so I might have difficulties in recalling facts and formulas – which can be a handicap.'

The highest academic achievements were gained by those who said their memories were best for facts.

Simon Powell (Highly gifted, aged 20, studying mathematics):

'I can't remember what I was doing yesterday. But machine code, I could remember all of about 60-odd totally abstract numbers all in hexi-decimal, which is nought to nine A.B.C.D.E.F. – that's to base 16 – and I could remember pairs of those as operational, and the whole lot, dead easy. I do have a good memory like that, but I was terribly upset when I had to ask a girl what her name was, and I'd known her for a year.

Textbooks are really boring. I prefer my notes, because when I'm revising, they remind me of what we did in the lesson; little things that the teacher said explaining it to you. It helps me remember a bit better when I read a factual text, to go through the first sentence or first line of each paragraph of a section. Then I go back to the beginning and read it again, skimming across the pages and picking out names, places, dates, classification of ideas. Then I will read it through in its entirety, and be able to think about it properly. If I remember something in an exam I will use it, but I never struggle to remember something because that never works, and I just end up getting panicky and blocked.'

Motivation to succeed

Assuming that there is enough intelligence and competence in learning to do the work, most differences in school achievement can be attributed to the pupil's motivation – their keenness. Yet, how is it that some are motivated in one area of schoolwork but avoid any effort in the others? Psychological theorists have produced different concepts of motivation, such as 'need for achievement' which can be distinguished from 'fear of failure', all kinds being affected by 'test anxiety' or 'effort avoidance'. It would be far too simplistic to say that motivation is just the result of reward and punishment, or even of more sophisticated conditioning by parents and teachers. People's behaviour depends not just on how they are treated, but also on how they perceive they are being treated and how they react to the situation.

Tony Steward, for example, was not gifted, but was a youth of well above average ability. He was the first generation to pull himself up from the poverty trap which had kept his family as labourers in Ireland. However, he was not inclined to pick up the middle-class mores that his school offered: his criteria for success were not theirs of academic achievements or money, but simply a job with a future. Almost all his friends were out of work and with little prospects of improvement. Some of them, he said, were very depressed about their situations. He wanted, above all, to be valued for his personal qualities, for himself.

Tony Stewart (Above average, aged 20, a trainee car mechanic):

> 'My grandparents were only educated till they were eleven or twelve-years-old, and then they had to go out in the fields to dig. There was no education for them, nor for my parents who had to leave school at about fourteen to earn money to eat. Just a continuing process. My mother was quite bright academically, but there was no way she could carry on in further education because she had to get out and work. She would've liked to pick some up later, except for having so many in the family. My father came over to England, from Ireland, when he was seventeen and worked in tunnels. Academic qualifications are not what really matter, but the type of person you are; how other people respect you and such.'

In their concern with children's education, by far the most frequently asked question parents and teachers ask of psychologists and educators is – How can I motivate them to learn? There are some answers available and they can often work, though putting them into practice calls for patience and understanding.

Encouraging motivation

- *Feelings of competence.* In general, motivation and the accompanying increase in the level of work, are encouraged by giving children a feeling of individual competence and a goal to aim for, even examinations. But too much adult pressure and control can actually undermine good motivation, because constantly being obliged to depend on someone else's decisions conveys feelings of incompetence to a child, an idea referred to as 'locus of control' (Stipek and Weisz 1981). This means that if pupils see control as located with the teacher or some other authority, they will be less involved and motivated in their own learning than if they felt more in charge of it themselves. So much experimental research in schools has shown that both motivation and achievement levels go up when children are encouraged to take more control over their own classroom activities. One wonders why it is so infrequently put into action. Poorly motivated youngsters find their urge to learn is increased when they are encouraged to help others, such as getting unsuccessful adolescents to take on the role of tutors to younger children.

- *Personal interests.* Children, like adults, do best what they are most interested in. This is the best kind of motivation – intrinsic – the kind which is generated by interest or relevance, especially when it is fired by the individual's belief in their own effectiveness. That energising assurance in one's ability to tackle a task comes best from positive personal experiences, especially from feedback that children have received on how well they did. Some of it they can see for themselves, but if other people's responses are to be effective, they must always be genuine, whether good or bad.
- *Praise and feedback.* Sincerity is the key. False praise, such as telling children they have done well when they know they have not, will not enhance their intrinsic motivation. Although a 'Well done' for following easy instructions may be pleasant on the ear and vaguely encouraging, it is not deeply meaningful. In neither case do the children feel in charge of what they are doing. Particularly undermining feedback would include telling a child he was just lucky in getting the answer right. Whether lucky or not, it certainly wouldn't enhance anyone's feelings of competence.

However, the situation is not entirely controllable by adults, as children can interpret feedback in different ways, depending on the psychological context and the child's personality. Telling one child he is doing badly may be interpreted as an excuse to stop work – 'It's not worth the effort', though for another, the response may be an increase in motivation – 'I'll prove them wrong!' Paradoxically, too much praise, particularly in a system of close supervision, may tell a child simply that he or she is doing the bidding of the teacher, rather than personally exploring the area of study and so developing competence. This can undermine intrinsic motivation, because it becomes psychologically impossible for the child to feel in control of his or her own progress in learning.

All children, whatever their ability, want to feel effective and engaged by challenge, which must include a risk of failure. The highly able need challenge at least as much as any others. Experimental work has shown that if children are given a superficial reward, such as money or sweets, they are far more likely to choose the easiest ways of succeeding, whereas if they are enjoying the activity for itself, they choose harder tasks, usually just above the level of previous success. No child can reasonably be expected to work hard in all areas of the curriculum, since individual interests are influenced by many things. But when children are interested in what they are doing, they have a natural tendency to take on challenges that exercise and expand their limits of competence.

- *Structure.* The advantage of looking back at the lives of individuals who have made outstanding achievements is that one can detect the broader influences on their progress, which might be missed by using more limiting methods of psychological tests or experiments, though the major problem is that people remember events differently. There are always very powerful motivating reasons why people have taken the paths which have led to their eventual success. For all high achievers, the most important influence in their lives has almost always been exceptional support and encouragement from their parents. There were plenty of incentives for learning from an early age, and any success was warmly acknowledged and rewarded. Also, their teachers too often took the same attitudes of ready and appropriate praise, which was particularly effective where pupil and teacher liked each other. As they grew up, the motivation of some may have been spurred by curiosity, while for others it was the desire for glory, fame or riches.

In America, Professor Benjamin Bloom and his team (Bloom 1985) phoned to ask 120 men and women under 35 years old, who had reached world-class levels of accomplishment in particular fields – pianists, sculptors, research mathematicians, Olympic swimmers and tennis champions – how they had done it. These achievers told them that no matter what their initial gifts, they had not reached high levels of achievement without a long and intensive process of encouragement, nurturance, education and training. Very few of the successful had been regarded early on as prodigies, so that predictions made in their childhoods would have failed, not least because of their unknown ability at that point to stick out the years of hard work ahead of them.

The parents of these high achievers said they were keen for the children to do their best at all times, and provided the role models with their own behaviour. Many of the parents were obvious perfectionists, setting high standards for the successful completion of a task. They worked on the maxim that if something is worth doing, it is worth doing well. Work was always completed before play – one did not idle in those homes. They checked their children's homework, and household chores were shared by all members of the family. Although these strictures may sound right – touching the guilt in all of us – it is hard to know what the effect of similar parental behaviour would be on children who did not 'make it', as there were no comparison groups of families in Bloom's study, nor the detail of ups and downs that could have been discovered by a more intimate style of investigations.

Yet the question remains – why did these youngsters stick at it at all? Why did they work continually at one type of activity for well over a dozen years and not rebel against their parents' designs for them? As little children, they said they had enjoyed playing at their particular interest, like the piano or the swimming pool, taking a great deal of pleasure from their learning. It was as that initial enthusiasm waned that their parents had stepped in. They'd taken the children to lessons and made sure they practised every day, rewarding them regularly with smiles, gold stars, or even candy bars. And the children had often formed deep relationships with their teachers. Practise became a routine habit like cleaning teeth, which in the end produced the shining feelings of competence and mastery. The high achievers described a lifelong interest and emotional commitment to their particular field, a desire to gain outstanding attainment in it, and a willingness to put in the great amounts of time and effort needed to reach their very high levels of achievement. However, the young people did not always remember that when they had flagged in their enthusiasm it was their parents who had kept them going.

Pressure

Parental pressure
In general, the higher the parents' occupational group in my study, the higher their child's IQ. This was also true in relation to both parents' levels of education, but especially for the father's. Higher-level parental occupation and education were also directly related to increased pressure on the young person to be academically successful, with the expectation that this would happen.

Fortunately, most of the high-flyers seemed to have minds which coordinated well with those of their parents', allowing them an easy and fruitful growing up. The rated estimate of pressure in a family was drawn from a mixture of objective measures, such as what the parents said they had done (e.g. choosing a school because of its academic results) and of my own impression. There were homes in which the pressure to succeed was almost palpable and I felt relieved as I closed the front door behind me that I was not a child in that house. It can be seen in Table 5.4 that the higher the child's IQ the stronger the pressure they were under to succeed.

Table 5.4 Pressure to achieve

IQ group	Strong pressure (per cent)
High	64
Above-average	28
Average	21

Self pressure

It was not just pressure from home that moved the High-IQ pupils to direct their energies into study and to do as well as they did. They were much harder on themselves than were their parents. Significantly, more of them than the other IQ groups described themselves as lazy.

This finding was unexpected and emerged spontaneously as the young people described themselves. There were two possible reasons for the gifted to have such feelings about their own efforts. Firstly, it is probable that they could well see the way things should be done, but when it is not within their power to fulfil those aims, they may blame themselves for their 'laziness'. The second reason may be that it was not a genuine laziness (as most of us understand it), but a form of 'guilt' for finding work so easy, when others had to struggle. This attitude was typical – 'I could have gone in for anything if I'd done the work. The fact is that I did no work and still got seven (Scottish) Highers, so I can sit back and say, yes, I was totally and utterly lazy.' Those with the highest IQs were the most likely to say they were lazy, although their parents disagreed strongly, as can be seen in Table 5.5.

Table 5.5 Perceived laziness

IQ Group	Parents say lazy (per cent)	Subjects says lazy (per cent)
High	6.8	20.3
Above average	13.2	9.4
Average	14.3	–

A few of the gifted young people were particularly hard on themselves, such as Vijay Patel, a tall, gentle youth. Both his Asian parents were cultured, sophisticated scientists. He and his sister, also both scientists, had written a novel which they hoped to publish, and his four A grades had secured him a place at Cambridge. His mother, though, said that she and his father had been somewhat disappointed by their son's results, explaining that he didn't do his best in exams because he was so nervous. Vijay and his parents agreed that he should have worked harder and he rebuked himself for inefficiency because he had followed some tracks in his learning which proved to be dead ends. He was even appreciative of the trouble that one of his teachers had taken in marking his work down to make him strive harder, but had the satisfaction of knowing that – 'They all said about me that I was self-motivated'.

In this study, there was a distinct relationship between academic potential and the drive to realise it from both parents and the highly able children. Both generations seemed to be aware of what the children were capable of academically.

As a significant proportion of the highly able were also in selective academic schools, it can be assumed that they were also given much encouragement there to do well at their exams. Thus, not only did those who were successful have the required innate ability, they also often had an educational environment from both home and school which promoted its fulfilment. Perhaps most importantly, they normally worked in harmony with their circumstances.

But harmony was not given to all, and heavy pressure does not always come from parents to children. It was the lack of balance between the strong pressure David Hancock put on himself, and the total absence of it from his parents, that caused him emotional problems. Both parents had left school at 15 and harboured few ambitions for their son. His dedication to work seemed self-generated, though he was well supported by his school where he had been totally focused in on his career, driving himself beyond most young people's endurance, eventually achieving A grades in five science levels. His latest move was to consciously modify his Northern accent to a Southern one, the better to achieve his career goals. His one creative indulgence was playing the clarinet in the university band. He could be described as a workaholic with dreams.

David Hancock (Gifted, aged 21, studying medicine):

> 'When I was at school, it wasn't that I wanted to be working all the time. Mind you, I always made a point of not working in the dinner hour, because I felt you should have a break in the middle of the day, but sometimes I used to think then that there must be something more useful I could be doing. So being bored in lunch hours was my own fault: I could have worked if I'd wanted to. I don't see any reason why I shouldn't be able to get into a position where I get high up in research and find a new vaccine, maybe for AIDS or rabies. I like to think that in my time I will do a bit of good as a doctor.'

Update 2001: David is an anaesthetist currently working on a year's transfer in the USA. Dreams can be fulfilled.

CHAPTER 6

The flowering of talent

To believe in your own thought, to believe that what is true for you in your private heart is true for all men, – that is genius.
Ralph Waldo Emerson, *Prudence*

Creativity is a part of daily life whenever there is a problem to be solved. It is involved in many if not most everyday decisions and activities, and although it is one of the most sought after features of mental life it is perhaps the most intangible – sometimes called the electricity of the intellect. It is a sensitive way of using knowledge for searching out problems, finding solutions and communicating results. In order to reach mature flowering it needs the means, encouragement, and plenty of practice.

Creative artists of any sort use the same two ways of knowing as everyone else – feeling and reasoning. No special mental skills are necessary other than those to which we already have access. Feeling suggests the direction, and what you feel to be right can be as valid in creativity as a consciously learned technique. Reason supervises decisions, checking that the impetus from feeling is workable. Although one form of knowing may be dominant – physically, mentally and spiritually – harmony in their use is crucial to the expression of talent. The ability to coordinate them develops with experience and it is moulded through sensitivity.

A talented violin student in this study obviously had the knowledge and skill to play her instrument, and she described how she also used her feelings to make the production of a score her own:

'Playing music is a very individual thing; the way you feel it and interpret it, and the way you express it in the instrument you play. I experience what I play; I feel very emotional, very compassionate towards the music. It's just a wonderful sensation.'

But perhaps this emotional investment can be taken too far. The great violinist, Yehudi Menhuin, was often said to be incapable of any intimacy or of emotion not 'validated' by music, and some critics with super-fine hearing complained that his too intellectual life diminished the quality of his playing. Menhuin himself explained poetically (Burton 2001):

'Taught from childhood to keep my emotion under rigid control, I early learned to sublimate into music-making everything that was in me of the dark free world of impulse'

Open flexiblity

Though the production of a creative work is controlled by the two forms of knowing, feeling and reasoning, the key state of mind is open flexibility. An artist has to be able to lift emotional repression and relax mental structures to get to the deep and sometimes irrational feelings from which the work springs. It calls for a strong tolerance of anxiety, because these feelings can be very disturbing in their ambiguous and conflicting meanings. There is also considerable pull between openness and control, between the need to keep the mind open to new information while being aware of inner experiences. It demands the ability to hold a complex mixture of ideas in the mind at the same time, to play with them and work methodically to resolve them to a new form. Indeed, creativity can be seen as a resolution of conflicts, in which the creative individual is able to see the extremes and manipulate them into a working unity. In fact, creative people often prefer complexity, such as asymmetrical designs rather than simple, geometrical ones, perhaps to impose their personal style of order.

Babies are creative
Creative life starts in the cradle. Babies show aesthetic preferences as soon as they can begin to select from the environment, which is soon after birth, reaching a reasonable stage of reliability in their choices at about eight months old. New-born babies, for example, show clear tastes for, say, green over red or different foods. By their first or second year, potentially creative children can already be seen to behave somewhat like creative adults. They are enthusiastic in the time and effort they put into their chosen activities with an uncensored openness to their experiences.

There are two major differences though between the child and the adult creative individual. Firstly, the child is much more tied to the here and now with a limited knowledge-base from which to work. Secondly, the child has not acquired the technical skills to carry out their dreams. Because of these two impediments, the lack of experience and novice technical skills, children's work is not like that of adults, even that of early geniuses such as Mozart or Picasso. It is, however, prodigious for a child (Radford 1990).

Jean Piaget, the great Swiss psychologist, emphasised that early childhood is the most creative period in life of curiosity, candidness and openness – until society starts to squeeze exploration into conformity. Understandably, parents usually teach their children school-type skills like numbers and letters to encourage school success, and so the natural creative interests of the child are not always recognised and encouraged. It provides a terrible dilemma for the highly intelligent child who is capable of nose-to-the-grindstone study to achieve high marks, but who also wants to explore ideas and techniques in a creative way.

How can a child remain both school-clever and creatively productive? There are many ways parents can help. Keeping track of a toddler's interests in a diary will provide a lead for parents as to which direction development should be encouraged, while still leaving the child feeling free to explore. Many other methods for parents are outlined in my book *How to Raise a Bright Child* (Freeman 1995a).

Creativity and intelligence

Creative behaviour is not totally different from the kind of intelligence measured by tests, although a high IQ alone could never be used to predict a creative bent. Indeed, to be truly effective, as distinct from a flash in the pan, all aspects of creativity need an above-average level of intellectual ability. Many studies have settled on a figure of about IQ 120 as a minimum basis or producing lasting creative work, for bringing ideas into a form in which they can be identified as worthwhile.

However, without a good input of intelligence, creative behaviour is so rare as to be a wonder. It is occasionally seen in slow learners (savants) who can draw or play music extraordinarily well, though experts say they merely reproduce variations of what they perceive, rather than working imaginatively. The exceptions are in the brilliant mature drawings by some autistic children, like nine-year-old Nadia who drew horses, though this ability faded as she grew (Selfe 1983), or Stephen Wiltshire who continues to make magnificent drawings of buildings, and even managed to attend art college to improve his technique (Wiltshire 1993). One theory is that these individuals do not use the normal verbal mental routes via reason to make their productions, and so they are free of its inhibition. This does not, though, explain their technical skills.

Research over many years into the lives of successful creative people has shown that they are indeed well above average intelligence and often also intellectual, in that they not only produce art but like to think about the problems and issues in their field. A major intellectual aspect of creative work is in the focusing on ambiguity and feelings, changing them into symbolic form such as words or musical notes, which the artist usually enjoys. This intellectual aspect of the arts was explained by Anna Markland, a highly talented pianist (aged 20, at university):

'There's a difference between music as a subject and music as a practical thing, and the two don't always meet. There were quite a few people at (music) school who were excellent performers but death on the academic side. The two must be combined, because if you don't know how music is actually put together and how it ticks, then what chance can you have of communicating something to an audience? You've got to actually know what it's all about. Thank God I'm doing a music degree.'

But the creative spirit can be crushed by an education which is too information-based, analytical and inflexible, and also by restrictions on the emotional development of children so that they become too fearful to express themselves in their own ways.

Update 2001: Jeremy Kramer – who now, at 36, plays jazz and soul for a living – insisted that his early promotion as a gifted school-achiever, in addition to his exceptionally high-level musical performance, had made him into an uncreative 'performing penguin':

> 'I can't even play jazz: I just learn it. My improvising skills are pretty poor. One can learn how to do it. You start with a chord and use the theory; some notes go with others. I have never gone to the piano to play for pleasure. It was always to impress someone. The pleasure was in the applause not the doing. I don't play for pleasure even now. In fact, I don't know how to create pleasure for myself. I even find it difficult to choose new clothes in a clothes shop.'

Ways of knowing

Even though similar learning experiences give rise to the acquiring of information and the flexing of creative ability, creative ideas must contain the seeds of change, of fresh ways of looking at things. However, the combination of knowledge, flexibility, talent, and intellect are still not enough for the truly creative person. The ability to derive a personal and unique understanding of experiences, then arrive at and stick to one's own conclusions, takes great independence of mind, as well as courage. To be creative is the reverse of being passive and contented: it means being dissatisfied with the status quo and in its fulfilment, and may at an extreme, involve rejection of one's own original style of life. The individual must have a personal grasp of distinct values, beliefs, ideas of self – and an awareness of opportunity – all of which are needed to provide structure for that person's particular sensitivity and perceptions of the world (Perkins 1995).

All studies of fine-artists, writers, etc., have shown them to have had a lifelong tendency to develop unique viewpoints, with enough strength of character to withstand social disapproval as they go on to define themselves in their work. But being creative is not the same as being pointlessly deviant. Real creativity is original and relevant to real life, even though it may take time for it to be seen as such. It also requires long-term effort, or the gifts might lie fallow and unproductive, even in the most potentially rewarding circumstances of the right place and at the right time. In a large American study (Goertzel *et al.* 1978), many artists said they had chosen that way of life because they felt clear about the way they wanted to express their feelings, as well as a strong need to put something right. They said they were sensitive to the way others thought and worked, but often had to work without the understanding of those around them, at times even in an atmosphere of distinct disapproval.

Going it alone

Laurence Turner had chosen to follow his star of creative artist as a fashion designer, with precious little to back him up. He was a tense, thin youth with a strong Liverpool accent. Yet at the age of 21, in just a year, he already had some national recognition, and occupied a whole floor over a shoe shop in the centre of the city, displaying his chunky, simple clothes. He had shown immense courage. His father said that Laurence sometimes went to the big stores selling his wares with apparent confidence, but once outside again, he'd head for the nearest lavatory to be sick.

Laurence's parents were easy-going, warm-hearted people. They lived in a poor area on the outskirts of the city, and had put up their home as security for a loan to give their son a start in his business. His huge debts didn't seem to bother them in the slightest. At our first meeting, in 1974, they told me that even as a new-born he 'hated to be swaddled', as a toddler he was 'determined in all he did, with a memory like an elephant, and an adult sense of humour, which didn't always go down well with other adults'. At 11, he only had just one friend, an 18-year-old boy. His parents had hoped he would become a doctor, with which he had agreed at that time. But he was also 'a bit clumsy', and had fine-motor problems which showed in his difficulties with handwriting: interesting in view of the fine, detailed work this very sensitive, creative young man had chosen.

Laurence's father:

> 'He wanted to be a fashion designer from about the age of fifteen. When he'd finished school he asked us – 'Will you allow me a year off to see what I can do?' He'd already started selling clothes on a second-hand stall. Mother taught him some basic stitch-work and I taught him a little bit about pattern cutting, and now *Vogue* (magazine) has called him a top young British designer. He showed great tenacity and he works extremely hard. I don't think anyone could have made him work as hard at any subject he didn't want to do. He wants to get rid of his overdraft so he can give us our deeds back.'

Laurence Turner (Highly talented, aged 21, fashion designer):

> 'Design is something you've got to have an eye for. Most of the people that come out of the poly here in Liverpool – the stuff they do is rubbish. Well, I was scared

of having my talent diminished by having to conform with what teachers wanted me to do, because that was what had happened in art at school. It was the cutting technique that I need to know, so I got a book on pattern-cutting, and taught myself to cut and sew the basics – arm, body, back, etc. Now I can build blocks for cutting out, and I can alter it to whatever I want.

I took some stuff to a shop in London, they bought it, and in about three months, it was in *Harpers* and *Vogue*. So then I was just caught up in it. Every six months, I do a collection. I go to the library and get the names of about twenty million fabric manufacturers, then phone or write to them, get the samples, and choose. I get really paranoid waiting for the reactions to a collection, and if I get slagged off I can get really depressed, because it catches my self-doubts about the work I'm doing. If I'd gone to a very good fashion school, I would at least have a degree to back me up, but I keep saying to myself – "They're wrong, I'm right".'

I started off really idealistic, head in the clouds about designing. Then I had some real setbacks because there was nobody to tell me about the pitfalls. On one occasion, I could have made fifteen thousand quid, and I didn't, because I didn't know about the production line, so the delivery was late, it wasn't accepted, and I was left with all the goods. I've learned by experience, and it's improving with each season as I get more professional. I think I'll try for the mass market soon.

My parents were very good, and when I got all this good press they said "You must go on". When they see me in all the magazines, my mum can say, "Oh yeah, those are our Laurence's clothes in them magazines". I think they'd have been happier if they hadn't had to put the house up for security, but I think they've got faith in my ability to pay this overdraft off. Making money enables me to buy books, to buy materials so I can do some art, things like that. If I'm good enough, I'll probably have to go to Italy, and I have this dream that I'll go out to New York as well. Right now, it's quite a good act; for the last four months, I've had a flat. But I never have any spare time; I just go to bed when the day ends.'

Update 2001: Lawrence worked abroad for two years, and returned to run his own establishment in Liverpool. He has had his ups and downs, but is now on a steady course making a living through his talent.

Insight

Taking the analogy of creativity as the electricity of intellect further, insightful thinking is the spark which appears to short-circuit reason in a flash of illumination! It is an ephemeral, satisfying joy with a magical quality (Bastick 1982). It is part of all aspects of life, an experience common to everyone, no matter what their level of intelligence. In its various guises it may take the form of just an everyday hunch offering a clue for making a decision, or it may be a deep 'Eureka' experience. That vital spark often comes at times of relaxation, during easy familiar action in the same way that Newton observed the falling apple while musing, Archimedes was taking a bath, James Watt was watching the kettle boil, and Poincaré, the great mathematician, was getting on a bus. Millions of other insights have been responsible for practically every innovative human creation to date. Even Poincaré said that logic alone could neither create anything new nor lead to anywhere but to tautology.

To be insightful is to be human. The computer, though it is a powerful tool used to analyse the most complex data, cannot ask even the simplest meaningful question by itself. Insight is basic to all levels of learning and the most effective teaching constantly seeks to develop it. Yet the thinking styles required for school learning and everyday life are different. School problems normally demand responses from an analytical and sequential style of thinking, such as arithmetic which has specific structures and answers. Everyday matters often require far more of the intuitive, flexible style of thinking with sensitive and free use of feelings. This is because life concerns – like who you marry and where you live – are rarely so clear-cut that they have only one right solution: sometimes several seem equally possible. In fact, just identifying the cause of the trouble, let alone the solution, is usually difficult, because it is part and parcel of the way you live. Everyday problems are very persistent too, one decision sometimes only seems to pave the way for the next set of problems. One cannot just close the textbook and go away. Furthermore, solving a life problem is one thing, but convincing people of the rightness of the solution is another.

At times, the brightest youngsters in my study caused some consternation in their school class with their flashes of insight, especially the gifted mathematicians who vaulted the recognised stages of computation. Although it is often a valuable exercise for such pupils to have to retrace their calculations in a more careful way, too much back-tracking can also act as an impediment for the creative aspects of their thinking. Understandably, teachers have some anxiety in knowing how to help their high-fliers balance the desire to soar with the need to check their working, as the following two boys found.

Simon Powell (Highly gifted, aged 21, studying mathematics at university) explained how it affected him:

'They thought I was only of average ability when we first moved to Scotland, so they put me in the bottom maths class to start with. But my parents complained. Then they moved me up and I immediately went to the top of that class. They were surprised because in maths I used to miss out the working, just write down the answer. One of the masters tried to stop me doing that, tried to make me more methodical, so I stopped making quite as many silly mistakes. Even now at university, I can do a maths question and get everything right, except the addition of two and two. I like to work with concepts, and I just go at too fast a rate. Where I make silly mistakes, other people make conceptual mistakes.'

It wasn't only in mathematics, but in the arts too, that a gifted young person would have a flash of insight, but fail to describe the reasoning behind it, leaving the listener wondering how he had reached that point. David Baker (Gifted, aged 17, at school) found it funny:

'The English teacher sometimes only understands what I mean three hours after – and by that time I can't remember what we were talking about. Once, I suddenly turned on the banks because they were investing in all the evil countries. That's evil invested in evil, which all seemed very relevant to `The Duchess of Malfi'. But the teacher didn't understand at all why suddenly I'd gone onto banks. I had to explain that Barclays was investing in South Africa and Lloyds in Argentina and then she understood.'

Insight springs from the heady stir of past and present experience, and because intuitive thinking involves the whole self, both emotion and intellect make up reactions to the mix of familiar and unfamiliar. Mild anxiety may build up before the 'flash', but after it happens and one knows the rightness of the insight, that confidence releases the tension. People have described the feeling of insight, but it can also be measured by changes in skin response, heart-rate and respiration. It produces a feeling of satisfaction and sometimes euphoria. The confidence which comes from insight also acts as a psychological reward to continue using the intuitive way of thinking, so that the more it is practised, the better it becomes. However, in a threatening situation like examinations, too much anxiety most often inhibits intuition. There was joy on Sarah Mortimer's face when she described for me one of her big mathematical insights:

'Last term, suddenly in the middle of one lecture, I understood the whole point of the course. It suddenly made sense, and everybody else was still sitting there in a haze, wondering what was going on. I'd grasped the concept and that was it. I was away. I could do the rest of it.'

Like any other pupils, the gifted need the enjoyable stimulation of variety, and the excitement that can come from the juxtaposition of ideas. That is why when lessons are too easy as in a mixed-ability classroom, the gifted lose what the other pupils may be getting from it – the satisfaction of tackling and resolving problems. To compensate, they may deliberately stir things up, either in their own minds or among others in the classroom, just to taste the spice of stimulation. Without that, school-work becomes just a rather boring matter of taking in and reproducing what the teacher says, and the flame of discovery burns low. The answer, of course, is to provide the gifted with a stimulating and challenging education appropriate to their needs. One highly gifted boy's mother (maybe assuming a stereotype of a gifted child), considered this the reason for her son's early disturbed behaviour: 'From when he started school until the age of eight, he used to cry and scream and have tantrums, because he wasn't being (mentally) used up, though he was teacher's pet'.

Which creative medium?

What makes one child choose the medium of paint and another that of words or sound to channel their stream of creative energy? Do the arts of painting and writing flow from the same source or have they different springs? Both my own and others' research have shown that general artistic ability does indeed come from the same broad source, but the form the surge takes is to a large extent directed by circumstances.

As soon as a baby first opens its eyes their senses have begun to be directed and, as the baby develops, what it learns to perceive becomes its personal truth. Small children accept what they are aware of as normal. This was how young Catherine Goumas had come to take up the violin. Her mother, a violin teacher, told me (below) how she had given her the musical expertise to get to a prestigious music college. It is very likely that there are millions of children like Catherine and her sister, who could be helped to enjoy a very much higher level of aesthetic awareness and the pleasure of practising it, with the right teaching.

The family lived in a bleak farmhouse, high in the Northern hills. The night I went to see them was pitch-dark, barely a quarter moon in the sky, and well below freezing. There were no signposts, just a right turn after the cattle grid, left down the next lane, right up the next, etc. The water in the bumpy ruts of the cart track had frozen and steep drops waited in the blackness for any careless twist of the steering wheel. On the way, my car became stuck in the backyard of the wrong farm, crashed into a metal wheelbarrow, the noise stimulating several Alsatian dogs to a barking competition. The first, with a great chain collar round its neck, came out of its kennel howling and several others followed. Then the farmer appeared, the pom-pom on his woolly hat wobbling in my headlights. Toothless and affable, he directed me out of the nightmare. I fantasised about the cosy warmth of the farm ahead.

Inside, however, it was not very much warmer than outside. We huddled around the only heat – a low open fire in a very small grate – though curtains, held up with bamboo poles over the doors kept out some of the wind. When the fire went out, which it did several times, Mrs Goumas held a sheet of brown paper in front to improve the draught and revive it. Only the kitchen and that little room were heated. Just once, Mr Goumas came in from working outdoors, clad only in a light sweater and slacks, carrying four small, welcome, pieces of wood, which he put on the fire. He seemed a pleasant if gruff man, but when his wife asked if we could have some more, he replied firmly, 'No, there isn't any more wood'.

Mr Goumas' own farm childhood had been very hard, penny pinching and the windows in his bedroom had been nailed open all year round. He had learned to be careful. His wife said that every penny he earned went into the bank – and stayed there. It was only now when his teenage daughters were performing to applause, that he was beginning to take some pride in them. Catherine was very happy with her mother's choice for her career as a violinist, though she did let slip: 'Sometimes, I felt it was all music, and I really wanted to try something else as well, but I was never given that opportunity'.

Catherine Goumas' mother:

> 'Jacqueline du Pré's mother did precisely the same with her as I did. She sang with her, and tapped rhythms out, frequently and regularly. This is how music starts, and any child, I reckon, could have done what mine have done, if they'd started in the same way.

> Cathy was always on my knee when I was teaching the piano, so she soaked up a lot of music. I usually have serious music on the radio at the same time every day. Both girls came in for musical bombardment one way or another. I teach a lot of bright children and I reckon that if I can catch them early enough, and with parental help, they do exceedingly well. The average child I teach, say from the age of five, can get into the (specialist) music school in five years.

> It was that early music training that got Cathy into the music school, because she was able to sing well in tune. She had a good ear. She could recognise rhythms. She could distinguish high and low notes, intervals, etc. It's the oral side that's very important at an early age, not the practical side, which is a skill only developed over many years – unless, like Yehudi Menhuin, they start off with it. Then when they're eighteen, they don't know what on earth to do and they have to start all over again because it doesn't come naturally any more: he had a terrible problem in his teens. As you know, somebody with a gift for something doesn't think about it, he just does it, and then if somebody else says, "How on earth do you do it?" it can sometimes kill it for them stone dead. They stop doing it because they start to think about it.

> There are very few people who are tone deaf. It's simply that that part of the brain hasn't been encouraged at a young age. The difference between the bright

children I've taught and the ones that aren't bright is that they find it easy, and so they just charge ahead. They're doing all the right balances and everything naturally, whereas with the other ones, you're continually saying "Balances...gently raise this, lower that".

We did get a colossal grant for their education, but we still have to pay out a lot of money, and that has hurt my husband. It's very hard on somebody who's been trained only to save. He has refused at times and I've had to take out a loan, or work extra hours and pay for instruments myself. I've really been the main support of the girls. What most people fear for musical children, except the few that have so much confidence, is insecurity. She's not good enough to be a soloist, and it's a case of where the opportunities come. My whole reason for teaching them music was because it was the one thing I could teach them. I know that if a child is good at one thing, even if they're stupid at everything else, they feel they've got a place in the world.'

It was a similar story for David Baker, but in quite another direction. His architect father had shared with his son something of his own love of nineteenth-century art and architecture, to which David had directed his exceptionally keen and creative self.

David Baker (Gifted, aged 17, at a comprehensive school):

'I like Manchester a lot, going sketching and looking at it. Sometimes I go into the City Art Gallery or the Whitworth Gallery and look round for inspiration. I really get a kick out of looking at things like the pre-Raphaelite paintings: Janie Morris is just incredible, and William Morris, Andy Warhol too, and other artists, they really move me.

My painting does a lot for me. Compared with my peers, it's the best – that's what the teacher said. My art work is original; I'm well into Fauvism; I like colour and I know I have got an ability. I do get a big kick at having spent my time creatively and developed a skill. I'm aware of beauty all the time. Just walking down the road sometimes, looking out of my window, and there's so much here at home – you don't really have to look very far to be moved artistically in here. Just look at the flowers, or the graphics on the record player, not that they're very good, but look at that carving. I'm not wild about the television – I think I'd take that away.'

Update 2001: David is 34 and has become a successful high-earning architect. After his long training, he worked for some years in France, for two rival big-name designer-architects (one after the other), both of whom he found to be hard drivers. But it gave him wide experience and travel all over the world. He returned to London and worked as a freelance for a while, designing restaurants and hotels, in which he is now an expert. He had some bumpy years, got fired a couple of times, and according to his father, cannot have been easy to employ because of his wide experience and learning. He is now in New York as Project Architect for a new big hotel on Broadway. When it is over he intends to set up his own firm. He is not married, other than to his architecture, though he does have a girlfriend.

But there are, of course, genuine differences between the technical production of the arts. The world famous guitarist Segovia once said that he could never have become so skilled if he had not had a strong thumbnail, not a problem for a writer. And though poetry once demanded some fine-motor skill for a readable script, the age of writing machines has alleviated some of those problems – on which hangs the following tale.

When I first met Mary Owen, she was nine-and-a-half-years-old. She played the recorder, loved reading, had a mature way with words and was about to take her national bronze medal for poetry. At that time, she wanted to be a musician, and described herself in her grown-up way as 'somewhat aloof' from her classmates' world of pop culture. Her great love was 'a quite authentic Victorian doll's house', that her father had made for her. However, her mother said Mary had problems at school, for which the headmistress had suggested remedial help.

The next time I met Mary was in the presence of Princess Anne, who was handing her the first prize for a National Poetry Exhibition. Mary was the outright winner from approximately 35,000 entries, chosen quite independently by each of the four judges – of which I was one – though I had not recognised her name. She came up to me and asked if I was the Dr Freeman who had done all that research with gifted children. 'Well' she said, 'I was one of your subjects, and you are coming round to see me soon for the Follow-up!' Of all the prize-givings in the world … as Humphry Bogart might have said.

Mary had also won other poetry prizes in her young life including that of the national Poetry Society. Here is one of her prize-winning poems which she wrote at 15 (*Cadbury's First Book of Children's Poetry*, 1983, p. 76).

Sea Swan

Swan flew heavy
over the sea
clapped white wings in the wind:
snake-neck straight.

Snow swan
settled pressing on the water

watching the faces
of young girls less white than his feathers.
    Grey against grey,
the sea and sky met dull as morning
upon Wales.

Low in the tide,
    two islands
echoed with hollow bird-cries:
January-bare.

Night-dark, in the hills
Fann swims among the reeds
neck gold-banded.
Present in dreams;
she calls to her mate.

And at Moonset
two swans dawn on the water,
ringed in blue-gold;
part of someone's madness.

Like the swan on our sea,
they unfurl their wings to fly,
    leaving only a ripple on still water.

Mary's background was typically Liverpool – mixed and somewhat exotic: one set of great grandparents were black, possibly from the West Indies, one grandmother she thinks was Jewish, a grandfather was Scots and the other from Liverpool. She had jet black hair, long, thick eyelashes, a fair skin and a lively twinkle in her eyes.

The family had moved up a couple of social classes. One of her grandparents had been in service (a maid), one was a bus driver, one a docker, and one did very little. However, their children, that is Mary's parents, had both had higher education in art colleges, and were now art lecturers. Their home was lined with a wide variety of books, including philosophy, poetry and biographies of painters. Mary had an unusually broad understanding of politics, her mind ranging far out of her own surroundings.

At the Follow-up it was clear that Mary's early talent and sensitivity had remained intensely verbal. 'Writing poetry', she said, 'has changed the way I experience life'. However, just as Lawrence Turner, a 'clumsy' child (described above), had moved into the technically precise work of making clothes, Mary had a similarly intriguing problem in view of her brilliance with writing.

Mary's mother described the problem:

'She's always had terrible difficulty with handwriting. When she was younger, she could cope by writing slowly, but by the time she was fifteen, under pressure, it was so bad you just couldn't read it. She also finds drawing and painting very difficult. Now, she types up a lot of her stuff.

At junior school, her needlework was a disaster, and we had to go there lots of times about it. They thought she was being difficult, but she just couldn't cope. She used to come home shaking, really distressed because she couldn't manage needles. The school sent her to the child guidance clinic, and they said her IQ was at gifted level, but the gap between her intelligence and her fine coordination was absolutely awful.

At first, for her, school was total panic and despair. She didn't want to go, so I used to make her, though I used to feel awful coming away. It was a nightmare, so in the end we took her out of junior school and tutored her at home for a couple of terms, until she went to the comprehensive school. At first, she did well there, but then at the end of the second year they began teasing her. She wrote well and her essays were read out, and she knew a lot of things that they didn't know – odd things that made her feel that she was a swot. It wasn't helped by her being a very late developer physically as well; she looked babyish and young. Then we moved, so she was entitled to go to the girls' grammar school (selective), where she could grow up a little bit more slowly, and she's been happier than she's ever been in her life.

The teachers say she's really exciting to teach because she'll stand up and argue and give ideas. The sort of thing she'll do just for her own pleasure is like when she wrote a critical essay on Tennessee Williams. When she only got a C for her English Literature O-level (national exam), the teacher wrote in her report that she'd probably written right out of the topic and gone on to something quite different, which was a bit too sophisticated for that level. Winning the Poetry Prize has let her realise that other people had actually seen that she could do it. I don't think she'll ever stop writing, which is nice.'

Update 2001: Mary went on to university to study English and History, but she said she was bored because it was too easy. She became very thin and dropped out after only a year. She then took a secretarial course and has had several jobs, but has not written a word of poetry since.

David Quinn has had a long hard struggle to be an artist. Even at his modest primary school his overriding interest was for drawing, and it didn't stop. His great interest has always been birds, and he took the plunge to be an artist when he began illustrating natural history books, specialising in bird identification guides and bird behaviour studies. At 41, he is now trying to make the difficult transition from the world of illustration to the Fine Art sphere of Wildlife Art – paintings, exhibitions and Limited Editions, etc.

Update 2001, David says:

'I suppose I come under the umbrella of Wildlife Art, a field which, generally speaking does not lie too happily in the bed of Contemporary Art. I am now known primarily as a bird artist, but it seems that I have depicted everything from a spider's spinnerets in a children's book, to a plate of spaghetti-like parasitic worms for a veterinary advertisement. The highlight of the last decade was, without doubt, the birth of our only child James in 1992. Although I had begun to establish myself as a bird artist, my wife returned to work as a bank clerk and I looked after baby during the day and attempted to do my work at night which, as you can imagine, was not an ideal or easy situation.

The field of Bird Illustration is highly specialised. Bird watching has become a very popular hobby and a real boom leisure industry. Despite receiving many offers of illustration work, I was driven to achieve the highest possible standards, resulting in extremely long hours of work, often to little financial gain and with the sacrifice of any social interaction. In addition, my own high expectations for my work and a feeling that I was somehow wasting my ability in pursuing this line of work, started to chip away at my resolve.

By the mid 1990s, however, I was being regarded as the best in my field by many leading ornithologists and peers. Their acclaim, for example in book reviews, was of little interest to me in all honesty, for I always felt I could achieve a greater sense of fulfilment as a Fine Artist. I began to resent not only this artistically limiting field of work, but also my inability to generate sufficient money for myself and for the security of my family. It was at this time that I began to experience episodes of depression. Although I could not motivate myself to work, our family unit remained loving and stable despite our limited income.

I was about to quit the bird illustration 'scene' but over the next few months, I turned things around and began to produce some of my best work in several books, though generating a sufficient income remained difficult. For a long time, I have felt that my 'future' lies in North American wildlife art. I was approached to join a team of artists on the National Geographic Guide to Birds of North America, which I did over a six month period. Last year I had my first public show of work at the British Birdwatching Fair, a massive event, and Joan and I were bowled over by the response towards my work. I also received an award, with the author for Best Bird Book of the Year – a book about the lives of Cuckoos.'

Musical talent

Music is probably the most popular of all the arts, important for almost everyone in the world – and it also had a special place in this research. All the twelve children who had been at a specialist music school in the first study had agreed to be included in the Follow-up (7 per cent of the whole), and their progression in the intervening years had been interesting. They had often found the competition fierce, and carving a route through to success had always demanded their exceptional determination and discipline, as well as an enthusiasm and dedication from their teachers, far beyond that of normal teaching. This keenness was not unique to the musicians, however. As a student actor said – 'I'd never send a sensitive child to a stage school – no way. I've seen people who were really talented come out of that place who did not have the killer instinct, and left within twelve months. But since the stage is such a competitive industry, perhaps that's the way it should be.'

At the specialist music school, pupils studied the full academic syllabus as well as their instruments and consequently the overall workload was very heavy. Several had found it so difficult to integrate their academic and musical work that they had given up the struggle with one. But for most, in spite of the intense pressure, the love of music and joy of playing were quite enough to keep them hard at work.

Deborah Lewis (Musically talented, aged 19, at music college):

'We were there to work. If you didn't do your homework properly because you said you had a rehearsal till quite late on at night – that was no excuse. And if you didn't get to a rehearsal on time because you were doing your homework, or because you had a lesson, that was still no excuse. Even in the time when it was getting close to A-levels, you could have rehearsals till half-eight at night, on top of a full day at school.

Can you imagine, having to go home and start your homework about half-nine, especially if you're tired? At A-level time especially, I was still at school till about eight o'clock in the evening. Then you'd be expected to come home to four hours of practice, homework on top of that, and it was often twelve or one o'clock before I was in bed. I was never able to rest. A lot of people skipped games, thinking that the two hours was a waste of time and they'd much rather practice, which made the headmaster worried about his pupils not getting enough fresh air and exercise. You had to feel sorry for the boarders. Some had been there since they were only seven, maybe because their parents wanted them to be musical whiz kids.

The standard of competition is so very, very high, and not winning can be so wounding when you're young. You've got to go in with the attitude that if you don't play well on the day it doesn't matter, it's no indication of your talent. But when you're up there playing, you can control your nerves because you're putting your whole self into the music.'

Many local education authorities in Britain had a system in which musical instruments can be rented at nominal cost, and music teachers would come to the school to give free lessons if there were sufficient pupils there. It inspired many a young musician, as Deborah went on to explain:

'I got my first oboe lessons from the Salford Music Centre; they helped me choose an instrument. Anybody could go free, if you were willing to learn. It's on Saturday mornings, and there's all sorts of wind bands and orchestras, and once you get to a certain standard, you can play in them. It makes it all good fun. The oboe is very difficult to start with because it doesn't make a particularly nice sound, but I plugged away at it and I really liked it in the end; in fact it's my whole life now.'

Update 2001: Deborah is a fine professional musician. Good provision allied with her talent and hard work has paid off.

The home support system
As concert pianists go, Anna Markland's background was far from promising, and yet she had won the most prestigious all-instrument, national competition in Britain, the BBC's Young Musician of the Year, before millions of television viewers. Both her sets of grandparents had come over from Ireland to live in the poorest, toughest part of Liverpool. Her father described his family as 'factory hands', but (and this is where detailed questioning pays) her great-grandparents on her mother's side had both been concert performers, her grandmother having 'got her music degree, her cap and gown at 14 from Trinity College Dublin'. Her grandmother's talent, though, seemed to have entirely skipped two generations. Anna also had an uncle who drove a motor bike in the Wall-of-Death, sometimes running a fairground booth, or at times simply dug ditches. Whatever genes had come through to Anna, it has cast her talent in fire.

Anna's parents now lived in a tiny house in the middle of a large, featureless, pre-war council estate outside Liverpool. It must have been designed to look pretty on the drawing board, without any idea that its inhabitants would own cars, so that there was a dark icy walk of more than a hundred yards from the road to reach the front door. Once opened, however, it revealed a gleaming, magnificent, full-size, grand piano which filled about a third of the entire downstairs area. Anna, now studying music at Oxford, had made the cultural jump to her present status as a nationally known figure with great assurance. She loved her parents, who had given her all the support they could, and visited them often.

Anna Markland (Highly talented, aged 20, studying music at university):

'When I was ten years old, my music teacher arranged for an audition for Chethams School of Music: great fun for about two and a half hours. They told me how I *should* be playing the violin, as opposed to how I *was* playing the violin – and they took me in to study the piano!

I thought there was too much emphasis on music there, music, music, music all the time, when people should have been going pot-holing, or playing sports. A lot of talented young musicians lose out on that. A lot of them also suffer from an adverse amount of competition, especially string players. They get so anxious, going round in kid gloves all day to protect their fingers. Maybe I shouldn't be playing hockey now, but I've never come to any harm, and I'm careful and look after my hands.

I use as many differing emotions that I can get hold of in my playing, and I gained from the experience of the BBC competition and all its ramifications with other people – like jealousy. It's useful being a pianist, whenever I'm feeling fed up, I just go and hit hell out of that piano for two hours. But during a concert I don't feel moved because I'm concentrating on communicating; it comes afterwards. The emotions are somehow inbuilt in a piece. Take the Liszt sonata I'm doing at the moment. I've thought out a particular theme for it and whilst I'm practising I'm thinking – yes, he's meeting her, he's taking her out to dinner for the first time. But then when I'm playing it for real, I'll play the whole thing through from beginning to end, trying to play it the way I think Liszt would have wanted me to.

I like to put in between four and six hours practice a day, though there's only room in my academic timetable for about three. But I'm basically a very lazy person, and anyway, there's more to life than doing academic work and music. I can concentrate quite easily, but when I've finished maybe four or five hours of solid concentrated practice I'm completely exhausted.

I'm very lucky to have an audience to play to, with, let's face it, national recognition. I've found something that I'm good at; it's marvellous, and I'm just incredibly happy. From the mercenary point of view, it is nice to be able to go out and buy what you want; I get professional fees now. I get days when I think – God, wouldn't it be lovely to take the musical world by storm – I'm going to be a performer.'

Update 2001: Anna continues to radiate exuberance for life and sheer happiness. Yet she has known despair. While still at school she was aware that her arms became tired after long practice. The problem reappeared at Oxford, but after two more years postgraduate study at the Royal College of Music her arms just refused to work any more and she had to give up playing. She was naturally very distressed and depressed. But, as she said cheerfully, there is no cloud without a silver lining. She had already started singing at university so she put serious energy into her voice. Now 36, she has made an excellent career singing in a group which was formed 14 years ago in Oxford. She loves it, but has also slowly returned to piano playing, and does 'only' about 20 concerts a year. She travels all over the world giving one kind of concert or another.

She says she has three different jobs, the singing, the piano and being a wife (to a management consultant who travels a lot) and mummy to two advanced children. 'A very hectic life. I love it all. No two days are ever the same. I'm a musical chameleon: couldn't imagine playing the piano for the rest of my life. I can safely say it has all been a success story.'

> 'John's singing in a concert on Friday,' Mrs Daszak told me. 'Wouldn't you like to come so that you could then say you'd heard him sing before he was famous?' She was a woman of passion, with absolute faith in her family, and had devoted her life to their achievements. John, a large, easy-going fellow, took it all in his stride, and agreed with her that because he was so clever, he didn't have to exert himself academically, and consequently he had not done well in his school exams.

John Daszak's mother:

> 'John definitely has a presence – a sort of aura. It was definitely proven by the time he was two-and-a-half that he was musically gifted. My husband proved it in as much as he tested him. First of all by the fact that he went to the piano and would sit there for over an hour, which is good at that age; concentrate and sit there. Not plonk, plonk, plonking, or banging, but picking out little notes, not definite tunes, but obviously a tune was in his mind. It was even obvious to me who's tone deaf.

> When he was between three-and-a-half to four, and hadn't yet started school, he used to carry around a small book about musical instruments; he'd point to the violin and say that he wanted one. We had a violin on the top of the wardrobe, which someone had given to us. One day when I was cleaning upstairs, I got it down for him, and he was absolutely thrilled trying to get tunes out of it. My husband felt that we ought to try and encourage this, and to that end, we asked a local violin teacher, but she refused to teach him, saying that he was much too young. We were at our wit's end because it was getting increasingly obvious that

he wanted it very much and was obviously able to do something. So I phoned up the School of Music and asked them could they recommend a violin teacher who would take on a very young child. They did, and he started having lessons just before he was six.

Even though he passed the audition for the Music School at six-years-old, the Education Authority said they wouldn't pay till a year later. So he had to wait. I'd like to say that Mozart was composing at four, but if he'd have come under our Local Education Authority he wouldn't have been acknowledged. It was a desperate thing for us to pay for these private lessons at the time, and also to get him to his lessons. We didn't have a car, and I had to take him on a bus and a train, and I had two other young children. But we managed, and he went on from strength to strength. That year, after he'd been refused entrance into the Music School, he entered various competitions and just wiped the board at all the local festivals. Eventually, he started there at seven.'

Update 2001: Mrs Daszak made great progress herself. She had gone out to work to support her children and with little education, rose from humble typist to be Personnel Officer of a large trade union. John's brother became a scientist of renown and honour by the age of 34.

John Daszak (a talented singer, aged 19, at music college):

'I gave up the violin when I was twelve because I hadn't progressed as well as I could have done, but it did give me a good background knowledge of working in orchestras and learning different sorts of music. Since then I've been singing, though I took up the double bass whilst my voice was breaking. You've got to wait for your voice to develop fully before you can really get anywhere, but whilst it's settling down, you can always work on repertoire and languages. I'd like to end up in either Italy or America, if I can get to the right standard as an opera singer.'

Update 2001: John Daszak's mother's faith in him has been entirely justified. He went from Chethams School of Music to the Guildhall in London, but found it deadening because he was obliged to study Lieder style for two years with very little performance, which is what he'd been trained for at Chetham's. He became despondent and thought of giving it all up. Fortunately, the principal there suggested he audition for The Royal Northern College of Music where he spent five blissfully happy years, and also met his future wife, another singer (they have two little children). He told me of the long struggle: 'As a singer, especially a man, it takes time to develop the voice and physique needed to sing opera. Performing as a singer is a part of life's experience. It's part of communicating with your audience.'

John started his professional life singing in an opera chorus for several years, then won a scholarship to study in Italy: 'They look at singing in a different way there'.

He sang as an understudy until he felt able to go freelance as a soloist. He says that because of his long years of study and varied musical background he is able to sing many parts that others cannot. He now sings with the English National Opera and has sung as a soloist in many of the finest opera houses in Europe, such as the lead in Peter Grimes at La Scala, Milan.

Stifled creativity

All abilities are promoted by the same general environmental influences – encouragement, example, and educational facilities. But at their highest levels, the emotional aspects of those influences may diverge, and may even be contradictory. Because creativity draws on emotional and personality factors it needs emotional freedom to flower, whereas successful academic achievement is more dependent on emotional control, as well as educational input.

Conformity and repression are the enemies of creative activity, but they are excellent for promoting high achievement in school exams, especially in science. The intense absorption of information that had been expected of many of the intellectually gifted pupils in this study sometimes left them feeling creatively and emotionally squeezed dry. Those university door-opening A grades demanded such single-minded determination that leisure activities were squashed by study, which sapped the young people's time and inclination for anything else. Even their critical thinking was dimmed; some saying wearily that it was simply easier for them to stick to getting through a hard day's travel, school and homework, without spending precious energy considering alternative points of view.

When you are gifted across the board, how can you be expected to know yourself so well in your early teens that you can choose which side of the educational chasm to climb? The problem is that almost all higher education students are selected on the basis of their school academic results, with the inbuilt expectation that somehow the brightest will be creative in their work when they get as far as research, whether in science or the arts. Several young people in this study who had been placed in that dilemma at school and had made the wrong choice, which they had then either to try and put right, or continue on the wrong track. Fortunately though, many did survive the selection system with both creative and academic traits intact.

In high academic achiever Donald Purdey's home, there wasn't a book to be seen. All he had known from his school was an indigestible diet of learning, more and more information. But now at university, his emotional shell was starting to crack with the new growth of his long stifled creative urge.

Donald Purdey (Highly gifted, aged 21, studying engineering):

'The school I went to was so far away, I couldn't take part in extracurricular activities. Anyway, it was a real sweatshop, so I didn't really enjoy it very much. I couldn't go to the local comprehensive because it's not very good; it hasn't even got a sixth form. Round here, you usually just finish school at sixteen and go into an apprenticeship, but my school was all geared towards university, so I was swept along in the tide. The trouble was that Oxford and Cambridge were the be-all and end-all, and I didn't make it.

Sometimes I feel disadvantaged in that I crammed a lot of science, but didn't develop myself culturally. I've never read novels or anything like that, and I've never bought a book in my life, even at university, though I intend to try and catch up on it. With having to do all that work, I was quite happy to be railroaded, and I didn't think a lot or question things. That's how I came to try LSD. I was just intrigued to know what it was like, because life is about feelings that you get out of doing something – pleasures and experiences. But it was hallucinogenic, horrible.

My dad's a painter and decorator, but he just puts up the paper that somebody else has chosen; I'd like to work out what would suit the room best, and maybe one day even design a house. One guiding reason for doing engineering at university was that I was sponsored. To have done another course would have been stretching things financially, and my dad wasn't too keen on giving the parental contribution.

I've been working with steam turbines. The way it's taught at university, you didn't have to be anywhere near one, but you do really have to learn its notes to know how it is running. It's through my analogies of where I feel it fits into the real world that I can see an application for all the maths I learned straight off. It is exciting to design. If I'm designing something that needs thinking out, and I suddenly realise that I'm getting there, I can't get it out of my mind. It's always there from morning to night. I just can't switch off it. I did it at work on one of my own designs; I hadn't read it in a book, I'd worked it out all by myself. I was concentrating on it all day, and time goes so quickly then.'

Update 2001: Donald has moved a long way from steam turbines. After his PhD he moved into medical engineering, making replacement joints, until his firm was bought out, then with his wife and two children, he moved to Cannes. Soon they will move to Germany, where he will leave practical engineering to work at the patent office. At 38, Donald is discovering the arts. He's bought oils to start painting, is intending to go to the opera, and has bought an annual ticket for the art gallery. But he is still a very hard worker and does not like to waste time.

Science or the Arts

Gifted youngsters do have a tendency to throw themselves into their chosen activities with such force that possible alternatives are left bobbing in the backwash. At school in Britain, young teenagers are often obliged to choose between studying arts or science. In my study, the idea was found to be popular, especially among parents, that if you chose sciences you could always pick up on the arts, almost as hobbies, but that if you went for arts subjects sciences would remain a mystery to you for ever. When earning a living was felt to be the most important goal of education, parents saw science as pre-eminent: 51 per cent considered science more important in education, only 8 per cent thought the arts were more important, and the rest made no choice.

An unskilled father voiced many parent's feelings: 'There's not really that much call for music or arts. Then again, some people do get a lot of pleasure out of art, but what you go to school for is learning, to get a job at the end of it, to get you out of the house.' And a gifted girl reasoned: 'There are a lot of jobs which are general, but jobs which are for scientists you couldn't get if you were an artist.'

Quite apart from the heavy academic workload which the high achievers in all subjects had to face, many of those who opted only for science had the additional distress of feeling aesthetically isolated and unfulfilled; their anticipated self-generating understanding of the arts had not after all materialised.

Raymond Grey (Highly gifted, aged 21, at university):

'I'm really an arts person, but I am also very good at sciences and that's what I chose at fifteen. But the timetable at school was so rigid you couldn't mix subjects, and it was a mistake. Taking science restricted me in a way that I didn't think it would. In the end I just never got the chance to try anything else, and that was when I began really to hate and detest what I was doing. They said that you couldn't possibly get through your A-levels (exams) if you were doing a subject that you didn't like. I didn't believe them, and I was right. I got all A's. Trouble was, I failed my Oxford interview when they discovered I wasn't very interested in physics. They nailed me when they started asking questions about reading around the subject, and I hadn't done any. But I'm still studying physics. I do like music, not that I'm ever moved to tears or anything, but it often stirs me. I'd like to spend more time with it one day.'

It could happen the other way too. No matter how much a talented and enthusiastic child wanted it, and no matter how carefully it was considered, to enter a specialist school and devote one's life to the study of an art was sometimes the wrong decision. An ex-music school pupil, had quite simply, made the wrong choice. He told me:

'I came to the conclusion that I preferred the sciences, which is why I left. It's a totally different type of person that likes music, from one that likes science. A musician knows things will happen, but he's not bothered why. He knows that playing his violin is going to make a certain sound, because he's holding his fingers that way. Whereas for a scientist, that wouldn't be enough; he wants to know why it's doing that. He'd learn all about nodes and wavelengths, and lengthening the strings. Musicians aren't worried about the wave-form in there; they're just happy with it as it is.'

Gentle Catherine Goumas (whose mother had organised her into the music school) said wistfully: 'I went there to do music I know, but I have a creative tendency and I would have enjoyed some alternatives, like fashion design, or textiles.'

The cost of high academic achievement

At times, academic research can be hard work, which then is given an added excitement by an unexpected revelation which lights up a whole new area. This happened in the Follow-up study with responses to the question – What gives you the greatest pleasure? It had been designed simply as a pleasant way of rounding off an interview of many hours. Table 6.1 shows how the whole sample answered

Table 6.1 What gives you the greatest pleasure?

	Per cent
Relationships	37
Achievement	24
A mixture of things	23
Creative/aesthetic activities	7
Nature	5
Physical activities	4

Using all the collected data from the whole long study, I made a statistical comparison between those who chose achievement as their greatest pleasure – the Achievers – and those who found their greatest pleasure in creative activity – the Creatives. (The statistical procedure allowed for the unbalanced proportions of the 41 Achievers and 11 Creatives. Indeed, what a small proportion of the 169 young people found their major satisfaction in creativity).

The results provided a clear picture of two kinds of young people in terms of their outlooks, personalities and scholastic success, all at high (1 per cent) levels of significance. Overall, the Creatives came from homes which gave them more aesthetic example and support, whereas the Achievers came from homes where academic success, especially in science, took precedence over aesthetic endeavour.

Important influences on the two groups

IQ: The most important finding was that there was virtually no statistically significant difference between the general intelligence of the Achievers and the Creatives. Both groups were at gifted level. The non-gifted had been less specific in their answers and so did not enter these categories.

Gender: Most of the Achievers (93 per cent) were boys and most of the Creatives (73 per cent) were girls.

Examinations: Although the Creatives had taken a wider range of subjects than the Achievers, they were considerably less successful in terms of grades.

Parental attitudes: The Achievers had usually grown up in families that had greatly encouraged them in their schoolwork from an early age, while their more creative urges were more often curbed.

Culture: The general ambience and decor of the Creative's homes were more carefully considered, and there was a wider range of books around than in those of the Achievers. But the biggest cultural difference was in the quality of music. The Creatives had a much more serious level of music at home and were far more likely to sit and listen as a family, almost never using it merely as background.

Emotion: The results of a test of emotional adjustment (Stott 1976) which had been given to children in 1974, was re-examined in terms of the young people's present behaviour. Even then the potential Achievers had been significantly much more troubled with emotion and relationship problems, and it still proved to be so. Ten years earlier the Achievers group had scored by far the highest hostility rating in the whole sample, 33 per cent, scoring above average on the nationally standardised test. But of the Creatives at that time, 91 per cent did not manage a single score on the hostility rating. It was a similar picture with relationships – the Achievers then had scored the highest peer-maladaptiveness rating of any grouping while the Creatives scored nil.

In the Follow-up the Achievers described themselves as significantly more often experiencing depression at times, and had much more difficulty with friendships than the Creatives. Although both groups had the same high intelligence, the Achievers saw their giftedness as a social handicap, an aspect of themselves which other people did not like (63 per cent) and on which they blamed their lack of friends. This was not so for the Creatives (9 per cent), who largely disregarded their gifts. The differences were clearly in each one's self-concept, and not in actual ability. The Creatives in this comparison also felt themselves to be empathetic twice as frequently as the Achievers.

Achievement does imply some competition, if only with oneself. It could be that the competitive element in the ambition to achieve runs counter to forming close relationships, especially with people of one's own age. Far more of the Achievers (17 per cent) said that they only had friends older than themselves, which was entirely untrue for the Creatives, almost all of whom had friends of all ages. The Creatives were also much more communicative; twice as many (40 per cent) described themselves as talking a lot, compared with the Achievers (20 per cent). To the interviewer, the Creatives were also livelier and much more fun to be with.

School: The Creatives were far more likely to be unhappy with their schools (36 per cent compared with 10 per cent) and far more of them (19 per cent compared with 5 per cent) had serious problems there. But they also had livelier, more individual attitudes to school, far more of them (55 per cent compared with 24 per cent) suggested more than three ways in which they thought it could be changed for the better. It looked as though the Creatively inclined either had much greater difficulty in fitting in with the system – or that the system was not flexible enough to cope with them. One creative boy explained:

> 'One of my great grudges against the school is that they only like people who conform – "Do your collar up", kind of thing. Well, I'm a bit different from the other people. They all tend to sit down and do work and I don't. I'm a bit more extrovert and they don't like that; I like to have a bit of a joke with the teachers – I don't go too far I don't think, though my hairstyle tends to provoke some "mention".'

Their discomfort in the system also showed in the Creatives' greater dissatisfaction with their careers advice because they more often wanted to tread an unconventional path. The vast majority (82 per cent) were unhappy about what they had been given, compared with the Achievers (43 per cent), who usually went on to conventional courses at university and so had far fewer vocational problems.

Leisure: Though the Achievers actually did have a greater variety of spare-time pursuits than the Creatives, fewer of those, such as team sport, could be termed personally creative. They also showed less involvement and perseverance in their chosen activities than the Creatives, and they tended to opt out and relax more into TV, 76 per cent of Achievers choosing mainly light TV, compared with 54 per cent of the Creatives. In childhood, though, the Achievers appeared to have enjoyed the same creative satisfaction as the rest of the sample, but as they reached the peak of intense study at 18, and certainly by the age of 20, few reported it, unlike most of the whole sample for whom there seemed to be little change.

The big pleasure for all the gifted teenagers was language. It showed in their floods of words in answers to my questions, though one boy admitted he talked in such torrents because it was expected of him as he was seen as gifted. It also showed in a great deal of private poetry, and in reading, as David Baker said:

> 'Balance is what I aim for. I do a little bit of drawing, and sometimes I write poetry. I'm deeply moved by poetry because it's very intense – far more so than novels.

Poets work best when they're depressed, and that's when I've written some of my best stuff. In the summer, when I've not got much else to do, I read about two library books a day. My own, I read over and over again.'

Most of the Achievers were well aware and also sorry about their loss of creative satisfaction in choosing to go all out for high examination success. But just a few had made considerable efforts to harmonise the academic and creative sides of their lives, like 14-year-old Dominic Thomas:

'I'm good at maths, chemistry and physics; pretty all round really, but I certainly have a leaning towards the arts, and I'd like to be far more artistic than I am. Balance is what I aim for; keeping my interests outside school, like with my rugby and singing. I do quite a lot of photography; I've got an enlarger and all that sort of thing. I do a little bit of drawing, and sometimes I write poetry. I'm deeply moved by poetry because it's very intense – far more so than novels.'

Update 2001: Dominic, at 31, had managed to accomplish exactly what he had intended at 14. He just missed a first-class degree in English because, he said: 'I enjoy having fun too much'. He went to Milan to teach English for a couple of years, having written his final dissertation on Dante, then qualified as a barrister (lawyer), a profession he is enjoying because as a self-employed person he can take time off. 'I am good at enjoying myself,' he explained. 'I get better at doing what I always did; I'm more of an expert at life balance. You get to know yourself as you get older and you get to know your limitations.' Because of the fun in his life he knows he 'underperforms as against potential', but he prefers it that way. He will marry his adored girlfriend soon with a 'happy inevitability'.

Many of the most ardent Achievers, however, had some difficulty in answering the questions which called for a touch of imagination, such as how they would spend unlimited money. The creative young people, though, took a more enthusiastic view of such a windfall, as Danny Smith (Gifted, aged 16, at school) imagined:

'I'd build a commune. It would be huge, really massive, and take millions of pounds to build, and the people in it would be totally good. There's a few people like that around, like me, you know, people who think like I think. It could be in a huge, secluded house, with really nice places around it, with lakes. Then you don't need anything else, it would be just like Utopia within twenty-foot stone walls with an electrified fence on the top. It would be great. I spent the whole of Sunday afternoon planning it when I should have been doing my homework.'

CHAPTER 7

Schooldays

And gladly wolde he lerne, and gladly teche.
Geoffrey Chaucer, Prologue to *The Canterbury Tales*

Schools in Britain range from large, highly organised, all-comer comprehensives to small private ones; from those with 95 per cent minority children to others where no minority child has ever been seen. While in some Local Authority schools the teaching of any foreign language is a rarity, others offer Urdu and Turkish and many more; while some private schools teach ancient Greek and Latin to seven year olds. To complicate matters further, each pupil reacts personally to the same provision. But it is only by asking those on the receiving end that it is possible to see where they find it irritating and useless or satisfying and valuable. This articulate sample of bright, sensitive young people had no inhibitions about telling me. Between them, they attended a great variety of schools, and their sincere accounts provide valuable feedback for those who will heed them.

There is no getting away from politics in education. Perhaps the greatest difference in outlook between the United States and Britain, is that in the former education is presented as a vehicle for opportunity in life and there are always chances to keep going in spite of any breaks from it. In Britain, however, children have to jump through state examination hoops at particular times, or face heavy psychological and financial disincentives from re-entering the educational system. This more black and white view adds pressure to completing the course at the appropriate time. In addition, centuries of continuous educational selection whether by wealth or ability, and of deference to those who have passed the barriers, have left their mark on a society where social élitism can still sometimes masquerade as high quality. (Details of the British system at the time of the Follow-up are described in Appendix 1, though educational provision changes constantly: and the sample's academic and performance in it are described in Appendix 3.)

School experiences

A normal classroom is a fairly structured place, activities focusing on the content of the lesson, which is designed so that the pupil's performance is correctable and thus improvable by the teacher. There is normally a dominant concern with information – which provides two problems for gifted pupils who are also interested in ideas for their own sakes and, the connected social problem, of how to adapt to the class while remaining intellectually alive and thus different. In fact, it is virtually impossible to show intellectually gifted behaviour without distinguishing oneself from one's school-fellows, unless the whole class is equally gifted, which does happen. Occasionally in this sample, pupils' efforts at serious thinking around the syllabus were treated with flippancy, but even more so were some attempts at creative work. This was even true at some rather rigid primary schools, graphically described by Adrian Lambert:

> 'In junior school we were told to write a book to take a week and I filled about three books in a day. But it wasn't what the teacher wanted, so, to make sure that everybody else was more diligent, she read it out then ripped it up in front of everybody, with some of my funny poems too, which everybody else appreciated. She'd rip them up to general amusement. If I'd say anything that the teacher didn't have knowledge of, I'd be seen as a real Smart Alec, and she wouldn't ask me again.'

The gifted may thus find themselves intellectually isolated, and need the frame of reference which is to be found in the company of people like themselves; as Rachel who had been accelerated too fast, said with feeling:

> 'If I have a child like me, I would definitely send him or her to a school where I knew they catered only for clever children. I would pay fees, and go without things myself to give my children that. Or at least, a school which had quite a lot of clever children, because then you get some sort of companionship, people to talk to of your own ability.'

Some children cope with their dilemma by behaving stupidly in class, such as shouting out silly answers to show how 'normal' they are. Others may become overly conformist, divert attention to someone who is an even more determined scholar, or become the class clown. One highly gifted girl explained: 'If I'm not in competition with people the same level, I get very lazy. Even with only moderate ability differences, I just feel superior, and so bored when we go over things so often.'

There is also sometimes a 'work-restriction' norm among pupils, which is more common in poorly cultured areas, though it can even operate at selective schools. There seems to be a strange classroom lore that it is acceptable to come top of the class – as long as you are not seen to work for it – as though achievement were predestined and that to work hard is interfering with nature. At some schools, it can mean that a child who wants to achieve high marks may have to study in secret to avoid the disapproval of schoolmates.

Unfortunately, although they are usually unaware of it, many teachers (even those who teach the gifted) direct the class to work at around its average level. Unifying the class in this way makes teaching easier, but can cause difficulty for a gifted child in a predominately average-ability school. A student teacher in my sample noted: 'From having been a pupil and having attempted to be a teacher, I see that the middle-ability band gets by far the most tuition, the top stream gets bored, and doesn't get stretched enough, while the bottom stream haven't got a clue what's going on.'

Many bright youngsters felt sympathy for the teacher in what they saw as the impossible task of teaching them in mixed-ability classes: 'It's just asking too much of one teacher to be able to cope with the diversity of abilities every single lesson'. Some felt a little guilty: 'Its not that I want to dominate people of a lower ability, but it's too hard for the poor teacher, having to teach at all ability levels.'

Some teachers coped with this problem by making 'assistant' teachers of the more advanced children, using them to instruct the slower ones. But for the brightest, who did not seem to enjoy the teaching, it really meant that they were marking time till the rest caught up. It was described quite spontaneously by several in the sample, as by Quentin Cooke:

> 'When I was about six or seven, we were divided by age and I was very, very far ahead of most others. Often, when the teacher got so overworked with children not understanding, she used to send them to me to try and explain it. Well, I felt partly flattered and partly annoyed, because it just took up my time when I could be doing something else; it was so unbelievably easy that I didn't benefit from doing it all over again. And some of my "pupils" were resentful, too, but I could take that.'

The Three-times Problem

In a normal classroom, the teacher usually says the same thing three times. First as an introduction – this is what I am going to tell you; again to boost it – now I am telling it to you; and then to summarise and make sure – that is what I have just told you. But the gifted remember it the first time round, which I have termed their Three-times Problem. In order to avoid the tedium of the three repetitions, they often devise a special technique. They teach themselves only to listen consciously on the first occasion and switch off for the following two. This demands a very high level of mental skill, which takes some practice to perfect. Highly gifted Caroline Hardman (aged 20) described how it was for her:

'In the lectures, I listen to everything the first time, but when they start going over and over the same thing, I use my automatic switch-off button. It started at school, where lessons were more or less handed to you on a plate. You can tell by the tone of the voice when it's coming again; it becomes a knack after sitting through hours and hours of lessons and lectures, especially when you keep having the same teacher. And it's the way they say, "Now, then", and I think, "Right, I've got five minutes to myself now". It can be really boring when lecturers say the same thing four times. We had one who asked, "Now has anybody got any questions?" and nobody said a word. So he said, "You've taken so long with nobody saying something that obviously none of you can understand it, so I'll go through it again." Ohhh!'

The danger is that before this technique has reached a state of reliability, the switch-off may go on too long and cause the child to miss some first-time round explanations. But the missing parts may be vital – perhaps a brick in the foundation of knowledge on which future learning has to be built. And skipping can get to be a bad, lazy habit. It becomes easier to slip into a dreamland of one's own than to adjust one's mind to new information. The learning of the gifted can seem erratic because of it, which is understandably confusing to teachers and parents. They seem to learn some things well – whatever they have listened to – then have the gaps where they have switched off. With bits missing they can reach the wrong conclusions, which nevertheless they may hold firmly.

Even in selective education, the Three-times Problem still holds true for those of the very highest ability because there is always some difference of ability between members of a class. A highly gifted boy explained: 'Even in our rarefied maths set, there were one or two people that found it intensely difficult, so the teacher would sometimes have to go back over certain points several times. I'd cut off, but I didn't lose track of what was happening, I would switch back in again when we got onto a new area.'

Types of school

Pupils with the highest IQs and thus the most academic potential, were not distributed evenly throughout the different kinds of schools (see Appendix 1 for explanations of schools). They were far more likely to go to selective (either private or state) single-sex schools, whilst the lower IQ pupils were more likely to go to mixed-ability comprehensives (see Table 7.1). Considering both the potential academic ability of their pupils and their strong focus on examination success, it was not surprising that the selective schools produce an overall higher level of examination success than the other schools.

Table 7.1 IQ and type of school

Mean IQ	Type of school
153	Selective
143	Private
134	Grammar
128	Comprehensive
127	Secondary modern

Selective schools

When they could, parents of gifted children, whether members of NAGC or not, often chose a school where the pupils were selected by high ability – selective schools. Although the majority of children at such schools had won scholarships to them, some were paid for by their parents. Several families had moved house to an area where there were free selective grammar schools. A mother of a highly gifted boy explained:

'Up to the age of eleven, he was standing out like a sore thumb. He used to come home from school and say "I won't put my hand up any more and answer questions". Now in this school, because they select, at last he's one of the lads, and it's such a relief. There's so much there that he enjoys. If he had to change school and go back into mixed ability, he would try to smother his talent again.'

When I asked the young people about their feelings on selective or mixed-ability education, to a large extent their attitudes reflected their own experiences, though a few would have liked an even greater degree of selective teaching than they had actually known, as a highly gifted boy explained:

'Even at this school, I didn't learn any new maths for about eighteen months because there was no streaming at all, and maths is one of those subjects where some people can grasp it and others can't. Now that I'm in the top maths set, I can state that having me in the same class as some of the people who are now in lower sets didn't help them, and it just held me back. I would have something worked out, conquered, and be ready to move on to something else, but I would have to keep on battering at it for three weeks because somebody else needed to take longer over it. What a boring year!'

Indeed, there was little intellectual democracy among the gifted in this sample. Of the High-IQ group, the great majority (80 per cent) preferred to be taught in classes that were pre-selected by ability. The only exceptions they would consider were subjects that were not examinable. One outstanding girl even described how she found some of the students in her computer class at university to be slow. She spoke without a glimmer of humour: 'It's mixed ability – everybody in one class'. However, going down the IQ scale, the other two groups saw selection by ability for education as significantly less attractive (61 per cent and 41 per cent). But one Average-IQ boy had reservations about mixed-ability teaching: 'It's a task to catch up with the others when you're doing your best and everybody seems to be getting away from you. The bright ones should tell you things, doing good for the people that aren't so bright.'

The cut and thrust

A substantial minority, mostly boys, thrived on the challenge of school pressure, hard learning, and the cut and thrust of keen competition. For them, a typical comment would be, as Dominic Thomas delighted in telling me:

> 'I like feeling a part of a big establishment, with uniform and Founder's Day and that sort of thing. Also it's a hive of academic activity, it's very stimulating. It's very competitive, which I need to work to my full potential. If there's an "A" to be got, then I want to get it. Exams are a challenge, and I would have liked to have been accelerated at school, again probably as a challenge.'

But a mother saw a different side:

> 'It's a stress reaction which shows physically. In the final year I had to go into school and say, "For God's sake, stop him working. I don't care whether he goes to Cambridge or whether he doesn't." His form master thought it was a rather odd attitude, but I felt that it was more important that he survived as a human being.'

Not all the gifted loved the pressure; some described in heartfelt terms how they saw the school abusing their potential and individuality, seeing themselves as just 'a cog in the school wheel'. Fifteen-year-old Justine Grayson at an all-girls' grammar school spoke of her school's restricted outlook:

> 'The style of teaching is uninspirational, uninteresting. The teacher talks and you take it down; homework is essays and more writing. They don't look for new ways to interest the class. They themselves are bored and of course, so are we. I'd like to be taught in a way that is more relevant to the actual world outside, to involve more personal experiences both on the teacher's side and on mine. I'm trying to fight boredom and frustration, just to get through my exams with good grades. I expect the teachers think I'm very lazy, but I don't actually know what they think because they don't really speak to me.'

Pupils were often expected to take in information and reproduce it on demand, which left them feeling intellectually short-changed. Many would have liked an easing-off from examination pressure from time to time and evidence of some concern for their own values and interests. As Justine added:

'There was no time to explore anything else outside your syllabus. I would have liked to have done things like computing, and more languages, to have explored more areas. The school didn't focus enough on the individual; it didn't bring out enough of what you've got to offer.'

Indeed, the most successful examinees of all, normally from the selective schools, showed a lack of broad concern for their subject area and a failure to read around about what they were studying. Maybe their natural curiosity had been sated because of the heavy spoonfeeding they had received, because a large amount of material has to be taken in very quickly in order to attain high marks in examinations. One father spoke sadly of his highly successful daughter, now at university: 'The disappointing thing to me is her lack of desire to find out for herself. She lacks the questing mind of a good scientist.'

But a teacher's enthusiasm for the subject could be inspiring, and when it happened the fortunate pupils responded with delight. Caroline Hardman was lucky:

'We had a wonderful teacher once. She made you sit back and think. It was her own enthusiasm, but she didn't so much inspire you as make you inspire yourself. She didn't sit there behind her desk like the big defensive mechanism, she'd sit on top of it. You couldn't ignore her. She'd never give just one side of an argument, she told you the whole lot then said "Right, tell me what you think". There was lots of debating in the lessons, lots of creative English rather than textbook English, like improvisation drama.'

Curiosity

Not all the high level achievers were as intellectually curious (or perhaps as fortunate in their teachers) although they had an extraordinary thirst for information. And contrary to what is often described as a characteristic of the gifted, they did not often enjoy finding things out for themselves. The effort of searching in libraries and museums was often described as too time-consuming and tedious, and some highly gifted youngsters even preferred predigested information in note form straight from the teacher's mouth.

In fact, over a third of the sample said they had never even been given the opportunity to learn through finding out via project work in the secondary school. But the high examination fliers who had tried it often made such comments as: 'Project work can give you a lot of satisfaction but it is a lot of work, and it does take up a great deal of time. I really do prefer to work in class.' Dedicated achievers felt even more strongly – 'God, what a waste! I could have done so much other stuff while I've been doing the work for this project. I want an exam to work for at the end.' When they reached university, however, it often hit such students hard as to how ill-prepared they had been for the independent study they were then faced with. Several had drastically reconsidered their ideas – 'More project work in schools would have prepared me for the sort of thing I'm having to do at university. Now I know what it's all about, I do wish we'd done more.'

But how the pupil felt about project-type work, and what they learned from it seemed to be largely a matter of how it was given and supervised. For the more thoughtful, such as Philip Bessant (Highly gifted, aged 20, at university though diagnosed as a toddler by his doctor as educationally subnormal), it was an intellectual challenge:

> 'Time is so limited in school lessons. Project work gives you a chance to do a lot more in depth on a subject that interests you. I can't say my projects were always successful, though, because I misconceived them. It would have helped to have worked more with the teacher first, to sort out the priorities of the problem. But it taught me how to plan better, and even more how to look through an idea, and what possibilities I'd have to research into and beyond it. It also built up my confidence to go out and find the information for yourself. If there'd been more of this at school, it would have been better.'

Comprehensive schools

The major benefit described by the gifted at all-comer comprehensive schools was social – that it had been a good thing to learn to mix and make friends with all kinds of people. Mary Owen, the gifted poet, disagreed with her mother, who thought she had been unhappy at the local comprehensive. Mary's view was:

> 'I've experienced both, and I really preferred the comprehensive system although the teaching was very patchy because the teacher had to flit across various intelligences. You did need some discipline there too because otherwise nothing would have got across at all. I can see that it's much easier with some selection. When I came to the grammar school, I found it quite amazing that most of the girls were studious and interested in the work, and they were all so well behaved.'

The major debit many described was their belief that they could have done a lot better academically at a more selective school. A university student was a little bitter about what he saw as his loss:

> 'At my Comprehensive there was absolutely nothing, not even the occasional ten-minute talk. I'd have liked some debating, say at an informal inter-school level. At Cambridge, I've seen that people from other schools have been more stretched. They've completed the syllabus a lot earlier than we did, and they were also taught much better how to tackle exams. Then they've done extra preparatory

study for the university course, which has helped them considerably. I didn't get any of that.'

Another debit in some comprehensive schools was the real lack of resources to learn with, including teachers and teaching. This sometimes led to some remoteness between staff and pupils, as one said: 'Half the time, they don't seem to know who I am'. Poor facilities are, of course, a considerable drain on the learning energy of all pupils, But it was particularly serious for those who had the ability to fly through the syllabus and go on to higher-level creative thinking, to be obliged to set their brilliant minds to the treadmill of copying by hand for hours. It is a terrible waste and a disgrace.

Fortunately for Geraldine Christy in Wales, unlike most of her schoolmates, her over-the-top-of-the-scale intellect would see her through the material handicaps of her comprehensive school. The range of the ten subjects she was studying in depth, however, would make the mouths of many children at selective academic schools water in envy. Her range covered chemistry, physics, electronics, design, craft and technology, music, English language and literature, Welsh language and literature, and mathematics. She was the youngest in her class, yet had been top in every one of those subjects since she started at the school. But it wasn't easy because of the school's shortage of money.

Geraldine Christy (Highly gifted, aged 16, at school):

'We haven't got enough textbooks to go round, so you have to copy about fifty per cent on to your files. I don't learn from it because I don't read as I write. We do get photocopied stuff in English, but they've been told they've overspent, so the English teachers pay for it out of their own pockets. I was going to buy the books, but the teacher said it's not worth it because you have to have a new one every term. We've got plenty of technical equipment though, like electronics and computers, because the school's been chosen by the Manpower Services Commission for this new scheme, Technical Vocational something. It's in English and maths that we're short of textbooks and stuff.

There are teachers that take our books in regularly and mark them, but there are some who have that many classes they don't have time to do it. The maths department – they can't hardly take our books in at all. In the sixth form, you might go nearly a year without teachers seeing your book. I'm glad we're streamed, though, because we can all go at the right pace instead of having to wait for other people. Even so, I think that if I worked hard it would cause embarrassment to some of my classmates, because I could really do better than I'm doing.'

Update 2001: Geraldine's concern for others continued. She left school with four A-levels, in Welsh, English, mathematics and physics, and even now feels 'absolutely delighted with my school experience'. After a degree in human psychology, she married, did teacher training for primary school children, but then worked in adult learning disability and behaviour problems. Since having her two children, she intends to devote her life to them as her mother did for her. 'She never had to worry', she explained, 'that her mother could not turn up to school events', and she wants it to be the same for her own.

Of the six High-IQ young people who had experienced the learning cultures of both selective and mixed-ability schools, their concerns were put most clearly in Andy's account:

Andy Spurgeon (Highly gifted, aged 17, at school):

'I had to leave the private (selective) school for money reasons and come to the comprehensive. It's been a very educating experience. There, I'd been in an intellectual environment where everyone was very outgoing with their talents. But at the comprehensive I started to understand some of those people who were less intelligent than myself and who weren't going to have as many job opportunities and qualifications.

But in order to stay sane, I had to make myself an average person within the school. So I refused to be in any sports teams or school productions, and I even held back on the academic side. But since I've been in the Sixth Form, which is a much more enlightened smaller group, I've been able to do more things, and they've started to accept me. One of the bad things that comes out of holding-back on the reins is that I've found it very very difficult to let go again. I do the minimum of work, because I was already at the top, and the force that goes behind the working kid is usually the competition, not the teacher. I would have been an abominable person if I'd stayed at the other school, but I certainly would have had better exam results.'

Harmony in education

Yet there were a few gifted young people from poor homes in this study for whom the comprehensive system had been the only one which could have helped them to develop their potential. Children who would have found it difficult to cope with the middle-class ethos of a grammar school and who could have been crushed by the snobbery in some private schools, could find their way with teachers who spoke with the same accent, along with their friends and with support from home. Whenever there are cutbacks in education, such culturally sensitive youngsters are bound to be affected.

George Booth was just such a youth who had no alternative resources but his hard work and his brains. Miles of drab, low-quality council housing surrounded his house on the outskirts of Liverpool. Of about twenty of the local shops, only one was open, and that was heavily defended with metal grills. The boards covering the windows of the others were heavily daubed with graffiti. People slouched by with bent heads. The area was surrounded by chemical industries – an Antonioni *Red Desert*. Fat chimneys with twinkling lights and black spiky towers silhouetted against the pink sky were topped by the everlasting flames of burning fumes. Even as the salt sea came over the land, it picked up heavy pollution and the whole area smelled of chemicals. It seemed like a very unhealthy place.

George lived there with his widowed mother who glowed with love for her two sons. He was tall and handsome, at the top of the IQ scale, and doing very well indeed in spite of being blind in one eye. He was at the local comprehensive school, in a mixed-ability class of his own age. The teachers there cared for him, giving him the kind of feedback and encouragement that youngsters at very much more expensive schools had never known, and it was there that he had learned to have ambitions to be an accountant or lawyer.

It was a situation, however, which highlighted some of the problems of gifted working-class youth fighting for a place in the professional world. Both George's parents had left school at 14, and the family income had to be supplemented by welfare benefits. But George's most obvious problem was that he was not articulate, and what he did say had a heavy local accent: there was no smooth flow of words to beguile the ear of a prospective tutor or employer. He was neither accustomed to talking to the full extent of his vocabulary nor reading. There were no books in the house and the only newspaper he ever saw was a tabloid, *The Star*. But he was fighting hard to overcome his disadvantages. The one paradoxical advantage he did have, though, in not being from an educationally aware home, was that he was quite free of the hang-ups of being labelled gifted. Nobody had made him feel different. He was very happy at home, and also with his neighbours and teachers, and was at one with his world. When someone is in such harmony, good things come out of it.

George Booth (Highly gifted, aged 17, at school):

'I give other people in the class help, and they prefer getting it off me, instead of them running to a teacher. Sometimes they'll ask questions in class that I wouldn't, so I just listen, and sometimes it helps me. I get on alright with my mates, and just leave the ones I don't like. I don't care what they think, but I don't think I'm any different from them. If my work's good I feel proud, and if it's bad it's my own fault. I can't blame it on anyone else. They don't tell me I'm a bright lad, but I know that if I've got an exam question, if the teachers give just a hint, I'd be able to give the answer straight off.

You don't feel confident if you come from a poor background, like going for a high-up job when there's someone else there from a higher family. You'd always feel he'd had the upper hand. That's what I'm working so hard at school for, to show them. I've joined the rugby team, and I play of an evening three times a week. If we get beat, and I know we could have won it, I'll come home and explain the whole story to my Mum. I keep telling her till I calm down. I think she's seen it all before.'

Update 2001: George was a shooting star. Because his school only went up to the age of 16, though he left with eleven O-levels, he had to move to a local college for his six A-levels, which he enjoyed. Then a first-class degree in economics at Leeds University, where he was also top of the year and won a prize for economics. Given a scholarship by Vanderbilt University, Nashville, USA, he attended the business school there for a year, and travelled around. He worked as a chartered accountant, moved into banks, and is now one of two directors at an investment bank, personally responsible for European software and IT services. Not a trace of his Liverpool accent remains. He is married and they are expecting their son in August 2001. He is just 32.

Teaching the gifted

The essence of teaching is in communication, and I am presenting a plea here for a genuine meeting of minds – the exciting minds of teacher and pupil. Education for the gifted is not just a matter of dispensing ever more refined pearls of wisdom nor of fitting pupils for high-flying careers. As with all children, it has a profound and echoing psychological impact on their feelings about themselves for life. And like other children, the gifted need teaching of a sufficient quality to promote their development – intellectually, emotionally and spiritually. All successful teaching for learning helps children to a sense of control over both the learning situation and themselves, and there is ample research evidence to show that this involves guidance by the teacher. And the gifted children in this sample knew they wanted it.

Significantly more of those in the High IQ group (87 per cent), compared with all the others (68 per cent), much preferred to work along with a teacher, whether to listen or better still as someone on whom to bounce their ideas. The gifted had a high regard for teachers who were willing to listen as well as talk. It was put succinctly by creative David Baker who really appreciated his teachers:

'I talk a lot, and so I talk to the teacher about what I think and what's going on, what I've read and seen on the news, what's happening in life in the world about us, and the actual theory that he's teaching us. It's much more fun than talking to my peer group, because teachers know so much.'

The value of different approaches to teaching is clear to most pupils, and the bright perceptive young people in this sample were extremely concerned about the way they were taught, the curriculum they were obliged to follow and the way the school was managed. Dominating their concerns was the wish that teachers should be sensitive to their needs, so that they could work better together. However, it did sometimes seem that many of the young people had expected high effort and commitment from their teachers, without being prepared to make the same contribution themselves. Perhaps, though, that was a fault of the questionnaire; I should have asked them specifically.

Of all the sample, only 76 per cent felt they had enough personal communication with their teachers, nearly a quarter saying they felt relatively unknown. A constant cry echoed through the interviews – Please treat us as individuals, not lumped together as a class. At times, these youngsters said, their grades seemed to matter more than they did. Some would have preferred smaller classes so that relationships could develop more easily. They felt it was too tempting to coast along in the crowd and would do less than their best. Just a few highly-achieving boys, though, did not want a close relationship with teachers at all; just the facts.

Expertise in teaching was very much appreciated by the gifted in this study, but not necessarily the teacher's specialist knowledge. They did not ask for nor expect super-teachers, but honest, competent individuals, who would do the job to the best of their ability so that respect could flow in both directions. One outstanding boy at a comprehensive school described such a situation: 'The teacher couldn't keep up with me, though she knew most of the stuff. But it was OK. She knew the syllabus, and had an idea of what was expected, so she kept pushing me and could tell me what to do.'

The best communication in the classroom must be two-way, so that teachers can also learn from their pupils. As one girl said:

'Teachers forget that no matter how young the kids are, they are thinking for themselves all the time. Pupils have a good idea of what works best for them, and they have a right to know and a right to ask. Flexibility is really necessary, so that the teacher can understand which things he'd taught well and which things needed going over again. Once in a while they should ask us how we think they're doing, and that way you'd get some positive results out of it.'

A recurrent theme from the young people was that honesty and two-way communication with teachers was particularly valuable to the gifted, as Samantha Goldman at a music school described with pleasure:

'I was the physics teacher's first A-level pupil, so she was always testing the water, saying, "Tell me, if I teach you this in a different way, would you understand it better?" She was very flexible and tapped into me. It was good fun. When I wanted to take astronomy, at first the school said no, but I asked again and again, and eventually the teacher and I learnt it between ourselves, and that's how I came to study it at university.'

Robert Fraser, a highly gifted 15-year-old wanted two-way communication:

'When a teacher can make a nice atmosphere to work in, one who can take the odd joke in a lesson, you produce better work. You've got the option to try and tell them what you think is wrong with their teaching style, and why they're not coming across as well as they might, and why their ideas are not being picked up.'

They hoped for respect for their abilities too, as 17-year-old gifted Dominic Thomas in a highly selective school pointed out:

'Class-time is so short and valuable, and writing is something that you can do at home, so the good teachers use it to do something else. We're interested in other things than the straight syllabus, so the best kind of teacher is willing to go into side matters. One of our best teachers very rarely gets round to doing any of the syllabus – we spend all the lesson talking. He's so interesting, I'll remember all the stuff from class, and then if I don't get any time to do revision, which is often the case, I remember it from the first time.'

Poor teaching

So much of the poor teaching which these bright young people had experienced, was due to teacher carelessness and laziness. The keen learners sometimes suffered unnecessary intellectual frustration.

This in-depth study has discovered a quite unexpected aspect of teaching gifted children – they were sometimes taught less conscientiously than less able pupils. Just because they were so good at learning (and often well behaved), some teachers clearly felt free to leave the classroom during lessons. A gifted grammar school girl was distressed: 'Most of the girls are pretty conscientious, so a lot of teachers just write exercises on the board, then go out and wander back in twenty minutes'.

This was not unique. Such teacher behaviour always took place in the selective schools. None of the average-ability pupils reported it. The gifted young people felt they were being cheated, rather than seeing it as a tribute to their competence in learning. It was a penalty of their giftedness and they were obliged to use their ingenuity to get round it, because it sometimes endangered their progress. Three angry young people had to resort to finding extra teaching: 'One of our maths teachers didn't always turn up and she had charge of our examinations. We presented a complaint from the whole class, but of course the school didn't do anything. So we had to go to night-school to get through.'

Others just managed with what was to hand, like Rachel Wallace (Highly gifted, aged 20, at university):

'You have no possible way of protesting about it, because most schools wouldn't trust the child. We had one maths teacher who would come into the lesson and say "Well, I expect you know what to do" and drift out again ten minutes later – never said a word – and there were only four of us in that A-level class. One of my friends was very helpful, he used to teach me while the teacher was in the staff room.'

This neglect of the brightest seemed to be mostly in mathematics and physics. As one gifted boy put it about his physics teacher, he has 'good, very good qualifications, but incompetent at teaching'. Andrew Spurgeon was not alone in saying:

'There are certain teachers that everyone in the whole school knows are very bad. The Head of the Maths Department is a brilliant mathematician with all sorts of awards and prizes for doing maths – but he can't teach. There are kids who are going to fail because of his teaching. Last year, they had to have another maths teacher in to teach his class at the last minute, but they still keep him on.'

Some teachers combined the two deficiencies of disdain for their pupils along with high qualifications. Nick Fawcett, gifted and long out of work, said:

'My physics teacher was one of the most intelligent men I've ever met. He'd got his PhD and really should have been in a university. But I couldn't understand him. He would come in, go through this, that and the other, set a problem for you, and then disappear to do whatever he did – most of the class failed.'

The more academic the school, the less likely it seemed that the pupils had any communication, much less a relationship, with its principal. The head was often a remote figure who didn't know their names, and whose instructions were either announced to the assembled school or came through the medium of a less exalted member of staff. This same person would be assessing their chances for university or a job, often filling in their reports for applications. Sometimes a single interview was the only one-to-one meeting between pupil and head teacher in a school life.

Some youngsters felt they might have been better off without any contact at all, though, such as imaginative Danny Smith (Gifted, aged 17, at school):

'I don't like the headmaster. Once, he suspended me – on a Friday, and told me to come back in on the Monday. He called me in to his study and said, "Smith, you look like a bloody cockatoo! It's going to go down in your report that you've been suspended" ... pathetic. I didn't do anything; just turned up with my hair still in pink spikes on Monday. Nothing happened.'

Feedback from teachers

Nearly a quarter of all the young people in the sample felt that they had received only meagre direct one-to-one feedback from their teachers on their work. Teacher 'comment' was usually a mark at the end of a written piece of work, with an occasional cryptic remark. But sometimes not even that, only a tick to signify that the work had been seen to be done. However gifted, pupils felt the need to be told when they were on the right or wrong tracks, and to feel that someone cared about their progress. David Baker had mixed feelings about it:

'My last maths teacher wouldn't let us know what we got in our tests. Fortunately, I didn't want to know, because in maths at that time I wasn't doing too well. But I don't know how they expected us to learn from that.'

Several pupils only found out how well they were doing from information filtered through parent–teacher evenings. One girl was shocked: 'The art teacher told my parents that my work was terrible. I wish he'd told it me to my face, because it came as a shock; I'd thought I was quite good.'

Perhaps giving praise is not part of the British culture, perhaps there is a little unrecognised resentment in some teachers towards their gifted pupils, because it seemed to be in very short supply in the classrooms. Teachers were not forthcoming in telling a pupil directly that they were very bright. However, the encouraging messages they did give were subtle, such as nuances of speech and maybe if pupils were lucky, a 'Very good' beside a high mark. Yet most of the gifted did get the message that they had been recognised as especially bright and that the teachers' expectations of them were high. Classic teacher sarcasm was pithily described by Andy Spurgeon:

'They write things in my report like, "His loud and flamboyant personality is perhaps justified in his results" – they never say, "Well done". We once had a mixed parents–teachers–pupils' evening, though, which was very interesting and very useful.'

Some had to find out about their abilities in other ways, such as Gina Emerson (Highly gifted, aged 20, at university) who felt that the petty and persistent criticism she had suffered was both pointless and destructive:

'They wouldn't let on if they thought you were intelligent, because they thought it was bad for you. In English I was told it would be a struggle for me to take the exams and now it's my subject at Cambridge. I used to be marked B and oceans of red all over my essays; it really discouraged me, so much that I started out doing Sciences. Then when I changed schools and had a teacher who used to rave about my essays, I thrived on his encouragement. It's probably a hangover that I still think it's a terrible thing to think highly of your abilities. I'd expected everyone at Cambridge to be brilliant, and that I'd only just slipped through the net, but I am actually very good.'

How teachers saw the gifted

In the first part of this study, in 1974, the teachers had been questioned directly about how they perceived their pupils. But in the Follow-up, there was no direct questioning of teachers because so many of the young people had by then left school. However, their teachers had shown how they estimated their pupils in three ways (given in detail in Appendix 2).

1. *By putting them in for public examinations.* So as not to waste public money, teachers are obliged to estimate each child's probable success before entering him or her for the free public examinations, and they were pretty accurate in their assessments. The pupils of higher IQ had been entered for more subjects and achieved significantly better grades than those of lower IQ. Their outstanding successes were apparent in level of examination, numbers of subjects passed and grades achieved. It is recognised that those who take science subjects are more likely to reach higher grades, and in this study, the brightest children were more likely to take Science or a mixture, rather than the Arts – a close reflection of their parents' preferences. Thus, the brightest had a double boost to their marks from both ability and science subjects.

2. *By accelerating pupils within the school system.* The highly able pupils were more likely to have been accelerated. Of the High-IQ group (141–170 IQ), 23 per cent were either accelerated or young for their school class.

3. *By somehow letting pupils know they were seen as bright.* The young people were asked how they thought their teachers rated their ability in school. Their answers corresponded well with the IQ measure, and, to a somewhat lesser extent, with results on the Raven's intelligence test.

On the whole, the teachers appeared to be good judges of the examination potential of their pupils and acted on what they found. But in truth, they were often judging future success on the basis of present success, and (understandably) had much more difficulty in recognising the gifted when their potential was undeveloped for reasons such as poor presentation as in spasticity, poor culture and lack of encouragement from home.

Discipline in school

Teacher–pupil relationships at all ability levels were beset with problems of discipline – how much, how little? No pupil wanted a weak teacher, and they made a clear distinction between those who were either easy-going and approachable or easy-going and slapdash. Ideally, particularly for the older, brighter pupils, there had to be respect flowing both ways – a bond between pupil and teacher. But this was not always so, in either direction.

Most pupils wanted the teachers to be concerned with their all-round well-being, as well as providing firm direction to see them through the examination hurdles. Teachers who could combine the two, knowing when to pull gently but firmly on the reins, were much appreciated. Sarah Mortimer the computer student, had benefited from this:

'The teachers who got the best out of me were the ones who knew when to say, "Look, come on, buckle down. You've not done enough." But when everybody was working hard, they'd relax the atmosphere and say, "OK. You've worked really hard, we'll do something a bit different for a while." They know what's going on and they know what's going to get the best out of everybody. You know where you are with those teachers.

Teachers who could communicate well like that did not have discipline problems, as the medical student, Jeremy Kramer explained:

'If the teacher was sensitive and could understand people, they didn't need to tell anyone off; everyone was immediately quiet. They understood. But I'd be silent as anything if there was an interesting teacher, no matter whether they were firm or not. A teacher that gains respect must give respect.'

It was not so much the examination system which the gifted pupils railed against, as rigid educational strictures, which they saw as sometimes pointless and unfair. The adjectives with which the very able described their highly academic schools were often those associated with eating – such as force-feeding or spoonfeeding. One boy put it in drinking terms: 'You can lead a horse to water, but you can't make it drink'. Indeed, the eating disorder of anorexia was described as prevalent at two high-pressure girls' schools, probably due to their overbearing strictness and lack of good teacher–pupil relationships.

Some youngsters, though, had learned to lean on their teachers or parents for work discipline instead of developing their own. As one boy said:

'Some of the best teachers we had were the strictest and most old-fashioned, especially the Latin teachers – heads down and get the work done – but they brought out the results. It's not that I like lessons with a firm teacher, but I work better under one. That's the problem.'

For others, too much strictness in the classroom could be negative, producing tension and detracting from the learning environment, especially for older pupils who were keen to flex their intellectual wings. A gifted schoolgirl found that:

'With a very strict teacher, I become more tense and can't think properly; my train of thought becomes chewed up. There's no two-way communication, just the one way. I might as well not be sitting there.'

Several of the brightest teenagers very much resented the old-fashioned discipline which seemed to go with the education provided in the more academic schools:

'On our first day the headmaster told us, "I'm a traditionalist, and I hope you'll leave here as traditionalists too".'

The gifted had different ways of dealing with unwanted discipline. One or two livened up their days by playing intellectual cat and mouse games with their teachers, some of whom handled it brilliantly as in this story from the highly gifted Andy Spurgeon:

'With a new teacher, I just have so much fun because they don't expect it. I run circles round them and do the most terrible things. I'll give you a juicy example. In the lesson one afternoon, I did a perfect act of the despondent person, completely down and slumping around, and I'm usually very cheerful and bright. The teacher sent me out of the classroom and asked my friend what was the matter, and he said "I think something is amiss, he's not been right all day". She came out and asked me, "What's wrong, Andrew?"

"It's personal."

"Is it your girlfriend?"

"Yes! She's pregnant" and I promptly burst into tears and flung myself on her. She wrapped her arms round me and said "Oh Andrew, Oh Andrew. Dear oh dear!"

For the next two weeks, I was smothered in sheets and leaflets about what to do. Then, I just couldn't stand it any longer, because I had to keep a fairly straight face every time I saw her in a lesson, so I told her that it was a false alarm. But she gave me A's for all the essays I'd done!'

Brief escapes

About a third of the whole sample – with deep questioning – said they simply removed themselves from the school premises for a break from the system when they felt they needed it. The proportions were about the same for different intelligence levels, 31.4 per cent taking an occasional lesson off, though 10.1 per cent measured their truancy in days or weeks. Some took the odd day off either to catch up with homework or to rest, taking a 'philosophical' approach to school attendance. (I had considerable, undeclared, sympathy with them because I had spent most of my school life doing the same thing.) At least in their early school years this was not an academic problem for the very brightest who could intellectually recoup the missed lessons.

But it could be too much and did catch up with a few, as gifted Adrian Lambert found:

'I nipped off whenever I wanted to. If you're clever enough, you can cope for years by sitting there and just listening in the lessons. Even for Maths A-level, for the first couple of months, if the working-out was still on the board when I came in, I could just about scrape through. But when it got to a certain stage, I had to either work or pack it in. So I would just pack it in.'

Parents sometimes colluded with their gifted children in this unofficial absence from school. Jeremy Kramer's mother said:

'He truanted from school quite a lot, and continued the habit at university. Nobody seemed to have bothered him about it at either place. The Latin teacher at school, whose lessons he always missed, chose to disregard it, possibly because neither of them liked each other. Still, he knew that Jeremy would come out with an A, and of course he did.'

Truanting could even be a positive educational experience for the gifted, as it was for creative David Baker:

'Last year, if I'd worked really hard in the morning, I'd sometimes take afternoons off with a couple of friends, and they'd just mark me absent. We didn't get drunk or play football. We used to write poetry quite a lot, and we'd read to each other. Say, if we'd done The Wasteland by T.S. Eliot in the morning, we'd have great fun in the afternoons, spending ages in the park with a bottle of wine, talking about it and eating oranges. We'd also talk about politics and the lumpen proletariat, and things like that.

I was learning more at the time in a different way about life and society, and was beginning to think about things, like injustice and the way human beings were, what people wanted, and why they behaved as they did. Then, towards the end of the summer, everybody had to have a long interview with the deputy head about school attendance and my cavalier attitude to registration had to stop. So, since the summer, I've been there all the time. You could say that I took a new direction in life, and I've even started gardening on a Sunday morning – money-wise, being Seamus Heaney (the poet) wears thin.'

Corporal punishment

In 1985, *The* (London) *Times* polled 604 varied parents with children aged between five and 16 on corporal punishment. They found that two-thirds approved of it in principle, and more than half in practice on their own children. Two-thirds had received some kind of corporal punishment at school themselves – nine out of ten fathers and half the mothers. In entire accord with those figures, two-thirds of these young people, boys slightly more than girls, were in favour of the short sharp physical shock – prescribed for others, usually 'bad boys'. This urge was not, however, based on experience, as less than a quarter of the group had actually been hit by a teacher. Those who had felt it were usually not in favour of it.

But several boys in this sample had been beaten quite strongly by teachers, though they said they had mentally brushed off the assault. But for one sensitive gifted boy, the caning, combined with lack of psychological support from home, had seriously curtailed his potential intellectual and emotional development. He had been diminished by what had happened to him, and was probably functioning at about average ability.

Peter Rhodes was his parents' fourth child, and his mother said he had been by far the most alert at birth. He could walk across the room unaided at 11 months, string a few words together soon after that and was a very easy child. When I had first seen him at nearly nine years old, I'd noted what a chatty and lively little boy he was, and how he loved school – no cause for concern there I thought.

Then at 13, he had been sent to an old-fashioned, high-status private school. Towards the end of his first year, he was severely beaten with a cane for, he swears, something he didn't do. His sentence was five strokes over his clothes, across his lower back and buttocks, causing great weals and fierce pain. He stood up after four strokes and pleaded with the teacher to stop, but the man pushed him down and gave him the final one. Peter said that the teacher who did it was skinny and small and it seemed to give him satisfaction. Though Peter was proud that he hadn't cried out, he was terribly shocked. His mother was away at the time, and his father didn't want to see the bruises. He blamed Peter, but said graciously, 'You've been punished enough – I shan't punish you any more on top of it'. Like any bruise, the weals turned red then blue, and lasted for a couple of weeks. But that was only the physical side of the incident.

Peter's hatred grew and grew, both for the man who had done this to him and the system that had allowed it to happen. Should anyone do that to him now, he said, he would give as good as he got, but as a slight 13-year-old, he had been powerless. Things went from bad to worse. He shrugged off the whole idea of school work, eventually leaving at 15. He seemed to me to find great difficulty in expressing himself, and obviously wasn't used to it. His father was a disciplinarian of limited interests, who had risen to wealth from a culturally poor background. His mother lived very much on the surface of life. She was astonished, for example, that I should expect her to know where her husband had gone to school, saying, 'Well, he was already 25 when I met him'. Of her gifted son's disastrous schooling, she said it was all his fault because 'He just stopped trying'.

Peter Rhodes (Highly gifted, aged 19, out of work):

> 'My parents wouldn't let me go to a comprehensive because it wasn't as respectable as the posh private school they sent me to, though they knew how I hated the place. It was awful. Either you fitted in, or you left, and there was no allowance made for you as a person. The teachers thought I was stupid. We were asked once in a lesson what our IQ was, and I said what mine was, because my parents had had it done – everyone thought I was lying or joking. Even when I did little spurts of work, they'd say, "How'd you do that? Did you copy it from someone else?" I failed everything so I'm going in the army, but my parents would rather I was here where they could control me. My Dad said, "You've had a very sheltered upbringing, you know".'

Update 2001: The army proved to be a good thing, providing Peter with a sanctuary to which he was committed for three years. As a bomb disposal engineer he was 'digging holes and driving trucks' and rose to be the youngest lance-corporal in his regiment. He loved the physical environment and mixing with lads from 'no-hope' cities and little education. At 21 he came into a multi-million pound trust.

Then his travels really started. Beginning as a garbage collector for seven months in Australia, he went on to the Far East, Thailand, Taiwan and Singapore, spending overall about six years there. He learned fasting to the phases of the moon and yoga, which cured him of his ME illness. But after four years as a simple monk, he felt that his social skills had begun to atrophy. Back in London, he fell in with drug dealers, but found the life 'very egotistical' and boring, preferring to go for the 'purity of the body'. In 1997, he met a girl with a Down's syndrome child and married her within six weeks, but she was violent and, he says, a gold-digger. He is now in process of divorce and concern for his beautiful and adored daughter, who has the same iridology as him. Peter runs a successful complementary medicine practice and teaches Thai kick boxing. He has made it up with his family, is happy, and feels that something good is just around the corner. 'Come and stay', he said, 'and I'll give you a free massage.'

CHAPTER 8

Goodbye to school

No more Latin no more French,
No more sitting on a cold hard bench.
Anon

It is often assumed that the gifted have some sort of inbuilt motivation to aim for high achievement, although this study clearly shows that personality and social circumstances have a strong sway on individual choice. For youngsters who do not have an intense urge to use their gifts – plus the extra energy it may take to beat the system in which they are growing up – their abilities may be under-exercised and unsatisfied. Even in this small sample, several found that their future depended on their own efforts: 'Apart from the class careers talk; sending off for the prospectuses, asking heads of departments and filling in the forms. If I'd lacked motivation, I could easily have ended up not getting in anywhere.' Of all young people, the gifted are probably the most likely to be sold short on advice for their after-school lives.

For most youngsters wondering what to do next, they turn to their families, which means that parents' own educational experiences and expectations for their children have a strong influence. So, lawyers tend to come from lawyer families or families with legal problems, doctors from doctor families or those having experienced serious health problems, and artists from artist families. In this study, parents' ideas and hopes for their children's futures were distinctly biased towards the sciences, though it was impossible for them to know the wide spread of current options available for their children, particularly as many occupations did not exist just a few years ago. Moreover, what is taken for granted in some families, like going to university, is unimaginable in others.

Careers advice

The wide variety of possible career routes for those who are gifted across the board can confuse even the keenest professional, as one gifted girl said of her careers officer: 'He came to school and said I could probably do anything!' Another girl was overwhelmed by the technology: 'I got a computer printout which was supposed to select the ideal job. It said "Cut off after 80, 127 remaining". I was supposed to select four. But there wasn't much point when I was suitable in attitude and qualifications for all of them.'

Jeremy Kramer had a much worse, in fact an insoluble dilemma. While full-time at a high-pressure academic school, in the evenings and when he could, he attended the (post-school) Royal Northern College of Music. His day school saw him shine in science and expected him to go on to a medical degree, but the music college expected him to take a music degree and aim for the concert platform. He explained:

> 'By the time I was 15, I'd finished all the music grades in trumpet, piano and theory, and the only other thing I could've done was a diploma, But that would have taken too much time from school. I found a terrible difficulty in choosing between music and medicine. I spent hours thinking it over, covering every aspect of why I should or shouldn't have done each one, and came to the conclusion I'd be better off doing medicine. I can do that and still do a lot of music, but I can't do music and any medicine. Also, while I was at music college I saw a lot of really brilliant musicians who didn't manage to find work.'

Update 2001: After much agony, Jeremy chose medicine but it did not bring him happiness. He missed his music, and at university found his fellow students more interested in beer and discos than the finer things of life. He became a psychiatrist, but told me: 'The reason I left medicine is because I became mentally distressed. I had to leave because I no longer felt I knew what I was doing and became scared of doing harm to people.' He'd missed his chance of being a music professional and set up as a music agent. He still plays at pubs and other venues, but now aims to help those who chose differently from him. His earning power is, of course, very much lower than as a doctor, which is quite a problem for him among his doctor and lawyer friends. From time to time he thinks about practising medicine again, but now feels very out of touch and lacks confidence. He could take a refresher course, but... well, maybe some time. He knows in is heart: 'At the end of the day I am achieving very little'.

The highly academic schools, like Jeremy's, which cater for gifted pupils, were unquestionably also the least flexible. The idea was current there and in other schools (as Deslisle (2000), found in the USA) that the gifted and talented do not need career advice and development. Many at high-powered schools found that the study area to which they were supposed to devote themselves for years, if not all their lives, was decided by teachers, sometimes without discussion: 'There wasn't any choice – so I didn't need guidance! You take the subjects allocated to you.' These were usually decided on the basis of school marks. Of the whole sample, over a third (33.7 per cent) had not been given a voice in these major life decisions.

But there were other school reasons which pushed gifted youngsters in the wrong direction.

Gina Emerson, for example, had attended a top boys' private school for her final two years. She had always been exceptionally good at mathematics and so chose to specialise in the sciences. But as the only girl in the class she found that the male physics teacher laughed when she put her hand up to answer a question and turned to a boy for the answer. She chose not to complain or fight this discrimination, but being a broad-based highly gifted girl, after one term simply changed to English. She got top marks in it and went to Cambridge to study it further.

Update 2001: On leaving university Gina took up her old love again on a postgraduate computer course, and now, at 35, has her own firm of graphic and web design. It is as though water has found its own level.

When a bright pupil was keen on a particular area of study, school timetables could be considerable hurdles. Although this is true for all pupils, it is a really big problem for one who has a real gift. The alternatives offered did not always bear any relationship to the pupil's choice, as for Caroline Whiting, who said :

> 'I wanted to do food and nutrition, but the careers teacher said no because it wouldn't fit in to the timetable – "Why don't you do French?" You see, I'd got a good French mark; so now I'm doing it for university.'

Some said they hadn't much idea of what was involved in the subject areas to which they had been directed. This could so easily have been built into preparation for the next stage of school work, and for several this lack had caused extra work and wasted time and money. Danny Smith, for example, had found himself months into the wrong subjects, though fortunately, being both gifted and a skilled learner he was able to catch up that wide gap of missing information, pass his school leaving exams with flying colours, and go on to university:

> 'I didn't get told about what was actually in the courses, just which subjects are usually studied together and which I could choose from. No one ever spoke to me personally about it, never.'

At times, study areas which were not considered essential, such as language or music to a scientist, were simply cut off a high-flyer's syllabus by the school as they were seen to be detracting from 'real' work. Not even the most dedicated achievers took delight in this sparse academic diet, though they did appreciate what it could bring them in terms of progress rewards.

Wasted time

The figures speak for themselves. Just under half (45 per cent) of this sample of young people – of whom two-thirds have a general intelligence in the top five per cent of the population – said they did not receive the careers help from school they felt they needed. Almost as many (42.6 per cent) said they received no personal, one-to-one careers counselling whatsoever. This aspect of education for the gifted (not unique to Britain) is at best very short-sighted in terms of national needs – and a scandalous waste of human resources from any point of view.

Even in this Follow-up sample of 169 young people, four students had been directed quite wrongly by their schools and the majority had been obliged to find their own ways, often by trial and error. It is only necessary to multiply this by the number of those who leave school each year, to get an idea of the immense waste of energy and talent. Each of those four misdirected young people had worked hard in the area they'd been directed to, even going on to study it at university. Mistakes can mean time, maybe years, working in the wrong directions. Stephen Kaye got caught in that way and felt bitterly that things could have been better:

> 'We did have an interview, but they were just interested to know what you wanted to do rather than to challenge. I'm a prime example. I've changed career and wasted a year, and if I'd had more insight as to what it was like to be an engineer, I'd have started with medicine in the first place. They could produce a set of standard video tapes which would give people a much better idea of careers, like what an accountant does during his day or a civil servant.'

Update 2001: Of that deviation into engineering, Stephen still feels that: 'There were better ways to spend a year'. He had a number of other rather irritated complaints about his comprehensive school, though in spite of that deviation he had done extremely well there, going on to study medicine at a good university. Long ago I'd recorded that he seemed destined to be a rather grumpy pull-yourself-together sort of doctor. He is now a general practitioner, believing himself to be a pragmatic all-rounder. It seemed that my prediction was accurate.

The academic schools normally made the assumption that their pupils would go on to university: 'It was just a matter of deciding which one'. Careers advice in such schools was most often a discussion of the best route, usually with the subject teacher – after the area of study had been chosen. Yet these bright students knew there were other things one could do, even if their teachers did not seem to recognise the possibilities: 'There are many different ways of approaching life and a career, other than the professions'.

Maybe this restricted view is due to the limited experiences of teachers in their own schooling and training – sufficient reason for obliging teachers to have some form of outside school experience as part of their preparation for teaching. Indeed, university could sometimes be a tragic assumption as the only place for the gifted, as Yvonne Barnett found:

'I never should have gone to university, but if you were capable of going you had no other choice. There wasn't anything I particularly wanted to study, and I would have been better off doing a practical course. I didn't even know about the interesting courses they do at polytechnics; the school didn't tell us because they thought they weren't good enough for us. I just wasted those two years at university before I left.'

The quality and quantity of the way the schools perceived their commitment to the post-school lives of their charges varied enormously. On the whole, the academically able were well prepared for examinations, with only a minimal gesture to their wider career concerns, so that for many, when the cocoon of school days began to burst they were decidedly on their own. At times, careers guidance was available in theory, but the pupil had to seek it out – not easy if you don't know your problem. Some schools offered an occasional lecture by an outside speaker, others had an evening or two with staff during the final year, and a lucky minority even had some human contact with a careers teacher. But that was rarely more than once and it almost never took the form of counselling. Too often, especially for the girls, it was advice on how to present themselves at interviews.

However, many bright ambitious pupils said they did not want help because they had already made up their minds. But when I asked them if they had ever been challenged in their choice or had the opportunity to discuss it, they were astounded. Genuine help from school for the rest of their lives seemed to be outside many pupils' frame of reference, neither being given nor expected.

The world of work
Without adequate guidance, too many young people pass through the school gates for the last time ignorant of much that would be useful in the world outside. Only a handful of the whole sample, and almost none of the gifted, had been given any experience of the world of work. One highly gifted boy spoke for many:

'We hardly relate any of the things we're doing to the real world. But something on banking or business, like how to manage your own finances, would be useful.'

Many found their schools very limited in communication with the outside world, for which they used terms such as 'an ivory tower' or 'a prison camp'. Another simile sometimes offered several times was of a train which ran on rails and so could not change direction easily, such as accommodating to a pupil's late development or change of mind. However, it must be remembered that success in school does not always predict success in real world settings, the influences of personality and motivation are essential. Werner von Braun, who developed the principles of rocket propulsion, failed in school algebra; Albert Einstein failed the admission exam in science to the Zurich Polytechnic (though some say he did it on purpose to give himself more freedom to think); Picasso could barely read – the list of successful school failures is almost inspiring.

Nor, of course, can any school assume that all super-intelligent young people will go on to some form of higher education, especially if they have experienced hardship in their social circumstances. It is a difficult problem to help such children overcome the temptations of quick easy money from low-skilled jobs to think of possible greater long-term psychological and economical satisfaction from putting in more years of study. Adrian Lambert, the milkman, had found difficulty in finding work on leaving school, and had a suggestion for both teachers and those who were considering dropping out:

'If you want to be a worker, it's actually better to have left school at sixteen. The worst thing is to graduate from school but not go on to get a degree. If only they'd taken us out on a bricklayers' course, taught us how to lay a brick wall straight, I could have found work within a day.'

Less than ten youngsters (5.9 per cent) had benefited from real contact with the world of industry, such as gifted Karl Sutcliffe, for whom the experience had redirected his ideas, so that he was very happily at work at university:

'I went on a fascinating three-day course on the science of paper. From that, I realised which subjects I'd have to take. Even if I didn't take up paper science, that combination gave me a very good choice – and it was my choice. The careers master at school was very helpful and still is. He's quite open, and we can go back and see him any time we want.'

Good advice

It was not all bad, though; about a dozen had moved on with sound careers advice. Some schools had a school careers room where students could browse, and a girl studying English at university had an interesting suggestion:

'They had good information laid out, and it was open all the time, but it would have been good if there'd been some standard video tapes on what people do at work. According to all the leaflets I read, it was – study English and be unemployed.'

Another girl trying to get out of the academic rut:

'I went through the art box in the careers office and the latest information was ten years old.'

Three schools had arranged a cornucopia of careers advice. Phillipa Longman was indeed fortunate:

'We've got a careers person, and a careers room, and we have lots of talks – different people coming on different subjects. Most of the sixth form go to the Area Careers Officer too, and we've met representatives from different universities. In the first year in the sixth-form, everybody is interviewed by a member of staff, and we have quite a lot of time with her; mine lasted about twenty-five minutes. She asked us what we wanted to do, and if we'd no idea, she'd give us some. If you wanted information she hadn't got she'd send away for it.'

The more perceptive young people, though, also knew that such matters as self-confidence and personal relationships were as important in their education as the often excellently taught mastery of skills and knowledge. They would have liked some help in developing that side of their overall education. There is a long way for the school counselling services to go in Britain.

Narrow advice

Even when careers help was available from school, it was often described as traditional, unimaginative and gender-biased, such as like boys being pushed into the professions, though they may be better suited to the arts, and vice-versa. A highly gifted girl reported:

'I've just had my first careers interview now at seventeen. It's a bit late because I haven't specialised, and now I've no idea where I'm going. I was asked, "Have you ever thought of becoming a nurse?".'

If the gifted found the advice narrow in the academic schools, it was often far off the mark in the comprehensive schools. Some, who were aware that their potential and personal aptitudes were being disregarded, were not even able to take it seriously. Andy Spurgeon, with a measured IQ well into the top one per cent of the population, said:

'The careers master told me, "Look, they want fifty bus drivers – here's the form". They just want to get us into jobs for the school statistics. I laughed at him.'

Andy's school did not find him easy. He had a mischievous sense of humour and a very different kind of ambition from most of the other pupils. Fortunately he had a sense of humour:

'When I told them I wanted to go to university they asked, "Have you considered other options?" and I said "Well, I had thought of being a toilet attendant; you know, work up from the bottom, start as a loo brush", and she said "That's glamorous!". Truthfully, I'd really like to become an actor, but I want to go to university first, so I chose a course which I knew I was going to enjoy, and which had a fairly low workload. You should have seen the careers people's faces when I told them I was going to university to do Honours Philosophy.'

Update 2001: Andy, now 34, explained why he did not get his degree. 'I left university due to two reasons. One was that I completed three final year theses all of which were marked as a first, and having done so, decided that I have really completed the learning required there and didn't have the time to hang around getting a bit of paper. The second reason was … I had been diagnosed as being HIV positive while at university and already knew many people who had died.' Meanwhile he became an important innovator in a well-known international software firm. He wrote to me (and I reproduce it with his permission):

'My sense of humour and lust for life continues unabated despite all of the issues. I have always had some sort of adversity to deal with in one way or another and I'm sure that my Mother would say that I'd have it no other way.

I still desire to learn and experience new things in the same way that I always did. As an example, while being ill this time round, I was going a bit mad sitting at home all day, so decided to learn how to program in the Flash web site development environment. Two weeks later I was writing tutorials for people on the net and am now one of the acknowledged experts at two of the web-forums where such programming is discussed.

All in all I'm very happy with how I turned out and am more than happy that I can pass on some of what I have learned to others. I've been asked to write pieces about discovering sexuality, a sci-fi series of articles, a book on learning Flash and various other things and am finally getting around to doing some of it. It's just another area of my talents that I have not yet really developed and am looking forward to plunging into when I recover my health (which I expect should be soon).

I still have some difficulty with dealing with other people who can sometimes be jealous of the facility with which I pick things up. However, I've found that as my circle of friends grows older with me, the difficulty associated with such tension grows less. Whether this is because I have grown softer and more understated with age, or whether it is because my circle of friends has become less threatened or more understanding … who knows?

I find though, that I am looked on more as a wise friend who knows a great deal and whose opinion is usually worth asking. It's the combination of a great deal of experience and deep general knowledge allied with an understanding of the human condition and how people work. I suspect that the knowledge and insight that I have always had is probably easier dealt with when packaged in an older body than when packaged in the body of a young upstart [grin].'

The perceptions teachers have of their pupils is well known as being affected by matters other than the pupil's ability (Hany 1993) This subjective appraisal of potential also affects the advice and encouragement which youngsters receive for their future working lives. Whereas poor children may be seen as suitable for manual work, a gentle girl can be directed to something which seems appropriate to her personality rather than to her gifts.

Caroline Whiting was a highly gifted, quiet and unassuming young lady. Although she was at a high-powered academic girl's school (Oxford High School), like so many of the gifted girls in this sample, they had not only directed her to a nursing career, but in addition had strongly dissuaded her from aiming as high as she could reach. But her delicate demeanour hid stern resolve:

> 'When the biology teacher saw my entry for a national biology competition, she said it was no good and full of mistakes, so I shouldn't disgrace the school by putting it in. But I didn't listen and put it in myself. It was runner-up, so they couldn't say anything after that. If only I had been given a tiny amount of encouragement I could have done a lot better, instead of wasting my energies fighting them.'

Update 2001: Undeterred by her school's lack of faith in her, Caroline went to London University to study Food Science with Physiology. When she received her excellent degree, she wrote proudly to the school to let them know, and they sent a standard letter back. Then on to a Master's degree in General Biochemistry to win a prize for biochemistry. Again she wrote to the school, and this time they bent enough to send her a personal letter of congratulation, which was better. By now she had overtaken some of her fellow pupils who had made it to Oxbridge. She worked on arthritis research for some years: her work was published and she spoke at conferences about it. Now married and with two advanced children, she has lived in different countries because of her husband's work. As the children have started school, she is looking for part-time work, because as she said: 'I didn't spend all that time studying to a high level just to drop it all'.

The gifted at university

The transition from the relatively structured and disciplined school day to the heady freedom of university life can bring adjustment problems to all students, and the gifted do not have a monopoly of such problems. But for those in this study who did succumb to distress, it could be much better understood by looking at their whole life situation. Their emotional problems were found to be of much longer standing and had simply been brought to a head by this big life-change. Many, for example, were associated with the circumstances which had bothered them as children, especially those who had been labelled as gifted by their parents in 1974. Sometimes when the deeply invested hopes of parents and teachers had put great pressure to achieve on their young shoulders, having reached their goal of university there were decided feelings of let-down. There was also a fear of being unable to keep up their previous impetus and results among their now more select highly able peers. It is a syndrome well known in business, the let-down which comes after a hard-won deal has been struck.

Some university students described feeling devitalised, overcome by inertia, with difficulty in concentrating, and a lowered motivation to study. Four of the students in this sample were almost clinically depressed or anxious. In every case they had tried to cope alone or with the help of their families. Their university teachers, who clearly saw their roles as purely academic, could be rather crisp when approached for help. Maybe it was bad luck, others maybe kinder. Only two students had approached the official university counsellor, but they felt their visits did not promise to meet their needs, and so had not gone again. Depression feeds on itself.

Although virtually all the gifted students had spoken of wanting to work with their intellectual peers, quite a few described an experience of shock at moving into an all-round higher intellectual gear. When coming top of the pile was no longer a matter of course, self-confidence was sometimes dented. But Jonathan Martin, at 21 studying for a PhD in Chemistry, still yearned for stronger competition at Cambridge – 'I'm so specialised that I'm not really competing against anybody. If I'm top it may only be out of a small number of people and it's a lot easier to do, so I don't feel that it counts.'

In the first part of the study, the highest IQ gifted children were found to be significantly more forthcoming in their suggestions for improving their schools, and indeed the education system (39 per cent suggested more than three changes, compared with 17 per cent of the others). One could say that the gifted also took a more stellar, metacognitive view, because they were less concerned with detail and more with the principles of how the system functioned. They suggested significantly far more organisational and curricular improvements than those of more average IQ, who were likely to suggest more personal, domestic changes (see Appendix 2).

In the Follow-up, when asked about higher education, not unexpectedly the gifted again gave a far higher proportion of lively responses, and they still saw improved organisation and management as keys to better provision. This was particularly true for the way they were examined:

'Surely at university, there was no need for the old-fashioned sort of exams that we had to take for finals. After all, everybody was pretty well at the same standard. A university should be a place where the student should have some say about how he's taught. They always seem to dismiss the ideas we put forward, and find excuses as to why it wouldn't be suitable.'

On the other hand, some dedicated and highly gifted students viewed their time at university as a rather nicer form of school. They did what they had to for their exams, were neither inspired by the teaching nor the atmosphere, felt no obligation to dip into any thought-provoking or even fun areas outside their own study, and had no comments to make on the system. That rather passive group was largely made up of science students of both sexes – who also managed to avoid most of the social and emotional problems – which they left to the students of the humanities and arts.

Prestigious universities

Every country has them, in the USA they are known as the Ivy League Universities (because of the ivy that grows on their walls, and they are private and expensive); in Britain the prestigious (yet low-fee) universities of Oxford and Cambridge are often seen as the holy grail of education by many parents and schools, and known as Oxbridge. The differences between these and other universities is often in their reputations and in the heavy investment the students made to get there. At times these differences seemed to have the effect of accentuating and compounding the normal problems of leaving school, of setting out from what is familiar and standing to some extent on one's own feet. A student's reactions to the new situation depended not only on their personality, but on their home backgrounds and the type of school they had come from. Sometimes the social divide was great and the competition frightening.

The greatest benefit many found at Oxbridge was the easy-going approach to tuition. The more mature students, those who were competent enough to use their tutors as resources rather than givers of information, enjoyed every minute of their time there. As one contented student said:

> 'The nice thing about being here is I've got time. I can toddle along to the library to follow an idea up, then go and have a chat to somebody or my tutor about it. I like learning like that. I find it a very constructive approach to work.'

Although most of the sample who reached there revelled in the new environments, some were decidedly less than comfortable amongst the dreaming spires.

The incentive system in most schools is extrinsically motivated, such as by examination grades or class prizes, and when those familiar rewards are either removed or become too distant, good school achievers can sometimes lose their way. This had happened to Rachel Wallace, whose enormous effort included seven A-levels for which she obtained A grades at two sittings, as well as special scholarship papers for Oxford. Though still only 17, she had secured a place at one of the most select colleges, for which she had paid with emotional exhaustion. Once there, dogged by constant fatigue, she could not muster the strength to become involved with university life. She cried a good deal and felt that she had lost control over her work and was a failure. When she tried to tell her examiners about why she had not done well in her examinations, they said she was simply a bad examination candidate – in spite of her long string of A grades all through school.

Rachel Wallace (Highly gifted, aged 19, a second year student at Oxford):

'My ambition was to get to Oxford. But when I got here everything fell flat. My brain went to sleep after about four weeks and it hasn't woken up since. I've worked about five per cent of the amount I worked before, though my tutors couldn't care less. My own tutor never looks at my work. I don't go to lectures, because I fall asleep in them. There's a lot that is quite interesting to do in Oxford, but I just go shopping, drink tea, read books, wander round the colleges – anything but work, really.

There are people here who are so much better than me that I could never have a hope of catching them up, and I no longer have the possibility of coming top, so that's rather a let-down. It seems a cheat to have to work hard to be third or fourth. The panicking becomes a way of life. I just don't know where to start. I get very bored and lonely too. I have one friend, but apart from her, nobody. Black depression is there. I just get days of it, and I try to keep myself busy, but I'm really powerless to do anything. I think it's getting worse, but I don't want to leave university. In a way it's quite cosy, and you don't have to think about tomorrow, because tomorrow you're just going to be in the same situation.'

Update 2001: Rachel at 36, told me she had considered studying medicine but didn't because, being accelerated, she said had made her 'big headed', feeling cleverer than everyone else – 'which is not an appealing thing in a person. Not a good preparation for life. But then, I might have been bored if I hadn't been. I don't know.'

Medicine, for someone as clever as her would have been too easy, she thought – like plumbing. And anyway, she was too young to start at 16. 'I chose physics because it was the hardest subject I knew. Now I think that if I'd done something I'd liked more I would have got on much better.' She was bored, failed to learn the basics, did not get a good degree and has never used it since. Boredom, or fear of boredom, continued to dog her. Of her acceleration she said, 'But then, I might have been bored if I hadn't been. I don't know. I get bored with nothing to do. Life seems to be a matter of getting bored and then finding something else to do.' (See p. 66 on boredom.)

Strangely, she now remembers little of her final year at Oxford, though blames her unhappiness at being dumped by a boyfriend. But things changed when she met her future husband. She worked in the civil service for many years, but with the birth of her two sons started a small business at home. Now she is very happy, but still feels the threat of boredom in her growing work which, she says, may not last for more than a couple of years.

Oxbridge and Cambridge Universities are made up of semi-autonomous colleges, each selecting its own students, and having its own social make-up. In the early 1990s the number of applications to these two universities from the private and state sectors were about the same, and accordingly each gained about half the places – even though the private sector makes up only about seven per cent of the school population. The situation in 2001 is slightly better in that the state sector is verging on a majority in some colleges. One comprehensive school boy in the sample said bitterly:

'Although they say they're trying to remedy that, they should really have something like ninety per cent of state school people there, instead of less than fifty per cent.'

Admissions tutors say this is due to myths about Oxbridge, and that they discriminate in favour of pupils from private schools, or comprehensive schools do not send enough applicants and additionally, since many of the private schools see other universities and polytechnics as only second-best, they are more likely to apply to Oxbridge as first choice. There are added stumbling blocks for candidates whose schools have not prepared them adequately because entry is not always entirely by state examination results. Not only are there interviews to be negotiated, but some colleges have entrance exams of their own design which need special preparation.

Several gifted and academically highly achieving Oxbridge applicants in my sample believed they had failed to gain a place because of inadequate preparation from school. There may not have been enough pupils there taking the special papers to merit the provision of teachers for the necessary tuition. Also, the gifted were in more of a minority at some schools: 'There wasn't enough competition to drive me on to do well'. Those from state schools who did gain acceptance, had usually received the kind of heavy coaching that is more common in private schools. One comprehensive school boy said:

'I've almost been on a conveyor belt for two years. But I was amazed when I got to Cambridge. I was expecting all these egghead types – it's total rubbish! Most of the people are the most amazing bunch of dossers the world has ever seen. How they got there, most of them, is beyond me.'

As at least six students from my sample had applied with a fistful of A grades at A-level, and had been turned down: it did look as though there were some non-academic reasons for their rejections.

Those who failed to get in sometimes felt that it was not so much their own as their school's social status which had been held against them. A student explained:

'Last year, I would have told you I wasn't affected by social-class, because at my comprehensive everybody was equal in a way. But then I was rejected by Oxford. It really shocked me. You get the message quite clearly here at Bristol, which takes a high proportion of Public (private) school types – they call it the poor man's Oxbridge. These people don't regard me as a Comprehensive school person; to them I'm just non-Public school. I've found it very difficult.'

The lifestyle of the prestigious universities would be daunting for socially unprepared students. These powerful effects were experienced in a tragic way by Alison Cranfield, an outstandingly brilliant girl who had attempted to jump the culture gap. But it was too wide for her and she had slipped and fallen. Even to think of it, nearly a year after the debacle, still brought tears to her eyes.

Alison was a tall, sensitive, hard-working girl from the far north. Even at our first meeting, when she was ten years old, I had noted how retiring and extremely polite she was. At Oxford, she described her fellow students as having too much money to spend: 'The boys got drunk, and the girls were too worldly'. Though her school had given her superb teaching and taken great pride in her achievements, they had not given her any preparation and personal help to see her through the great changes of pace and style which she faced alone – nor had the university when she reached there. Not one person had ever reached higher education in her family, no example to give her courage and know-how. She only had her belief in God.

Alison Cranfield (Highly gifted, aged 21, a bank clerk):

'I felt looked down on because of where I came from. They would tease me and imitate my accent, then say they couldn't understand me. It was very upsetting at the time, but that wasn't the whole reason I left. I failed my first year exams because the course wasn't right for me. No one at school had ever discussed it; it was just "OK, off you go". My background knowledge wasn't sufficient, because I only knew what I'd been taught in school, those few books I'd read for my exams. I had so much catching up to do. I was taking French, though I've never been to France, yet other students even had second homes over there.

When I left, I felt I'd let down my school and the neighbours and the church. The college agreed that it was best for me to leave. It was galling when they suggested I should have done a different course or gone to a different university.

After I got back, for the first six weeks I'd go to sleep at night and pray for the bomb to come. I didn't have the courage to commit suicide and I wanted someone to do it for me. I stayed in the house all the time because the neighbours would ask me about Oxford. But I was just ending up self-pitying, so I started going to places where people hadn't known me before. I took up new interests, started going to a drama group once a week and made new friends there. And I went to a different church.

I felt very much that what I'd done was wrong – to step out of my caste, to think that I could be like one of them. My reaction was to hate the students, higher education, and everything that I associated with Oxford. If I have my own children, I wouldn't encourage them to go on to higher education. I'd rather they were on the loose for a few years and sorted things out before committing themselves to something like that.'

Update 2001: Alison's route continued to be rocky. Still living at home, she resigned from her job as a clerk and enrolled for a BEd. at a small local college. But she found the lectures pitched at too low a level for her: the slow pace 'drove me berserk'; at times she was so boiling with frustration that she couldn't wait to get out of the classroom to pour cold water on her face. She cannot have pleased her lecturers when she told them 'that the concepts they were trying to teach us were so simple to grasp that the lesson could be completed in a fraction of the time'. Also, as she was two years older and very much brighter than most of the other students she felt removed from them and did not socialise much. The simmering pot finally overflowed and she left in her second year – the second academic course she had quit.

After a few other false starts, Alison took a polytechnic BSc in Mathematics, Statistics and Computing, gaining a Distinction. She is now steadily moving up the ladder in the secure atmosphere of an insurance company, in the statistical/computing arena, where she has been since 1989. Alison is happy, married to a man who is 'educated way below his potential' with three bright children. Her view on being labelled gifted is well worth quoting:

'I have realised as I've got older that intelligence matters for very little, which has been a hard thing to learn, as it's the one thing on which I was consistently judged as a child. Every day, people around me are more successful (by whatever measure) than I am, and the fact that I could probably "better" them in an IQ test doesn't make the slightest difference, nor should it. I don't even think intelligence is that apparent outside of a classroom environment. Not many people that I deal with now know that I went to Oxford or that I was considered bright as a child, and I think most of them would be astonished. I think that there are times when I deliberately recall that time of my life through some sad vanity, to remind myself that I did have the ability to "make something" of myself, even if I lacked the imagination, determination, etc., etc. I must try and put it behind me for good.'

More support needed

Samantha Goldman had risen in her brilliance like a shooting star, then fallen to earth again. Even in this sample of exceptionally high achievers, she was quite outstanding in her breadth of ability and enthusiasm for life. Her six A grades at A-level taken at one sitting were in widely varied subjects. They did not even include music, although she was an outstanding pianist at Chethams School of Music and had been expected to reach the concert platform. Strangely, her immense talent and vitality in her playing became a problem in her study. Out of school she had been without any guidance: her enthusiasm for the enticements of university life carried her away, leaving little time for her studies. Some support and advice from both school and university, taking her personality and background into account, could have made all the difference to her future.

Samantha Goldman (Highly gifted and talented, aged 19, at university):

'Cambridge was my first choice, but I failed the entrance exam, probably for lack of preparation, and anyway they probably wouldn't take people from a school like mine. In my first year at London I played in the orchestra, in the second I was orchestra manager, and in the third I'm President of the Music Society. They still tease me a bit, like when I come in someone says "Oh look, the working-classes have arrived!" I think of myself as working-class, and obviously all the rest of them do because of my accent, so they tend to treat me like a pet poodle, and it can get a bit irritating. I'm going to go back north as soon as I can.

I didn't go to the lectures after the first couple of weeks in my second year because of the musical I was directing, 'Oh What a Lovely War'. It just snowballed. I wrote the score, organised the costumes, and did just about everything else. I spent all day in the theatre from about eight in the morning till midnight, and then extra hours on the phone. It's the thing I've enjoyed doing most ever, and it was a smash. But it was staged the day before my first exam and as a result I did very badly. I hope to do something like that when I leave, but I don't know how to get into it.'

Update 2001: Samantha failed all her final exams and returned north to work as an assistant housemistress at her old (part-boarding) music school. She re-took and scraped through her finals, and then a teaching certificate specialising in secondary maths with subsidiary physics. They wouldn't allow her to take music because she had no A-level in it – her 'huge amount of background knowledge and experience' counted for naught with the university. So, although she was employed to teach maths at a big comprehensive school for 12 years, she also taught most of their practical music. Unfortunately, she was effectively obliged to leave because she was treated badly, which seemed to me very much a case of the 'tall poppy syndrome': she had very much more to offer than is usual among specialist teachers, and it could have caused jealousy and the desire by the others to cut her down to size. The trauma caused her to become clinically depressed and to loose her exuberance and confidence, but she rose above it and now teaches in a primary school for children with problems, very happily. She has never married, but feels content with her life and cat, singing in several choirs, including a group she organised herself, and keeping up her interest in science. Additionally, she told me: 'I seem to have spent a significant part of the time since I last saw you being interviewed by newspapers/magazines/radio/TV programmes about what it's like to be a "gifted failure".'

Although most intellectually gifted students are happy and do well at university, it is, to say the least, a waste of human energy that those who are more sensitive, or still immature, or who find themselves taking unsuitable courses, may fail to thrive there. Though universities were certainly not set up as caring agencies for the emotionally fragile, they do want to get the best from the students they accept, for reasons both humanitarian and economic.

Gifted students often come to university with the special problems of extremely high expectations of family and teachers, added to which they may have a greater clarity of vision of what might be done. They have often experienced put-downs, may have grown up feeling different, and are short of praise and reassurance. They need someone to turn to who understands their situation and how they feel about it, who can help to make them feel more comfortable in a sometimes strange alienating place. It may be, for example, that a smaller university would be more suitable for an individual, such as Alison Cranfield, which might have saved her years of real distress. This would help the gifted student to continue to develop at his or her own pace – and eventual exceptionally high level.

It is true that we all make mistakes in finding our ways in life. But much of the emotional and financial cost of setting out on the wrong path is avoidable. In theory, help is available everywhere – in school and in higher education – but is often too remote and not always very effective. Greatly improving the universities' counselling services need not be a financially extravagant move; for example, suitable faculty could be trained in counselling skills and paid extra for their time. Indeed, in economic terms, stemming the loss of bright young people from these costly places of study would more than pay for the extra help they might receive. It would, however, require a refocusing of university outlook from only teaching to include some caring too.

CHAPTER 9

The wider social world

Be good sweet maid, and let who will be clever;
Charles Kingsley, *A Farewell to CEG*

The most pervasive social influences on an individual's education is family outlook. Although this applies to all children, its effect on the gifted can be different and more powerful because the stakes are much higher. Because of the in-depth approach of this research, the parents were able to tell me about their own parents' background and how these had affected the sample children, which helped to untangle the web of circumstances in which these young people grew up.

Social mores clearly affect people's lives in Britain, as indeed elsewhere. Unwritten social rules hallowed by time, at times appeared to radically change the life chances and progress of these young people. It was not primarily a question of money, because the families ranged from very poor to very rich, but rather people's ideas about themselves, their self-concepts. When Derek Girling, a highly gifted boy, refused to go to university (at no cost then) because 'it's not for the likes of me', he was listening to past social values, not the reality of the time, yet it did change his life. But in 2001 he says bitterly that he was wrong then; he had chosen to do everything the hard way.

The idea that gifted children from all backgrounds can make sturdy growth without special help is fading, if slowly. In many parts of the Western world, diminishing numbers in many schools due to a lower birthrate have narrowed the curriculum and thinned the educational nourishment. High unemployment has meant that bright youngsters, the ones most likely to get the jobs, sometimes see little point in staying on to take more exams at school, and leave to take what work they can get. Far more British children leave school before 16 (82 per cent) compared with other nations, such as Japan (4 per cent) Germany (10 per cent), and the United States (10 per cent). Proportionally fewer too take up further training; a great loss for late developers.

Social status

Home outlook is effective in enabling gifts to grow in not always obvious ways. It shows, for example, in the amount and quality of homework a child does (Hallam and Cowan 1997). In every country, children who are set homework, do it, and have it marked, perform better at school than those who do none. Even though there is a wide variation in how much different schools set, parents who approve of it often see a heavy load as a sign of a caring school, and some keen successful children set themselves extra problems to do at home. Schools in poor areas sometimes make the premises available after hours to those whose homes are not conducive to study.

Family outlook and style of living was highlighted in this study, for example, in the young people's television watching habits. When those who watched more than three hours a day were compared with those who watched less, a number of significant family aspects emerged, though there were no differences in the children's sex or intelligence. The lighter viewers described themselves as distinctly higher up the social scale, more likely to be at selective schools than at comprehensives, had longer concentration spans, and enjoyed more outside activities. When they did watch television they preferred more serious programmes.

For gifted children, a modest family background could have a more profound effect than on those of more average ability. This was because they were more likely to change their educational environments and thus have to swim in a somewhat different social soup. The move could come in childhood via a scholarship from the local primary school to one which was selective, private, specialist, or boarding, or it could come later with entry to one of the more prestigious universities. Whenever it happened the gifted individual would be well aware that it was made because of his or her brain power or talents, and that their social background was not the same as that of most of their classmates. Most did settle well, some being explicit:

'I couldn't be bothered with anybody who was prepared to exclude me in terms of background. People put far too much energy into maintaining distinctions and barriers.'

Others, though, shied away from confrontation:

'Going to Oxford, you meet people who are definitely in a class above you. They are friendly enough, but never too friendly. Well, that's fair enough, because they're of that class and I'm not.'

The difference between state and private schools in all countries of the world is not only material but social. A highly gifted boy at a Liverpool comprehensive school described the gulf: 'I've only ever met boys from private schools in passing. You can spot them straight away. It's two different societies, them and us really.' It was echoed by an equally able boy from the other side of the valley: 'One would assume that if people cared enough, they wouldn't send their children to those extremely limited state schools.' The snobbery at some of the private schools could be hard to take, as one girl found who had clearly let her school (Oxford High School) down: 'At speech day they only called out the names of the girls who'd made it to Oxbridge, not those of us who'd gone to other universities.'

Private and selective schools

Their lower social status was held to be responsible by at least six highly gifted youngsters for their failure to obtain scholarships to selective private schools. This seemed to be the case for Karl Sutcliffe, for in terms of measured academic potential he was more than merely suitable for academic education. Indeed, the secretary of the school he had applied for had told his parents that he had done extremely well in the entrance exam. Karl concluded bitterly that this was because 'his face didn't fit', and in truth, there were very few boys of his social status at that school. He felt that this blow to his ego had caused him to lose interest in school work, causing his mother many tearful nights. But he was determined that never again would he be socially rejected. He was a dominant young man who would interrupt many of my questions to redirect me to what he thought I should be asking. Socially he saw himself as having already made progress, being: 'mentally upper-middle, but held back by my parents', a shop assistant and a mechanic. He was trying to smarten himself up, beginning with an expensive sweater with the Pringle mark clear on the front. I feared for him as destined for embittered middle management, his enormous potential intellectual power dissipated in pub philosophy.

Karl Sutcliffe (Highly gifted, aged 22, a bank clerk):

> 'People I know socially talk behind my back, but I tolerate them, put on a show. They've got a use, and perhaps one day I'll need them. I'm going to make something of myself. For the next couple of years, I'm going to follow the bank's career structure and then get myself in a situation where I can go out and say, "That's the job I want; I'm having it". I'm going to educate myself, but not in formal education – I am in life – I'm trying to diversify my interests. I'm going to start playing golf, because these are things you need, like joining the boss on Sunday in a game. Try and get myself in with the right people, that's what I'm aspiring to do. One day I'd like a nice castle with a moat in Surrey or some old county, as an investment. I can get rid of my accent; I can carry that off. I'm not thinking about elocution lessons; it would sound odd to the people I'm currently in contact with; it's got to be a gradual thing. Mind you, the way really is to tie yourself to the top of the Empire State Building and say, "World, listen to me".'

Paul Nash had the opposite problem in a sense, and found his life 'schizophrenic'.

Because his local education authority had forbidden any child to be advanced at school, he had ended up with a free (assisted) place at an expensive boarding school. His home was small and drab, a little bit run down, on a housing estate amidst hundreds of others like it. The other boys at school were largely from rich families who he felt rather looked down on him, so he never brought them home. In spite of having been at the school for seven years, he had clung to his original strong local accent, perhaps as the one bit of him that he still owned. Although his examination results were outstandingly high, Paul refused to try for Oxbridge, fearing yet more snobbery, and so felt that he was letting everyone down. 'Despair' was the word he used to describe his frequent long spells of depression, which were sometimes so bad that he felt he would never re-emerge. He saw himself as trapped, not knowing which way to aim. Dark clouds hung about his future. He felt he would have been much better off at a mixed-ability day school, especially one with girls in it.

Update 2001: Although he now remembers the school as OK, Paul is not enthusiastic about it, and says, 'I don't like the idea of sending my children there. I don't like the idea of boarding schools.' He graduated with a good degree in linguistics, and combined this with his work as a programmer for a cancer charity, currently bringing it together in his work for a PhD in the evolution of complex meaning structure. This will increase the understanding of how children learn language and possibly how robots learn language too. He is married and very happy.

The effect could be almost as distressing when the move was from private to state school, as Andy Spurgeon found: 'Some of the people at school, they make you think that you're just a turd on the sideboard because you're middle-class.' Another boy came across it at Cambridge: 'I'm meeting people for the first time from comprehensive schools. They seem to be such nice people. In fact, I'm the only public (private) school person in my group, and they think it's very amusing, but they don't hold it against me – I don't think.'

Suspended between those different social worlds, Yvonne Barnett was never quite sure where she fitted in. Coming from a poor home which was also emotionally disturbed, she had been given a scholarship by her local education authority to an expensive boarding school. Her experiences had left this highly gifted, sensitive and very beautiful young woman with a problem of insecurity.

Yvonne Barnett's mother:

'We thought it was a good idea at the time, going to that posh school, because she needed the push and the competition. But then she saw how the other half lived and she couldn't compete. We did have such hopes for her.'

Yvonne Barnett (Highly gifted, aged 22, out of work):

> 'I've got a very mixed-up family background, but it means I can cope very well, because I've been through that and nothing else ever seems so bad. When I first went to the school, my accent was really strong, and kids used to rag me and make me talk so they could laugh. I got very jealous that some of them could buy anything they wanted and had loads of clothes. Also, I'd never done French at junior school like the people that had been to private schools. Consequently, I was hopeless at it. I would never bring anyone home. They would have been embarrassed at coming to such a little house, and my manners were so different. I don't think I should have gone. When I heard about my local comprehensive, what they've learnt, and the kind of courses they were applying for, it made me really jealous.'

Update 2001: Yvonne left university in her second year, worked as a waitress for several years, then took some business courses. She became an administrator for a small firm, but seemed to go on from job to job.

Derek Girling had an IQ over the top of any scale, and the ability to do almost anything, were he not intellectually crippled by the social shackles in his mind. As a teenager, he often said to me, 'Well, that's the way I like to put it – blunt like a working man'. He had left school at 16 with all A grades at A-level – 'in my worst subjects'. But, he told me:

> 'At the time of the choice to do Oxford or Cambridge, I believed that I wouldn't have got in, mostly because my father wasn't a suitably employed person. That would make a difference to my credentials; they'd ask more of me than somebody whose father was say a doctor. That's how I feel. I would like to have gone in a way, but I don't think I'll lose out by what I'm doing.'

His mother filled me in: 'He'd mixed with them boys for six years at school, and he wasn't that struck, especially the moneyed ones. He didn't want to mix with them for another three years. He's much happier on the ground with "real people".' Indeed, he was working for the local Electricity Board, doing a part-time degree, wiring houses, 'knowing what it's like with his finger-ends frozen, trying to dig a solid piece of ground'. His mother approved, adding, 'Bringing my kids up, I've had some "brick-bats" from neighbours, because I let them play out and get dirty, and because I had a piano for them instead of new suits and posh clothes. It really hurt at the time. But I looked at them and they were happy, and they were thriving. They were achieving what was in them. You're not a bad mother if you don't have the latest microwave oven.'

Update 2001: Derek gained a first class honours degree in engineering and is now a Development Engineer in a major electricity company. He and his girlfriend of 18 years have bought their own home, and have, he said 'found out what it's all about'.

He works long hours, to the extent he had to give up years of singing in a top chorus, and is feeling that perhaps he made the wrong decision all those years ago to leave school at 16. But then, as he said, 'Careers guidance was decidedly weak'. He knows now that had he stayed an extra year he could have gone to a good university, instead of doing it the hard way via a five year 'apprenticeship' followed by years of slow arduous climb. He says he is 'loathe to blame', but now realises the great demands that had been made of him. He was young for his high-pressure school and then accelerated by a year, which meant he was effectively two years ahead. He calls it 'an unseemly rush'. He now realises that he wasn't mature enough to act on his own in his decision not to go to university.

But he's not prepared to sacrifice his life any further to social mores, whether of social class or the fashionable 'rat-race'. The latter is what would be needed to get to the top of his career ladder: 'working all hours, staying away from home two or three nights a week in hotels. No thanks.' Derek is 36, and they have delayed starting a family long enough. Their strong temptation is to cut loose; maybe save up enough money to emigrate to somewhere warm and sunny.

However, some of the young people were sure that social divisions were here to stay and would affect everyone's life chances no matter how gifted. This view was expressed vehemently by Samantha Goldman:

'It's in everything, absolutely everything. All your life chances are restricted if you're born into the working-class. You can never escape from it. You can never completely con yourself or anyone else in trying to change your class. You're born and brought up into a certain set of people, who have certain attitudes towards society, each other, and education in particular. It makes communication between the classes quite difficult in either direction. You can see it happening around you. For instance, in the (primary school) staff room, where I teach, teachers think that children are stupid because they come from the council estate. They use it to explain why a certain child's misbehaved in a classroom, though it's probably just that he thought their lesson was boring.

You can even see it in marking the work, because I went through a lot of their exercise books, and if they had the right name or the right accent or the right dad, they tended to get a better mark than I would have given them, not knowing who they were.'

Gender

Very many studies around the world have shown that from earliest childhood, boys receive more encouragement than girls to be independent, self-reliant and assume responsibility, and that it alters their approach to both school and work (Freeman 1996). In this study, over 30 per cent of the boys, compared with five per cent of the girls, found their greatest satisfaction in achievement, a basic difference from which many others stemmed (see Chapter 6, under heading 'The cost of high academic achievement'). In addition, the boys were more likely to take their success as their due because of their own ability and hard work, whereas the girls often looked upon it as something outside their control – luck – though they claimed their defects as their own, as had been found in other studies (Heller and Ziegler 1996). For many girls, being successful could threaten their image of their femininity, which one gifted girl at university kept at bay by her display of good-little-girl behaviour. Her only hobbies were knitting and sewing, and she insisted that I inspect her neat child-like bedroom – dolls, teddy bears and slippers in their places. She explained in her sweet way: 'I do care what other people think of me, and I always try to be nice'.

By chance, there were significantly more boys in co-ed comprehensive schools and girls in selective, single-sex schools, where they worked harder. Parents were significantly more satisfied with their daughter's school and progress there than their son's school and performance. At the first hurdle of state exams at 16 this seemed justified, since the girls passed relatively more subjects, but the crunch came 18 at A-level – when the boys obtained twice as many A grades.

More boys had gone on to university, the girls often settling for colleges and polytechnics, some even told of being discouraged by their teachers. Every one of the girls in this sample who had gone to university had been at an all-girls' school for most of her school life, and every one of the 17 boys who had gone to university from a comprehensive school had studied science. This extraordinary division may be coincidence, because the sample is not large, but it is in line with evidence from much larger studies.

Update 2001: gender and achievement
What a change in only 13 years: the gender scene in Britain has changed radically. By 2000, girls were outperforming boys in all public examinations at school in all subjects other than physical education. This covered all the Standard Attainment Tests taken at the ages of seven, 11 and 14, and national examinations at 16 and 18. What is more, girls' grades were higher, scoring a higher proportion in the top three national examination grades, and they had a lower rate of failure (9 per cent compared with 11.9 per cent for boys).

In 2001, for the first time, women are gaining more first-class university degrees than men. This has trebled in just ten years, with women now leading the field in 12 of the 17 subject areas, including medicine, law and business (HESA 2001).

Cross-cultural comparison, though, presents a different picture. An investigation of 8th grade mathematics achievements covering 38 countries showed that although 'In most countries the gender difference was negligible' (p. 48), there were significant differences among the highest scoring 25 per cent of students – the gifted ones (TIMSS 1999). Only three countries stood out against this trend of girls doing at least as well as boys, as reported: 'In Israel, Tunisia, and the United States, the percentages of boys reaching the upper quarter level were significantly greater than the percentages of girls reaching this level' (p. 48). For those three countries, there appear to be considerable cultural differences affecting girls' high-level mathematics achievements. There are thus enormous differences for the gifted between countries with supposedly similar outlooks, notably the USA and Britain – the transatlantic waters are muddier than we had thought.

Teachers and academics are struggling to understand what lies behind this reversed gender divide in British attainment. One possible reason is that the boys say it is difficult to study because other boys might laugh at them if they behaved like 'teacher's pets', which is by definition unmanly. Possibly it is because of the change of style of examination from risky last minute short-term memory and multiple-choice questions to continuous assessment. But their advancement is also bringing some strain to highly achieving girls. Early career planning has been found to be a cause of stress for some, which merely delays rather than resolves the conflict between family and work (Lucey and Walkerdine 1996).

Equal opportunities

When asked whether boys and girls should have the same opportunities in life, virtually all parents said they should. But deeper questioning and observation sometimes exposed the old division – science for the boys and art for the girls. In fact, three times as many boys as girls specialised in science, and more than twice as many girls as boys in arts subjects. The parents of the girls were decidedly keener to have music appreciation taught at school, and indeed five girls went on to study music though no boys did. For all girls at school, as they get older, the likelihood of being taught science by a woman and so seeing a woman in a scientific role, becomes less.

However, not all the parents would even pay lip-service to the idea of equal opportunities. Julie Knight glowed with youth and beauty. She dressed with care and style, smiled as she spoke, and at 16 was much sought after by young men; her father fielded her constant phone calls from boys while I was at their home. Her mother and father fulfilled their gender roles to an extreme; her mother said little and always agreed with her husband, who pronounced with great authority. He considered it a complete waste of time for girls to have anything to do with science. His message for Julie's future was clear, and although Julie had been a keen scientist, and had overridden the school's pleading for her to do what she was best at by directing her to take French, History and English. She dared not tell him how she felt, but said to me in an impersonal way, as though it bore no reference to her own life: 'People should have more say in their own careers, because it's their life'. Julie Knight's father:

> 'Let's face it, you can be all the women's lib you like, but there are no jobs for girls in science. The female mind works more on intuition, and the male reasons things. She's going to get married anyway and have children, so there's not much point in her studying further.'

It was much more complex for Gina Emerson, a girl who seemed to have every facility to fulfil her intellectually quite outstanding potential. She had been to one of the most exclusive girls' schools in Scotland, and lived in a large, beautiful home, the walls lined with good books. But her brilliance had added greatly to the intensity of her gender conflicts. Her father, who loved his daughter dearly, was a somewhat old-fashioned man, brought up in a patriarchal system. His expectations of his daughter, which had been tragically compounded by her mother's death, included the old-style female role. From childhood, her conflict between trying to please her parents and wanting to enjoy the excitement of using her mind, had brought her guilt and distress.

Gina Emerson (Highly gifted, aged 19, at Cambridge university):

> 'My mother died over a year ago, and it changed everything instantly. I was suddenly responsible and in charge of things. I was 16. I spent nine months at home before university and got the frustrated housewife syndrome. Mummy's friends became my friends, and I took over some of her voluntary social work with them, which is all right up to a point. Daddy said I was having a kind of marriage without the good bits, just doing the housework.

> Rationally, I know I don't have anything to be depressed about, but I still cry quite a lot. And when I cry, I really cry. I can't turn to my father, because either he'd not understand why, or he'd feel guilty, thinking it was all connected with Mummy's death. At university I see my boyfriend, it's wonderful. But though I'm quite happy to be superficially cheered up by him, I feel kind of guilty because it's not really a solution to my problem. During these holidays I've only been out twice, and after both times father said, "You left all this washing-up to do, and I had to do this, and we didn't have enough potatoes on Saturday night" or something. I want to be a student and I've got to be a housewife too. He doesn't ask my brother because he's away at school: he's different somehow. Day to day, I never seem to have enough time to do the ironing or the meal or whatever.

> I suppose I am growing up a bit, though, because I'm feeling more responsible. When I go back to university, I tell my father he's got to feed himself properly,

leave him instructions as to how to do his washing and ring him up to check if he's all right. I picture myself marrying an alcoholic or something, and having a really tough life, but satisfied because I've redeemed that person.'

Update 2001: Gina, now 35, left Cambridge with a 2:1 degree, which she felt slightly ashamed of because she knew was below her capabilities. The reason, she recalls, was too little work because she was having such a good time. On leaving she took up left-wing causes, running the journal *New Socialist* until it closed, then worked for the Fabian Society until she had to leave because of clashing with a 'very ambitious, massively sexist general secretary'. So she freelanced from home and did trade union newsletters, then worked for an educational publishers for a few years. Now she owns a firm doing graphic and Internet design, along with her brother James. Gina lives with her boyfriend from Cambridge who is a university lecturer, though they are not sure whether to have children or not. She adored and misses her father who died, and cares for her rather lonely younger brother. She told me: 'I think I could be doing anything really. It's important that I do something for sympathetic people. I need time for my extra activities.' These are almost impossibly numerous. Gina is currently standing for election as a Labour councillor, is a school governor of a primary school, does the soup-bus once a week, sings in a choir, works for the credit union, is an executive member of the local board of trade ('Fascinating, most of the others are over 60') and has a strong Christian faith. She said: 'The challenge of the twenty-first century is to increase the pool of volunteers'.

Should girls and boys be educated together or separately?

The gifted in Britain are far more likely than more average children to be educated along with their own gender because they are more likely to be selected for highly academic schools which are usually single-sex. Although single-sex education was common even 25 years ago, it now seems a little odd, and did not help the very bright children to make easy relationships with the opposite sex. In fact, when asked what they would have preferred, only 14.2 per cent of all the sample would have chosen single-sex education, and those were mostly girls (23 per cent of the girls) who felt that they could be placed at a disadvantage with boys in the class. They often looked forward, however, to a more balanced life at university, though it did not always happen, as one girl complained: 'I'm living in an all-girls' hall of residence, so I've never really spoken to boys'.

Those boys (9.2 per cent) who did prefer single-sex education still worried about missing out on the social aspects of growing up, and with reason, because it usually affected them more than the girls. It was described by many boys, as here:

'There's a certain sort of veneer you get at an all-male school. Everybody was always quick to put everyone else down and quick to make jokes at each other's expense. You come out very hard-bitten, cynical, and quite quick, but very dry. It would have been a lot better if it was mixed.'

But some of the boys could see what the girls feared: 'At my comprehensive, the girls did very badly in science, though they were probably about even in the arts subjects. I'm sure they would have been better off in an all-girls school.' But the price the girls had to pay for their greater opportunities at single-sex schools was at times decidedly Victorian:

'We weren't allowed to talk to the boys, even though the boy's school was next door, and you got a bad mark against your name if you got caught. The only allowed times were either in a joint choir that came together once a year, or in the orchestra. In the Sixth Form you did have some lessons with them, but our biology mistress said that all boys were very bad and they would want to get you "into trouble". Girls from my kind of school may flip when they get to university, and be off with the boys every night.'

As some prestigious highly academic boy's schools now take very bright girls at 16, several girls in this study had the experience of both girls' and boys' schools. However, they were not always made to feel at home. Rachel Wallace was one:

'At my girls' school, they just didn't seem to have the same enthusiasm and competition. But when I first went to the boy's school, they'd say, "Good heavens, a girl doing physics – can't possibly be right". There were four girls in the class and the teacher used to just teach to the boys, and if we didn't know anything he used to say, "Oh, don't ask. Don't ask." Even on my school report he wrote that I asked too many questions. He didn't want to know the girls. He just talked to the lads.'

But for girls from the more rigid type of selective girls' school, the new mix could come as a great relief, as Gina Emerson found in her expensive boarding school:

'The boys' school was much more relaxed; no uniform or regulations about bedtimes, which were ridiculous for 18-year-olds. Before, the mistresses used to get so uptight about petty things, like your hair's sitting on your shoulder and it's not tied up with a blue ribbon; they think it's the end of the world. It could go on for a fortnight – "That wicked girl in the second year". You go to bed at night, and you've got to face it all the next morning, and you haven't been able to tell anyone or go home and get away.'

Many gifted young women, enjoying an education and positions that would have been denied not only to their grandmothers but to their mothers, took it all as their right, with never a backward glance. Some at university saw the feminist groups there as irritations and felt that they were spoiling the female image with their aggressive behaviour, and often disassociated themselves from any taint of relationships with them. About a quarter of both sexes thought that feminist 'extremists' had gone too far. As one girl put it: 'It's quite funny, at the beginning of term the feminists put little leaflets in all the fresher girls' pigeon-holes asking "How do you feel about being one in four at Cambridge?" I'm very happy: I like it like that.'

Family influences

Opportunities in education have been improving over the generations across the Western World, especially in Britain, but some families have managed to make better use of opportunities than others. One of the advantages of this long-term study, has been that the accumulating influences of family outlook on the education of this sample could often be identified. This difference in approach and outcomes showed very clearly in looking back at the almost parallel lives of two Liverpool families.

Across three generations, the two families had a great deal in common, though they had never met. The four sets of grandparents had been poor, unskilled and minimally educated. Then, caught up in the benefits of the post-war welfare state, their children, today's parents, had been selected for free selective Grammar school education, and each now had a highly gifted son (even bearing the same initials). Both boys had been to state primary schools and had been picked out as gifted by their head teachers, but each family had reacted differently and the boys' stories had forked. Though both had then aimed for Cambridge University, one made it and one did not.

Neil Cope's family took a fatalistic attitude to life. His parents' feeling of lack of control over their own destiny was not far removed from that of their own parents. Against their deep doubts, they had accepted the head teacher's advice and sent their son on a scholarship to a private school. Neil's father had obviously been a very bright boy, remembering: 'One day I came home and said to my mother, "I've got eight O-levels" and she said "Great", and carried on with the washing. It just didn't mean anything to her.' But in spite of their Grammar school educations, neither he nor his wife felt capable of making decisions about their son's education: 'We feel the teachers should guide the children, because our own education wasn't sufficient for us to do it. So when Neil was ten, they took it out of our hands. Yet making him so different, he had such a difficult time.'

Neil Cope (Highly gifted, aged 20, at university):

'Nobody at the school came from my area of Liverpool, and I felt a bit inferior because of my accent. I also got bullied because I was getting my homework in on time and they weren't. Some of the boys there really weren't very good. I knew I was intelligent, but if I didn't do well, then nobody else would know. That's why I got my head down and worked, and also I'd be letting a lot of people down if I didn't.

When I went for my Cambridge interview I felt slightly out of place, because I thought a lot of the people there would have money, and I didn't, but I really wanted to go when I saw it. For a lad like me, I'd have to do better than a person from Harrow or Eton, and if I had been at a comprehensive school, I would have had to do very much better still. If I hadn't tried, then I would have regretted it for the rest of my life, and at least I know now that I didn't get in because I wasn't good enough – or at least I wasn't good enough on the day.'

Although he was from the same social background, the attitude of Alistair Lund's family was completely different and wonderful. His was a line of fighters. His parents declined exactly the same advice that Alistair's parents had had from his head teacher, and instead of sending him to a private school had plumped for the local comprehensive.

Alistair Lund's mother:

'We had great pressure put on us by the headmaster of the primary school for Alistair to go to the independent school, but we wanted him to be in a more natural environment. Obviously there were children there who weren't interested in learning, but we backed Alistair to rise above that, and he did, staying with his own age group. I can't complain of his results at all, with 15 O-levels, can I? But at the independent school they were geared to the Oxbridge exam, and there were no facilities at all for that at the comprehensive.

At the last minute, we went to Cambridge as a family, and Alistair and I hoofed it round at least 20 colleges to see which ones would take him without special entrance papers. Some, like Magdalene, wouldn't entertain boys from comprehensive schools. He had to go through very rigorous interviews, and he's very modest. I don't suppose he told you that he was head boy in both his schools, and he got an A grade in O-level computer studies without any lessons. We're just waiting to go to the Palace for his Gold Duke of Edinburgh Award.

My father was a man of great strength of character. When he was a boy, he ran away from home to avoid working the copper mines in Anglesea. He told me he walked barefooted through the snow to the nearest port, saving his good boots strung round his neck – it was in January – and signed on as a cabin-boy in a sailing-ship. They went round the world for about 12 years, and when he came back to the village he found his mother had died of a broken heart, the year after he'd left. He bought her a decent headstone. He'd gone from being the dogsbody on board ship to being the captain.'

Alistair Lund (Highly gifted, aged 20, at university):

'In the Sixth Form at the comprehensive, I admit I became rather intolerant. I know that sounds big-headed, and I'm sorry. They weren't talking about anything that was worth talking about, it was all "Did you see Top of the Pops last night?" and "Do you want to come out to the pub tonight?" There was nothing else. I desperately wanted somebody else to talk to. And that was really bad. In the end, I just switched off a bit. Since I left school, I haven't really maintained much contact with them at all.

I've had no social problems at Cambridge, but then I keep away from the droves of Sloane Rangers (upper class). One of my closest friends is from a Public (private) school. I keep telling them about people in Liverpool and how they speak. I took a Scouse (Liverpool dialect) dictionary down with all our words, spelt in the same way they would be pronounced, and also a book of short stories written in this sort of dialect. They find it quite hilarious, especially if they hadn't met any before.'

Moving up in the world

It was clear that many of the parents and grandparents of the young people were very bright though relatively uneducated. So often in their youths they had been keen to study, but their chances had been blocked. Sometimes the hazardous route to higher education needed several generations to overcome. Very few of the parents in this sample who had left school at 15 still assumed that their offspring would do the same, and most made every effort to help their children to post-school education.

For some, usually the mothers, their own experience had added considerable impetus to their efforts for their children. In the first part of the study, the mothers who had joined the National Association for Gifted Children had been significantly more dissatisfied with their own education, at whatever level, than the mothers of both the Control groups. As one mother said:

'I passed for the grammar school, but my mother, who was traditionally Irish, didn't think it was a good idea for a girl to start there and go on to university. And so I wasted all those years after I was eleven. It's made me more determined that my children are going to have the best.'

I heard some remarkable stories of how families had changed their lifestyles across just a couple of generations when the opportunities for betterment were presented, after perhaps hundreds of years at a basic level. Another mother said:

'My mother went into service (a servant) at about fifteen, so she had no education. But when I failed my eleven plus (see Appendix 1) I wasn't allowed to forget about it. My brother, though, he graduated and got a PhD.'

Even among these stories, the rise of Angus Cameron's family was exceptional. All four grandparents were Scottish crofters, but it was the stalwart men of his father's line who had pushed upwards. His father's father had struggled via night-school to become a schoolteacher, then his own father, through apprenticeships and night-schools, had become a qualified pharmacist through an apprenticeship. Now Angus, as gifted as his forebears had been, had reached university. The family had become middle-class city folk, which affected how Angus had experienced his school, as his father explained:

'Here in Edinburgh, Angus went to one of the largest comprehensive schools in Britain, in an area which has a reputation for being one of the roughest, dirtiest areas in Scotland. They speak fairly rough Scottish "Dinnae ken, Jem" sort of thing, and my two spoke in a rather posh accent. We all had a rough time, with anonymous phone calls at home. It was a bit hurtful, but Angus is quite a tough character, and fortunately he got into the really top class, and emerged unscathed out of a school like that, with excellent results. His sister suffered a lot though.'

Update 2001: The Cameron graph continued sharply upward. Angus was the first in his family to earn a degree, and then a PhD in Organic Chemistry (synthesis of sugar compounds), and on to a life of high-level research with major international companies. He is now Environmental Chemicals Laboratories Manager, dealing with for example air analysis, occupational hygiene, water, effluent, soil analysis. He and his wife, a primary school teacher, are still hoping for children. Their standard of life is very good: Angus loves his involvement with sailing and has completely rebuilt a £25 dinghy.

In the old days, difficulties in obtaining education had often been due to financial poverty. Taking up a 'free' Grammar school place meant buying a uniform, games kit, outings, etc., unless the local education authority had a fund for poor children, and it was more than poor people could manage. As a Welsh mother described:

'I was brought up in a mining valley in the depression. My father was out of work for six or seven years, which is why I left school at fifteen, having matriculated a year early, though my parents would have liked me to have gone on. My brother got a County Scholarship to university. They wanted us to get out of the mines.'

Sometimes, though, determination paid off, as one father described:

'My father was a brilliant scholar who was forced to leave grammar school at fifteen to earn the family bread. He got a Degree and a PhD on his own externally at London University in economics, though it was never really any use in his career in the bank, so he stayed frustrated there all his working life.'

Girls, even between the 1950s and 1970s, not infrequently had to give way for their brothers' education: 'My father's attitude was that education for a woman was a bit of a waste, and took a very detached view of me then as just a girl. But my brother obviously had to earn a living and keep a wife, so he could go on to college.' Several of the mothers had actually been told to fail their exams, as one said with understandable bitterness: 'My mother told me to fail the grammar school examination, because being a divorced parent at that time, she couldn't afford to send me, although I was the top of the class. I've had a raw deal.'

But shockingly, it could also be teachers who halted both boys' and girls' educational progress:

> 'The day before we were due to sit the scholarship, the headmistress came in and said that too many people had passed the prelim, and that these girls, even if they took the scholarships, wouldn't pass. She read out about ten of our names, and I was one of them who weren't to take the exam. I had a sister just two years older who did go to grammar school and she's done very well. She ended up at university. I still feel cheated.'

Teachers, however, were less likely to discriminate for reasons of sex than for social class, which is how this father lost his chance

> 'I was at a small village school with just two teachers, and if your face didn't fit with them you didn't get your rightful chance. Three or four in the class that were nice were given lots of extra tuition and pushed to get to the grammar school. The rest of us were nowhere near ready for taking that exam. When one of the "outcasts" actually passed for the grammar school, the sheer amazement on the head teacher's face was something I remember even now.'

In spite of difficulties like those above, passing the eleven-plus to the free Grammar schools provided the opportunities for many others to move up educationally and socially. Mary Owen's mother, who is now a college lecturer, had that springboard:

> 'Thanks to the 1944 Education Act I went to the grammar school. But my parents hadn't a clue. They were very nice and supportive – honest working-class. There was never really anywhere at home to go to be private, to do my homework, or to think things. We all lived in one living room, and I used to do my homework on the bus. All the middle-class kids, whose daddies worked in offices, tended to be in the A form, and the rest of us were second-best in the B form. I didn't know how to cope in the system, and I was terribly overawed by these middle-aged, Oxford educated lady teachers. The only thing you could do with all that din at home was paint and draw – the soft option – so at thirteen I went to art school part-time. Quite a lot of the people who were gifted that way did the same.'

Gordon Bailey's four grandparents and his own parents had had minimal education. Although his mother did win a place at the grammar school, she wasn't told about it for years because her parents wanted her to be useful about the house. She looked away as she said, 'My father wouldn't even let me go to the girl guides because he thought it was middle-class and that I might have met people there who would give me ideas beyond my station.' But she and her husband were determined that their children should have something better. It was a long and difficult trail for them to find out about schools and scholarships, but now two sons were at Oxford with Open Scholarships and the third, Gordon, was on the way there, though it was at times a little rough for them all. Gordon was at a selective school and told me:

'At school there's a really awful middle-class social circuit, which excludes working-class boys like me. Of course they wouldn't exclude me if I tried hard to be like them, but I don't want to be. There's very little mixing really between the social classes, which is a shame.'

Pressure

Strong pressure on the academically gifted to strive to their utmost came from three sources – the family, the school, and sometimes it seemed to spring from within the child, while parents looked on in amazement. It is a danger for some gifted children who become seduced by the social rewards of learning achievement – of honour and improved self-esteem – that their zeal can become excessive, virtually taking over their lives. For a few schools, it did look like a means of collecting the hunting trophies of examination successes, and both schools and parents did take advantage of it when it seemed that it would have been better for the youngsters to develop other areas of themselves, such as making friends.

Family pressure

There are parents from every walk of life who want their children to fulfil their dreams, and are prepared to spend great amounts of energy and money to make them come true. A handful of the gifted young people in this sample seemed to be squeezed to the last drop of effort to do better and better. The fact that he or she could achieve the results without much obvious effort wasn't good enough; they had to be seen to work for them. For such parents, a 'good' school always 'stretched' their children and had a record of high exam success and Oxbridge entrance. Some of the private schools had obligingly directed themselves into turning out well-primed examinees, though parents were usually aware of their children's lack of all-round education. As one said: 'I wasn't happy with the fact that he didn't have a cultural education at school, and in the fast stream you miss out on all the sports too.' A father who had knowingly over-pushed his son was sympathetic:

'I pitied him going there, but I had to take him away from the other school because they'd gone on to mixed ability-teaching which is absolutely diabolical. It would certainly have ruined him, because he would have taken the opportunity to just drift along. But he never did make any friends.'

Some children, however, were strong enough to throw off parental pressure, as the mother of a gifted girl described;

'My daughter once told me that she concentrated on music because it was one way of getting Daddy to herself; he would do music with her endlessly, because he loved it. Then she stopped because she was terribly afraid he was trying to make her into a professional musician, and she knew she didn't want to be.'

But others, for whom the pressure had accumulated to an insupportable level, might suddenly opt out of school – making a leap to freedom and fun, as a boy at a high-pressure school explained:

'In the final year of the sixth form, it came to me in a flash why certain people would "jack it in", just suddenly get fed up of the whole thing and leave school. I know quite a few people who've done that, only a few months away from their A-levels. It's disillusionment, when they've spent all their lives in education and it doesn't seem to be getting them anywhere. Some of them went to (community) colleges, taking another two years, when they could have finished them in four or five months at school.'

Sometimes a young person was subject to pressures from all sides, like Mark Stubbs. Unlike many of the boys at his academically powerful school who resented the limitations of the curriculum, Mark was filled with pride and delight at being there. His striving, which was much stronger than a normal desire for achievement, seemed to give him great satisfaction. He smiled with pleasure as he described the demands his mother made on him, and the firmer his teachers were the better he liked them. He beamed when he told me that they had lowered his marks to make him work harder (as Vijay Patel's teachers had done) because he saw it as a sign of esteem – he was, after all, top in both science and arts. His wide range of reading matter was carefully chosen for educational value rather than pleasure.

At nine-years-old, Mark had seemed to me to be withdrawn, with noticeable difficulty in making eye contact. At that time his one great joy was his little dog, and his eyes lit up when it came into the room. His pleasures were divided between 'going for walks with my dog' and 'playing indoor games against myself'. By the time of the Follow-up he had developed an academic, professorial manner, considering small points in detail before allowing himself to move on, and often returning to earlier questions when he felt his answers had been less than satisfactory. He rebuked himself several times for being 'lazy'. He was an only child, living in a large emotionally cold house, and obviously the apple of his parents' eyes. But he still wanted to be made to improve himself. I found him sensitive and sympathetic, and very lonely. He had yet to feel moved, he said, by any artistic experience.

Mark Stubbs (Highly gifted, aged 20, at university):

'In the express course at school, you learned something once and then you were expected to remember it. It was good for me. The only disadvantage was that we didn't have time to go over much work. I was pretty near the top all the way through because it was hard to slack at that place. There was a lot of pressure to get good marks every half term, and you really had to work to try and improve each time. I enjoyed the pressure. Most managed to cope, though a couple of boys cracked. The science teacher tended to mark me down a bit if I didn't do everything word perfect. He'd probably give me a B instead of an A, because he knew I could do the stuff and wasn't really trying. It was good for me because it pushed me on. They only do that for people who they think could be getting full marks every time, and I was around the top in both arts and sciences.

Mother always says, "You should have done better" whatever I do; she's never satisfied and always finds something wrong. I only got two A grades and a B at A-level, though I did get to Cambridge, but she said, "Why didn't he get three A's at A level and a scholarship?" At school, it was better for me when I got the cane rather than detention, because then my mother wouldn't find out about them. There's no way I could hide the fact when I arrived home late at five o'clock, whereas if I'd had a caning I could hide it. She'd be very angry and I'd get an extra punishment from her, then she'd keep it going over dinner with sarcastic remarks. That sort of thing would go on for a day or so.

Sometimes I get angry about my work and call myself a fool, saying, "Look at this work. You've only got ten for this work. You should have got at least fourteen. Absolute fool." After a little while I calm down, realise what I've done wrong, and try to mend my ways. With friends, I try and assess what's wrong with me and then try to change, force myself to be different from what I really am sometimes. If I wake up in the morning and think I've actually learned something the day before, that I'm actually wiser, that gives me a lot of pleasure.

God's an all good being, a person who's really perfect in all ways and is just aiming for the good of the world. The final state of the world is the best possible state the world can end in. He just exists watching over the world. I don't like the idea of my fate already being written out, though, I like to have the idea that I've got some free will, somehow or other.'

But it was not always possible to tell the direction from which the pressure came – how much from the young people themselves and how much from outside. For example, Stuart Carter's determinedly achieving parents were both scientists who said they simply couldn't imagine a family where people were concerned about the arts. Neither could Stuart, who spent all his energy on scientific study, to the clear detriment of his emotional development. His self-esteem appeared to hang on the academic rewards he could present to his parents. But his father could not see that he had had any influence on his son's life and said rather peremptorily that any problems were inherently Stuart's own: 'The relatively academic education he's had and his choice of subject (computer science), are absolutely ideal for a person like him, and have gone some way to minimising the effects of his personality.'

Stuart Carter (Gifted, aged 22, a computer programmer):

'I always want a piece of paper to be proud of at the end. If you've done a subject for a few years, and you end up with nothing, apart from knowledge – which of course is valuable in itself – it doesn't give you as much to be proud of. Even a school exam which says "You got such-and-such a percentage", it finishes off the achievement. I've been working fifteen years continuously in education, and now I'm working as a computer programmer. But I need a rest. I'd like to be a bit irresponsible occasionally, not in the nasty sense, but I want to feel that there is a lighter side to life. Other young people seem to have it.'

False parental hopes
Pressure from home was also imposed on young people who were seen as gifted but who were not, so the children could not live up to their parents' hope and expectations, and failure in their parents' eyes was the only possibility.

Marion Steele's environment had been carefully structured for climbing the academic ladder. Both her teacher parents had pushed her hard to study, as had her old-fashioned Grammar school. She was dutiful, worked hard and had done extremely well with her above-average abilities, getting into a polytechnic. But within weeks of leaving home she had fallen in love. When she and her fiancé were no longer constrained by home and school to put in the hard work necessary simply to pass they had promptly failed their first examinations. It was love on the dole for them. When I arrived on a glorious summer's day, Marion was watching a television soap opera behind curtains closed against the sun – held down by books. She knew her problem:

'I really need to be forced to work and I missed that pressure when it was gone. When I didn't pass my exams, the course leader had me in his office and said, "If

I were you, I'd do the decent thing and withdraw now. You've got nothing up here" (she pointed to her head). I've got to pay back the grant now.'

Louise Brinscombe too, described the pressure she had been under, saying: 'My Mum was never satisfied', though her mother put the blame in an unexpected place in a rather confused way:

'I joined the Society for Gifted Children after reading an article in a magazine, because Louise fitted in with so much of what it said. When she was very small she did all sorts of unusual things, like teaching herself to read at three. But if I hadn't joined this Association and then been part of this survey I wouldn't have really felt that she was very bright. I was sorry I did, because then I put a lot of pressure on her, and I think that's one of the reasons why we're not close. My expectations of her caused quite a bit of antagonism with the teachers too, because I thought she could do better, when from their point of view she did quite well. If I hadn't known she was quite bright, I would always have been pleased and encouraging to her when she did quite well. Perhaps it's an emotional thing, a problem that I've got, that I still find it difficult to say I'm pleased with her. I feel as if she's resented me expecting too much... I suppose, though... in actual fact, your survey didn't have anything to do with it.'

Pressure from home could alienate gifted children from their parents, but it could also hold them captive. In spite of the fiery red hair and sharp blue eyes of his Scottish ancestors, Alec Spicer's quiet personality appeared to have been additionally subdued by his mother, who had brought him up with an intense concern for what she saw as right and wrong. Consequently he had put his very high intelligence to use by more and more study at home, while his school fellows were out enjoying themselves. After a handful of A grades in his school-leaving exams, then university, he had returned to the nest to carry out her moral teachings, by becoming a policeman.

Alec's mother had placed him in an intolerable intellectual dilemma. If he had followed his school excellence at university by obtaining a first-class degree, he would have been obliged to leave his home to work in the city and would be in danger of not returning. So, quite unconsciously at the time, he had lowered his final marks and could then continue to live with his mother.

Alec Spicer's mother:

'I was 42 when Alec was born, and he's always been with adults. He didn't have many children of his own age as friends – well, not any that we wanted him to play with. Not because of social status, but because of standards of behaviour. His only friends were the son and daughter of a minister actually, but they were little devils. I wouldn't let Alec go into a house where I felt the influences were bad. I wouldn't let him eat school dinners, because they fed them on fat, so I always gave him sandwiches. He didn't like school dinners anyway.'

Pressure from school

At the time of the Follow-up, the then government had devised The Assisted Places Scheme in 1980 to provide fees and other expenses for low-income parents who wanted to send their bright children to private schools. It was to be allotted £180 million in 1997 to serve just one per cent of the school population. Some private schools filled more than 40 per cent of their places that way. However, the recipients were found to be mostly the children of parents, such as teachers, who would have helped their children educationally without the scheme. What is more, the scheme, only paid for *already* highly achieving children, relatively few places going to children from culturally poor homes (Edwards *et al.* 1989). The scheme has now been scrapped. Several children in this study had received this award, involving them in lengthy travel to a distant school, which took a heavy toll on their energies and relationships.

Neil Cope's father (above) described with evident distress that his son had gone through:

'Neil used to leave home at seven, then do two hour's journey each way by public transport. Then, he'd have homework on top of that – about two to three hours a night, every night. He used to have to turn-in Saturday mornings as well, till twelve. That's six days a week, four hours a day travelling. When he was tired, or when there was something emotional he couldn't deal with, he used to just cut off completely and sleep. In the school holidays he'd just sit and not do anything, or read a very light book.'

Being a high achiever, Peter Amos, also a recipient of a distant Assisted Place, had no difficulty with the academic work, but because of it had carried an exceptional physical and emotional load from the age of 11. Although there was a very similar school nearby, his parents had chosen the further one in their pride at his 'place'. They had a copy of the newspaper report of local lad makes good, framed on the sideboard. After a lot of talk he eventually told me that he would have preferred to be in a mixed-ability, co-ed school where he could be more involved, and probably happier. Coming from a working-class home, he felt different from the other boys at the private school.

He was of slight build and at 15 could have passed for very much younger. He did what was expected of him and slept a great deal in his remaining time. In talking to him his eyes sometimes drooped and I was concerned that he couldn't work up enough energy to talk. He found it quite impossible, in spite of a great mental struggle, to say what was attractive or unattractive about himself. His father said that if told to, he would put the kettle on, but wouldn't check whether it had water in, and laughed delightedly that this was typical of the professorial mind. To me, Peter was emotionally impaired, but it was hard to tell whether it was a defence against his demanding world – or simply exhaustion.

Peter Amos (aged 12 at school):

> 'I have to catch three buses each way, about three hours travelling a day. I do about two hours homework every single night, and weekends too. It's too much, I could do as well without that amount of homework. There are one or two other boys at school like me, but not many.'

Though it had taken a different form, school pressure on brave little Emily Saville had also taken a heavy toll. She was undoubtedly well above average, but neither quite up to the school's aims, nor the performance of her highly achieving older sister. On the surface, she was the most positively happy schoolgirl one could ever meet, insisting how much she loved her school, how dearly she looked forward to going to it every day, how many friends she had there and how superb it all was. She played the violin in two school orchestras, the piano in between times and lacrosse for the school. But the protestation methought was too much. Her mother described what would happen:

> 'Her sensitivity is acute, far above the norm, quite extraordinary. She hated the school to begin with, though it's small and friendly; a lovely school. But she felt she was in prison. She became claustrophobic; you could see her clamminess and her heavy breathing. She couldn't stay in the classroom and had to be sat near an open door. Then there was an awful phase when she couldn't go out to play, even down to the bottom of the school field, without being absolutely terrified.
>
> The way that school measures things, she's middle of the road. One night before an exam, she had a giggling fit, which I think was hysterics. I heard this terrible noise from her room, went up and found her with tears rolling down her face, and she was saying, "Well, I just can't remember. I can't remember." She couldn't stop. It went on and on. She sometimes tidies up the counter of a shop she happens to be in. She's been thanked once or twice. It's all things like that that make you think that she's very insecure and wonder why. She seems so happy and uncomplicated.'

Pressure from acceleration

The easiest and most frequently chosen way for a school to deal with an academically advanced pupil is to speed up their education by advancing them a year or more. This procedure has many names, such as 'grade-skipping' or 'being put up': it is sometimes more euphemistically called 'vertical enrichment' or more commonly 'acceleration'. Some educationalists believe that the emotional problems it may bring are overrated.

Psychologically, acceleration focuses a child firmly in the direction of achievement. The major reason given by schools is to alleviate the child's apparent or anticipated boredom with the work their age-mates would be doing, and so is expected to encourage their continued enthusiasm for learning. But in my study those – of identical academic giftedness – who had not been accelerated, were no more bored in school than those who were. Quite the contrary, the gifted with same-age non-gifted classmates became far more involved in the non-academic aspects of school life and seemed happier. They had statistically significantly more friends (one per cent), enjoyed school more and had achieved at least as well academically.

This study is the only one I know of in which the long-term intimate effects of acceleration on children have been investigated with regard to personal development, relationships and careers. While at school, it could be seen that very few had benefited from being accelerated. Seventeen of the Follow-up's 169 young people had either been accelerated or were young for their class. Many had found this presented them with such difficulties that were at times detrimental to their greater well-being. Paradoxically, acceleration may even have been responsible, as some parents thought, for lowering their children's final examination marks.

Only two of the young people who had not been accelerated, would have preferred it, at least in their area of ability. Stephen Kaye was in a difficult position, and in his case, it looked as though acceleration or some other form of enrichment for mathematics would have helped him a great deal. I wondered why his school would not allow this quiet boy to work on his mathematics in the school library, instead of having to endure that classroom tedium day after day.

Stephen Kaye (Highly gifted, aged 14, at school):

> 'Most of the things I've been taught in maths I knew anyway because I was very interested from a young age. The lessons are OK, but the work is boring. I used to finish it quickly, but then I ended up getting more and had to re-do the same work over and over again. So now I spin it out. Sometimes I do what everybody else will be doing next, so when they come to it I just have to wait. The problem is that I can do it more quickly because I know it better, but because of that, I end up doing more work instead of less. It's the others who ought to be doing more really, because they're learning it and I'm usually not.'

Update 2001: In fact, the school allowed him a few lessons a week with older, more advanced learners. But he did not jump a class. He finished his A-levels with his own year group, though slightly young in the class, and did very well. He had adjusted by the age of 18 and got on well with his classmates after all.

Parents who had to watch their highly gifted children struggle socially among older and more mature pupils so often suffered with them. As one father said: 'He didn't tell us what he was going through at the time. He had a few stomach-aches and things like that on going to school, you know.' They often felt obliged, though, to take the opinion of the 'experts', the teachers. A mother described how her slightly built but highly gifted son had been unhappily accelerated by two years: 'Both the head and the deputy head wanted it. They said, "If he can't make it, who can?".' But it did not always have even the supposed benefit of giving extra time for work, as one accelerated boy said: 'I didn't try for Oxbridge because it would have meant staying on at school, and even though I was so young, I'd had enough.'

Of course, parents and teachers were not always in agreement on this, as one mother complained:

> 'Although Iain passed the entrance exam to the grammar school a year early, the junior school headmaster wouldn't allow him to go on the grounds that he would be socially immature. We, his parents, would have liked him to have had the advantage of the extra year later in his school life, but they made him repeat that year and take the entrance examination again. It was degrading to him in a way, because it was a feeling of failure. Now we know that the headmaster's judgement on his social standing in his class was wrong and Iain is too mature for his year.'

In making the decision to accelerate the children at school, both parents and teacher acted in true sincerity and in a way that seemed right to them at the time, No one, though, had asked any of the children what they themselves would have preferred – I checked on that. But the decision was never taken lightly, as a father explained of his son who was normal in size for his age:

> 'We did a lot of heart searching, then and now. It was a great pity in some ways; he wasn't mature enough. When he was sixteen, there were men of nineteen in the sixth form. He played football very well. People used to talk about it, this tiny little boy who played like a tank.'

Growing-up effects of acceleration

For some of the highly gifted pupils, normal growing-up problems had been exacerbated by being accelerated in school, as expressed by a 14-year-old girl:

> 'Some of my class at school have changed beyond recognition, leaving me behind. They like going out and drinking and things like that, and only last year they were staying in, or just going round to each other's houses, having a laugh. I don't think I've changed so much.'

Talking to the whole family sometimes picked up the two sides to the story. Robert Fraser was a tall 15-year-old highly gifted youth. He had laughing eyes and an air of supreme self-confidence, anticipating the success he considered his due. However, he spent little time in study, and saw his modest exam results as unimportant, consciously relying on the powerful reserves of intelligence he knew he had to bounce him over the next more significant hurdle. Though socially his acceleration at school had caused no problems with his classmates, it was different at home. Yet his father's strictures dripped off Robert like water off a duck's back. Robert's father understood the problems of his son's two-year advancement in school:

'He feels he should be able to go to places for eighteen-year-olds like the others in his class and be treated like someone of that age. But though he seems very mature in some respects, in others he's still a little boy. There's been a lot of trouble because of the influence of his peers. This final year, it's not been easy at all, because I'm not very good at keeping my temper. When I see that he's playing around, and he pulls the wool over his mother's eyes, then of course, it starts a row.'

From Robert's point of view, however, life with his parents seemed to be even more of a struggle of being misunderstood and his maturity underestimated, than it was for other adolescents who had not been accelerated.

Robert Fraser (Highly gifted at school and accelerated by two years):

'Growing up has only been difficult at home, not elsewhere. My friends are all older than me, but they're quite proud to know me. My parents don't understand; when all your friends are going out, you want to go out with them. Next year I'll be learning to drive, and after that I'll have the use of my parents' car. And it won't just be the odd day trip here and there; it'll be a long weekend away. Being young in the class like me is quite a rarity, quite special. But there was a bit of resentfulness from some people who thought I might have taken their place by going to that school early. It's done me more good than harm. I think anybody would jump at a chance of missing a year at school.'

Update 2001: The acceleration had an unexpected benefit because Robert decided to change courses at 17 and so had that extra year. He did not find the company of his true age peers to be any different. His cavalier attitude to work continued with the modest outcome of his 'enjoyable degree' in Economics. But it was no handicap and he is now, at 32, Managing Director of his district branch of a large people promoting organisation, which aims to avoid people 'hanging up their brains with their coats' as they get to work. He is married, and the second child is on the way.

Even in a selective school, where the whole class works at an advanced level and differences in maturity are not a problem, advanced intellectual stimulation can still be at some cost, as Vincent Jacobs described:

Vincent Jacobs (Gifted, aged 16, at school):

> 'Old friends at other schools still haven't taken their O-levels, and I've done them already. Now, I'm working for my A-levels and then there's the six years for medicine. I know I've got to slog for the future, but I feel as if I've lost my youth. Life comes in one headlong rush; it's going to hit you in the face tomorrow, and you don't have any time to take stock of what's happening.'

But it was very much worse for others. A two-year grade-skip had put a considerable strain on the natural pace of growing-up for highly gifted Damien Bradley, to the extent that I felt could leave him unhappy for life (a prediction which proved to be only too accurate). His father had great ambitions for him, but seemed only to see what he wanted. When Damien was ten years old, his father had described him as an outstandingly happy child with many friends – though that had not been my impression of Damien at the time. I had noted his withdrawn manner and how his eyes seemed to lack the responsive sparkle of fun and challenge in the testing sessions that virtually all the other 209 children in the sample had shown. In fact, he already looked bored with life. His intellectual ability was so advanced that in spite of being at a highly academic school, he had been grade-skipped by two years – and then placed in the express stream. The result of putting him among much older boys, with neither regard for him as a developing person nor for the two years of learning he had missed, had lowered both his expected examination results and his sense of worth. To try and right the difference, he had taken a year off to work between school and university, so that he was now almost the normal age and size as his fellow students. But the psychological pattern had been set. He had very few friends or outside interests.

Damien Bradley (Highly gifted, aged 18, at university):

> 'Being smaller at school, I wasn't going to stand any chance physically. I was never good at sports, and I was hopeless at athletics and gym. It used to embarrass me. At the time, I used to think of it as just me, but later on I realised it was probably that I wasn't as well-developed muscularly – mind you, I've never found sport that important, so it doesn't bother me. If someone said, "Why are you so small?" I used to just laugh. It just became a joke, so I had to beat them verbally and usually it worked. It got to such a stage where I would do it to just anyone – put up a defence straight away. It's automatic now. I've taught myself not to get angry. I get bored sitting around the university, but then, I've always been bored. I don't think it's been any advantage, being younger, apart from the fact that I've had a year out. It wasn't right at all. I'd have been much happier in my own age group. I wouldn't do it to my kids.'

Update 2001: Damien's still remembers his grade-skipping of about 20 years ago with some horror, even though he is now 34. He told me: 'I felt like a fish out of water. It altered me psychologically, and not in a positive way. It made me defensive and closed-off, and the effect has lasted. I've been depressed and I think it had something to do with those few bad years. It was all about statistics for the school, for Oxford and Cambridge; they didn't consider me at all. I didn't want to go to Oxbridge, I wanted to go to a more normal university. At that time, Sheffield was the premier place for architecture, so that's why I went there. But I took ten years over it.' The reason was that in his second year Damien had kicked off the pressure of home and school, spent too much time in the bar, did no work and failed his exams. He recouped over time, then, almost at the end of his qualifications, he'd taken off with his girlfriend for Central America for two years. Now he is working in an architect's office and trying to regain some lost ground. He has been in a happy relationship with his 'partner' of ten years, and has joyfully rediscovered his lost self.

Being smaller than their classmates affected girls too. Her mother called Julia Morley 'a nine-out-of-ten girl', as she had never quite reached her potential. She had been advanced a year, but as she continued through her girls' selective school, her marks sank lower and lower. She was socially immature in the class, and had considerable relationship problems – the older girls would give her the brush-off very crudely. She told me:

> 'I was always very self-conscious about looking younger, especially at first, and I was very small compared to the other children, although not compared to my own age group. I still think of myself as short, even though I'm average height.'

It was not a sudden move-up at school which had disturbed Rachel Wallace, as she had been taught with classmates older than herself through almost all her school life. Her examination progress had been accelerated to an extraordinary degree – to her parents' great approval. She had taken three A-levels at 15, moved schools, and taken a different four the following year. She described with pride how she had worked so hard that a teacher told her she'd been up till two in the morning marking the extra work Rachel had volunteered. The teacher, she laughed, had begged her to slow down. Yet separately, both Rachel and her parents told me that she had not been fully stretched! Her mother described some of the results of the pressure on this brilliant girl, who had reached the golden goal of Oxford:

Rachel Wallace's mother:

> 'She's obviously outstanding in her abilities, and therefore she couldn't find her intellectual peer group, except somewhere like Oxford or Cambridge. There's no one round here able to have a conversation at the intellectual depth she wants; she's a very deep-thinking girl. She's told me that her mind thinks independently of her – it goes on racing and racing, and you can't stop it; it's got a life of its own.

Sometimes she hates herself with a deep anger, and she can attack herself, which is very difficult to handle. She scratches herself and makes herself bleed, and then this morning she was banging herself. I wonder whether it stems actually from when she was very tiny and she couldn't do the things she wanted to. Her arms and legs wouldn't do what her gifted mind ordered, like she couldn't control the pencil and so on.

We had an incident with her. I can't remember what started it now: it all happened in the middle of the night. First she sat on the landing and threatened to throw herself down-stairs. We tried to talk to her to calm her down, and eventually she went outside into the garden, barefoot in her nightdress, sat down in the flower-bed and screamed. When Rachel screams, she really can; she used to do it as a baby in her temper tantrums. She screamed about three times at the top of her voice, so much so that several sets of neighbours phoned the police thinking murder was happening, and three police vans arrived outside. One of them talked to her; I don't know what he said, but eventually she came in, somewhat subdued, and went to bed. It was obvious she'd been under enormous pressure.'

Rachel Wallace (Highly gifted, aged 19, studying mathematics at Oxford):

'I've had no regrets about being accelerated; I found the work interesting, and I might have been bored if I'd been further down. I came out equivalent with girls of eleven when I was seven, but they thought they couldn't really put me with others of that age, so they went half and half, and I was two years ahead instead of four. I had absolutely no confidence at all, and I didn't have any friends. I don't think it was my fault, or that I was spoilt, but the others would spend their time teasing me because they said it was fun – nine-year-old little girls are so cruel.

It didn't make it easy for me to grow up, though I think I did gain something while I was going through that. Even though I now have friendships that I feel sure are not going to disintegrate, at the same time, there's always the lurking fear that they don't really like me, that they're only tolerating me. It's not really rational, and I'm quite negative about myself. To a certain extent, I've been a bit depressive and melancholy in temperament from the time I was very young. My mum tells me I used to come home sometimes from school crying my eyes out, being so unhappy. I don't remember that.'

It can only be concluded that moving children out of their age group did not appear to be the best for almost all the gifted young people in this sample. It should be restricted to the physically fit and the emotionally stable; and even then, only as a last resort.

CHAPTER 10

The challenge

Wherefore have these gifts a curtain before 'em?
William Shakespeare, *Twelfth Night*

The big question which pounded in my head throughout this long was why so many of these bright eager children had needed to struggle so hard to even partly realise their gifts. It was not only unfair on them but a wicked waste of everyone's energy and future. Far too much of their energy went into fighting the educational establishment, supposedly there to help them, or dissipated into wrong channels because of poor guidance. The social pressures which can diminish a growing child's feelings of worth ran rampant, even though schools and universities could have helped. Why did Oxford University not reach out a hand to Alison Cranfield, the highly gifted girl from a poor background, before she fled her higher education in tears? Why had her school not offered her the slightest preparation for the social hurdles she would have to jump alone?

For some youngsters, their lives were like a pot with a hole in it, so that only a portion of their wonderful gifts could grow and enhance their lives. And if this study did, as I believe it did, throw light on some of the reasons for this terrible waste of human endeavour then it should also be possible to draw conclusions as to how the situation can be improved.

No formula

If there is one sure thing, though, to have emerged from the thousands of hours of this investigation, it is that the influences on individual happiness and success are like love – many splendoured – and though it is possible to tell others how it feels and what happens because of it, there is no sure recipe for success. And although educational institutions cannot be responsible for the infinite interactions of individual personality and ability, there is a great deal that they could do about improving opportunities, and caring enough to see that they are taken up. Of course, no institution has the power to direct the lives of its students, nor would it be ethical, but without some help, especially for those without a firm home support, the essential link in a delicate chain can be broken.

There are many theories on abilities, notably intelligence, but at times I felt they were decidedly removed from the subtle realities of real life. Does it matter in the end if a beautiful new baby was born with a general intelligence with strengths and weaknesses or 13 distinct 'intelligences', when in primary school his teacher shatters his dreams by tearing up his poem in front of the class?

Negative social pressures had negative effects. So many young people had learned and accepted that some good things in life, such as a professional career, were not for them, although the tests has shown they had the ability to do almost anything they could imagine, and more besides. Yet they did not even attempt to fulfil their early dreams. Whereas some might argue that this is simply a part of growing up, of maturation, I hope I have shown that it is far too often more a matter of pressure to conform. There are people of all ages who seem to feel a need to put the liveliest and more creative in their 'place', and this, alas, includes educators.

Since the 1991 edition of this book, at the invitation of the British government (Office for Standards in Education), I have overviewed the international research evidence on gifted education (Freeman 1998). I found that many activities carried out with gifted children could not be justified in terms of measurable results. Things that adults do for and with the gifted, giving their time with good heart and the very best of intentions, may have no effect at all, though they do often give pleasure to everyone concerned, both adults and children. Where possible, though, it is important to have a basis in evidence before taking action. This chapter overviews the conclusions from this long study along with information from other sources. It is concerned with helping not only the gifted, but other children, overcome some of the obstacles which life throws in their paths. Some of these obstacles are inevitable, and can even be stimulating and a challenge, but others as we have seen, are destructive, soul destroying – and avoidable.

Emotional development

By the end of the first survey in 1978, many of the then current myths about gifted children had been exposed for what they were – false. Because of the careful system of double controls and the in-depth interviews with children and families, it could be seen that the emotional problems often expected of the gifted, such as poor relationships or temper tantrums were not due to their gifts at all. Of itself, a high IQ did not cause emotional problems for the children, nor were exceptionally high IQ children found to have different personalities from the rest. The children with some emotional disturbance, coordinated by reports from parents, teachers and measurement, had ability levels spanning the sample range from just under average to the top of any scale.

The idea that gifted children were bound to be 'odd', and accordingly unhappy, circulated among parents and teachers, so that some looked for it and found it, and at times even seemed to encourage it. When a bright child was unhappy it was often the gifts that got the blame. Yet there, in the same class as the labelled gifted children, loaded with expectations, there were unlabelled others – of identical gifts – who were neither expected to be nor were emotionally disturbed.

Where the gifted were distressed, it had not acted like the grain of sand under the shell of the oyster – none of those unhappy children looked ready to produce any pearls of art or poetry. In fact, they generally achieved less well than those of the same ability who had enjoyed peace of mind. Some young scientists appeared to be entrenched in a poor self-image for life, and I hazard a guess that for that reason, in spite of their brilliance and extremely hard work, they will not mature into an Einstein or a Linus Pauling.

The Follow-up showed that although some children's advancement and promise appeared to have faded when others caught up, most early problems had entirely disappeared. Sleep in young children, for instance, had brought complaints from the parents who had put their children forward as gifted. But when I asked them about this many years later, most seemed to have forgotten all about it. I reminded them. 'Oh', they would reply, 'he just grew out of it'. So much for what is often said to be a defining sign of giftedness.

Another supposed problem for the gifted is that of inevitable boredom in class when they are obliged to study with others of lesser potential. But looking back, most of the gifted young people felt that any boredom at school had eased off as they became more in control of their learning. As one teenager said: 'The further back I remember school, the more boredom I remember, because I was enjoying fewer subjects then.' Others expressed longing for their earlier, simpler lives: 'When I was younger, I used to be very happy sitting down with a book. Now, I haven't time to do that, so there's more potential for being bored.' But the boredom they described was well within the normal range, even for those who had it badly, as one boy described with feeling: 'I get bored at school, I get bored at home and I get bored in the holidays because since we moved to the country, there's nothing to do.'

The serious problem of retrospective studies is that memory is well known to play tricks. It could be seen in this Follow-up. For example, the girl I interviewed while she was a university student in the 1980s told me at the time how unhappy she was and so often in tears, but in 2001 she described her student years as all fun. Nor could I recognise the demanding father who, looking back, described his son's childhood as blissfully happy and carefree, glibly attributing his present misery to his gifts. But checking the notes I took the first time round revealed that the little boy was decidedly unhappy, and at ten-years-old perfectly aware that strings of high-level achievement were attached to his parent's love and approval.

Physically, other than fulfilling their reputation of being more likely to wear glasses, I could not see any difference between the gifted and other children. (And yet, subjectively, I thought I saw a special brightness in their eyes, and what I can only describe as a 'pulled-together' look of competence.) The real differences lay in their abilities, particularly of concentration and memory. When added to keenness and hard work, allied with educational opportunity and a stable home, their potential could reach astounding heights.

All long-term studies on the development of exceptional talent have shown the cumulative effects of the interaction of family attitudes with the gifted child. For example, a four-year investigation of talented American teenagers (Csikszentmihalyi *et al.* 1993), found that learning to invest in difficult tasks was very dependent on social support: the stronger the support the more developed the skills. Most studies of high achievers have discovered that they are emotionally stronger than others, with higher productivity, higher motivation and drive and lower levels of anxiety (Holahan and Sears 1995). High level creativity, in particular, requires notable strength of character to overcome the forces of conventionality. Post (1994) found that in his study of 291 world-famous men, with few exceptions they were sociable and 'admirable human beings' ... 'Genius as a misunderstood giant is one of the many false stereotypes in this field' (p. 31).

Life and measurement

To many people intellect and emotion are understood as different things. Intellect is usually seen as being a higher state, a rational brain activity that only humans can do, whereas emotions are of a lower, more primitive, level. The assumption is often made that whereas the intellect is controllable, emotions are still wild, like sudden anger. But intellectual activity and emotion cannot be separated. The intellect is affected by all the emotions experienced, from sadness to joy, and unquestionably by the extremes of passion. The volunteer, for example, who wants to help a poor village in a developing country must think intellectually about how to provide a supply of clean drinking water, but is inspired by feelings of compassion.

Research ideas in developmental psychology are moving away from dependence on specific measures, such as tests of abilities or classroom experiments, towards more naturalistic assessments. I chose a unique combination of in-depth interviews with observations, along with measurements of the young people's intellectual, artistic and emotional life. However, the intellectually gifted did present special problems of measurement. Firstly, an extremely high intelligence is rarely fully exercised and so cannot be observed in action in the everyday world, and secondly, there is uncertainty at the very highest levels about what intelligence scores are describing, and that the scores do not go high enough. In fact sixteen of the youngsters in this study hit the ceiling of the IQ test at 170, since it is not possible to score more than 100 per cent.

The two intelligence tests used in this research provided different viewpoints: the Ravens, measured only with patterns, whilst the Stanford–Binet tapped into language and school-type learning. Neither test, though, was designed to find out how the final scores were reached. In identifying high ability in music or sport, though, expert judgements are always employed along with an observation of the way a child learns – looking at the process as well as the product within the context of the child's development.

Relationships

Social cognition is related to intelligence. I found in these independent interviews that the higher the child's IQ the more likely each one was to say they were able to understand others, to be empathetic. But understanding is not the same as actual social behaviour; and there can be a difference: the way each of us behaves comes from learning in a variety of social situations. Positive attitudes, such as being sensitive to the feelings of other people, were more frequently shown by the more confident youngsters, who were also better at seeing adults as both resources and friends.

Although overall the youngsters in this study with exceptionally high IQ scores were found to be as emotionally stable as the others, no matter which experimental group they were in, they were described by parents and teachers and measured on tests of social adaptation as being more sensitive. This sensitivity seemed to have stayed with them as they grew up.

Social experiences also help determine what we notice or fail to notice, and there is a strong relationship between this and how people process information. Attention is always selective. It affects the extent to which people feel in control and responsible for the events in their lives. Julian Rotter's original idea of Locus of Control proposed that those who feel in control of their lives, who have an internal locus of control, are better placed to succeed in the world than those who feel under the control of others, that is with an external locus of control (Battle and Rotter 1963). There has been much investigation of this idea, though with mixed results. But overall, it seems that people who feel in control of their own lives are more likely to seek information, process it more efficiently, spend more time making decisions, and have better memories for what they have learned. They have more task-related thoughts and are better at concentrating, so they are more likely to achieve more highly, especially when that achievement depends on original thinking. It would follow that highly achieving gifted children are more likely to have an internal locus of control.

Lessons from home

In growing up, each child has to learn to assess the capacities and predict the behaviour of other people around. It is social learning, demanding individual sensitivity and awareness, and is an important part of intellectual as well as emotional development. In everyday life, one can see that the way an individual tackles a problem can change radically with a different social context. For instance, it is well known by both parents and teachers that what a small child appears to be capable of doing alone at school may not hold true for home, and vice versa. This study provided many clues to ways in which parents had been able to help their children develop to a very high level both intellectually and emotionally. (Practical advice emerging from this are published in my book *How to Raise a Bright Child* (1995)).

After the home influences had been rated, statistically analysed and 'boiled down' to their essentials, two highly significant and vital keys to home educational advantage emerged, parental involvement and provision for learning.

- *Parental involvement:* There is no single type of parent–child interaction which is critical to the development of children's high level abilities. Whatever the economic situation, interaction is complex because parents and children each have their respective intellectual capacities, as well as their own personalities. But genuine, regular interaction of parents and children is decidedly effective. It starts with the 'conversations' with newborn babies and moves on to a variety of mutually pleasurable activities and experiences, such as listening to music and exploring interests. For example, a child may be interested in sea shells. Giving her a book with pictures is very nice, but how much better when parents set off to look for them together using the book as a guide, maybe with a picnic, and certainly with enthusiasm. The beneficial difference in outcome of that kind of involved approach was plain to see in this study.

  It was example rather than expectations which made all the difference: the way parents conducted their own lives proved to be a very powerful way of teaching their children. Parents act as models for their children, and in their love the children neither simply imitate them nor even swallow their ideas whole, but rather each child absorbs and then evolves its own values from what has been seen and experienced. The parents who had the most positive effects on their children's high level development were not those who told their children what to do, but who did it with them.

- *Provision for learning:* Material to learn with involves both physical equipment and tuition. Would-be artists need far more than a few scraps of paper and a pencil stub, a mathematician needs a teacher, a linguist has to hear the language and a budding violinist needs a violin.

Children need to be taught specific skills and be given the opportunities to practise them. For example, it has been seen many times that when children are learning to read, those who read out loud to their parents regularly at home have markedly higher reading attainments than those who do not (Rowe 1991). The ways which are the most likely to enhance children's high-level learning, which will last through life, do not, however, depend on a great deal of money. Education authorities in many parts of the world provide extras virtually free, even if parents have to seek them out. The public library service is but one shining example. But parents have to be both willing and able to make the effort for their children take advantage of the opportunities around – and some parents in this study who had very little money showed that this was entirely possible and greatly advantageous to the children.

Stress

Stress is brought about by a situation which demands too much adjustment from an individual. It is rarely due to a single trauma, but rather to an accumulation of stressful events. The myth says that gifted children suffer more stress in their daily lives because of being different. This did not, however, appear to be true for the majority.

There was the danger, though, that some insecure individuals took their self-esteem from their achievements, rather than for themselves as rounded individuals. They were sometimes under extra pressure from parents and teachers to be continually successful, so that their time to find out about life at their own pace and in their own ways was drastically reduced. This situation was often complained about by the subjects of a follow-up of 1964–1968 Presidential Scholars in America (Kaufman 1992). Although the ex-scholars continued to do well, they often described how they relied on school-type achievement, not only to provide them with an identity but also a feeling of worth. What is more, being a 'know-all' is not perhaps the best way of attracting friends.

It depends how pressure is applied, though. Nathan Milstein, the distinguished pianist, was not noticeably talented as a boy, hated his lessons, but was forced to practice for long hours by his mother, with little thought for his emotional development – which nevertheless appears to have occurred normally (Milstein and Volkov 1991). But others subjected to a pressured 'hot-house' regime, such as William Sidis (Wallace 1986) and Jacqueline du Pré (Easton 1989) were emotionally damaged by it.

Youngsters who have a heightened perception of what can be done can set themselves impossible expectations. An example is a young child whose hands are not big enough to span an octave on the piano. She knows what it should sound like, but has to make a little jump between thumb and little finger, rather than bringing both down together – so that the sound is wrong. This can be intensely frustrating and stressful. Perceived failure is inevitable, which can be discouraging. Without adequate emotional support, even the most potentially talented may simply give up.

Although some in this sample had specific gifts and could plan their career route, such as John Daszak in music or Johnathan Martin in physics, there were others who seemed to be able to do almost anything to an exceptionally high level. For them the stress of deciding what to do could be severe. Before he left school, Jeremy Kramer's degree-level music qualifications and top marks in science brought the stress of what to study next (see Chapter 8, under heading 'Careers advice'). In fact, neither path could be entirely satisfactory because the other would be neglected, and so it proved. By 2001 the roots of this problem had become thick and unmoveable.

It can be a downward spiral; when a child is exposed to family stress he or she may become emotionally disturbed and thus 'difficult', which then causes further detriment to the parents' own relationship bringing guilt all round. Over time, the emotional turmoil can eat away at the child's feelings of worth, the burden continuing long after the initial problem has gone. But when parents become irritable, aggressive and quarrelsome it does not impinge equally on all the children in the family. In fact, it seemed to me that parents had sometimes focused on just one of their children for special treatment as gifted – and difficult.

However, not all children are equally susceptible to stress. Research evidence suggests a higher level of intelligence is more likely to safeguard the individual who may have a more advanced and wider variety of coping strategies, reinforced by success. In a longitudinal study of a group whose life circumstances were traumatic, Werner and Smith (1992) coined the term 'resilient' children for those who managed to reach a happier and more competent adulthood, compared with their peers. One important feature of the successful children was that they were 'engaging' – able to command the attention of adults in their lives, especially someone outside the immediate family circle. But they were also more robust and sociable and had an external support system of responsive schools, religion – and above-average intelligence.

The gifted in my sample told me of the special pressures they experienced, such as feeling obliged to conform to the average by way of teacher 'put-downs', and the influence of their classmates. Even greater pressure, though, came from parents and teachers who, maybe for their own vicarious satisfaction, pushed them very hard to achieve. Some youngsters did their best to oblige, subduing their personalities (if not their souls) in blinkered striving for academic excellence. For them, healthy emotional development, including the freedom to play and be creative, was severely curtailed; the glazed look in their eyes said a great deal as they worked doggedly on to achieve their A grades and first-class degrees.

As in the first part of the study, the Target group had described themselves as more sensitive than the equally gifted first control group, and they were also distinctly more lonely and depressed, their bouts of misery being far worse than for either of the other groups. However, there is no empirical research evidence to show that depression and suicide among the gifted is greater than that in the general population (Gust-Brey and Cross 1999).

The message for those who are likely to bring that stress about, teachers and parents, is that such pressure usually has the opposite effect from what was intended. Far better results in human terms were found when the gifted were treated with respect, allowing them enough responsibility to make many of their own discoveries and decisions. However, there were others, especially those in the arts, who seemed to have an inbuilt impetus, a spark, a 'psazz', which could light up their personalities, bringing them great inspiration and success.

Emotional defences

In their exceptionality and their sensitivity, the gifted sometimes construct complex, inhibiting psychological defences against expected hurt. A common variety is to hide behind intellectual walls of their own making, implying that they are too clever to have normal relationships with ordinary people, a situation too often encouraged by parents. This attitude encourages boredom at school, and so some never acquire the discipline of learning, which can be difficult to pick up later. So this defensive boredom becomes a downward spiral, getting worse and worse, eating into their happiness and achievements. It happened to several of this sample, mostly girls, who had ended up with relatively modest and long-delayed qualifications because they had avoided real intellectual challenge which might have exposed them, as one girl put it as being, 'only average or less than average'.

The gifted do face particular situations which others do not, such as never-ending very high expectations. They too have a need to relax from giving a superb performance every time. Additionally, if their gifts are developing at uneven rates, or as often happens they are receiving less praise for their achievements than other children, it can be difficult to produce at top level. In this study, there was the young boy who produced three funny 'books' a day, when the teacher wanted a serious effort, and so tore them up dramatically in front of the class. He often thought of that single severe emotional trauma, in addition to his very disturbed home life, and blamed them together for his sustenance addictions, which he has spent a lifetime fighting more or less successfully. Having to keep quiet about one's surging ideas all the time is more than distressing; it is destructive of future ideas.

Two valuable routes to helping right the gifted's feelings about themselves are specialised counselling and being with others like themselves.

- *Counselling:* Most teachers are neither trained to find out about developmental details, nor have they always the time to do so. A helpful move would be for the gifted to be sure of frequent one-to-one interviews with a specially trained teacher or counsellor, who keeps good contact with the parents. The counsellor should understand the kind of pitfalls the gifted may encounter. Regular visits away from the subject teacher would enable an advanced pupil to find out about different areas of interest with a view to future occupations. The gifted have special needs for guidance as they may not only be advanced in their learning capacities, but they may be exceptionally able across the board, or, like other children, lopsided in their development. Comparison of age-norms on measures of social and emotional development, as well as in specific subject areas, can provide valuable guidance.
- *Being with others like themselves:* It is true for everyone, that to be with others like oneself is more comfortable. For the gifted, it allows them to stride out intellectually, while continuing to learn the social skills of making relationships. It demonstrates that hiding behind their brilliance is a false defence because even among their intellectual peers relationships are not necessarily smooth.

It has been suggested that talented boys with sensitive artistic traits, which are regarded in the West as feminine, may only be able to find their comfortable mirror in similar males, and that this might be a possible reason for homosexual relationships. But the great majority of the highly sensitive, artistic and aware young people in my study who felt they were different from others had simply grown up with it as a part of their personal make-up. It did not seem to have affected their sexual identity.

Where pressure on these gifted young people was unyielding, their studies all-consuming, the incompatibility of their circumstances too strong or their own sensitivity too difficult to handle alone, they did have emotional problems. The gifted too need time to 'stand and stare', to find out about life at their own pace and in their own ways. To be healthy, there has to be a balance in everyone's life, and for the gifted adolescent that includes good relationships, developing interests outside study subjects, and taking part in school and many other activities.

For most normal schools, it is not always possible to meet the needs of these special children, especially those who have non-school-type educational needs. For instance, most academic school education is biased towards verbal skills, rather then the visuo-spatial ones such as fine art or sculpting. But there are very many different places outside school to which children can be directed to learn new skills, for example places of work, specialist out-of-school activities, museum activities, archaeology digs, and even spending time in other kinds of schools.

Gifted learners

All schools design educational experiences to develop the minds and behaviour of pupils in certain ways, and a school which is beneficial and effective demonstrates this in the care the teachers provide, notably in their concern for the way the pupils learn. This includes the means of teaching, such as feedback on pupils' work, as well as what is taught. It shows in the encouragement for pupils to be involved with the design of their own education, both in and out of school. It is there in the school's atmosphere, both physically in the state of the buildings and emotionally in the way the pupils behave.

An education for the highly able should not be, as it so often was for the sample in this study, a matter of acquiring astounding exam successes early, culminating in a PhD at twenty. As with all children, it should encourage a genuine feeling for learning and considering, and should stimulate curiosity – 'knowing how' rather than 'knowing that'. In the long run, the goal of education must be to equip all children with the means and motivation to continue learning, after they have left home and school. The only way to find out whether the gifted do need a change in their education is to look at how they are managing with what they are receiving, which is what this study has done.

Why some learners were more successful than others

Those selected by virtue of their ability to do well in examinations are a particular group, with very specific mental skills, and they do not represent all gifted individuals – Pablo Picasso had difficulty with reading and yet was obviously highly intelligent as well as being an artistic genius. Highly achieving examinees must be able to concentrate and remember large amounts of material, as well as having access to the higher-level skills of drawing their ideas together in the examination time. This is not simply exam technique, such as answering the question accurately and timing answers, but concerns the use of high level mental facilities. There were in fact clear reasons why so many of the young people in this study had achieved at such exceptionally high levels.

To begin with, they did have the potential – sheer intellectual ability – to work at a gifted level. As very young children, they had often begun to acquire the essential broad knowledge base, usually because they were keen to know things and searched them out. Their parents had told me about their earliest development, and in the first part of the study I saw it for myself. It was a statistically significant feature throughout the study that for the successful children, their home educational environments had usually included what they needed for learning, including material provision, the example of their parents' behaviour, and the good communication that parents, teachers and child often shared.

As they grew up, the more successful young people had found personal ways of organising their powerful mental abilities, which were different from those of the less successful because they were more aware of and made more use of their personal learning styles. To help their understanding and remembering, they used methods such as searching the material for its principles, then focused more on the substance than on the tiny details of what they were learning. This not only helped them to reproduce the material, but to elaborate on it. They were also more aware of the nature of the problems they were tackling, and through that awareness, were already a long way towards solving them. The less successful had remained with more immature, less effective, shorter-term techniques, like memorising their lesson notes and hardly ever looking things up in books or using other resources.

In addition to their own efforts, the teachers and parents of the most successful youngsters had mostly judged their potentials accurately, and had helped and given them encouragement. For the high achievers, there was often a mutually rewarding situation both at home and school, the young people feeling comfortable with their desire to learn and parents taking pride in this. But the less successful pupil was less likely to enjoy that kind of harmony, sometimes seeing school lessons as irrelevant to his or her personal needs and future life.

However, what teachers have always said – that hard work brings results – is undoubtedly true; a significant proportion of keen pupils of moderate ability had studied hard and with good results. The strength and direction of their motivation was influenced by its goals of doing well academically and what that meant to them. When intellectually gifted children are unmotivated, it may be that they are either avoiding threats to their self-image from possible failure, or are aiming for different goals from those which have been chosen for them. For many of the highly successful examinees, the goal which had influenced them was not just the examination successes, but the acquisition of knowledge, and the promise of further use of that learning. This goal was appropriate for their abilities and interests, and they had worked towards it with efficient study strategies. Were less able or less motivated youngsters to be offered lessons which appeared to them to be personally valuable and meaningful, these would be more likely to inspire them to take part in them.

Lessons from gifted learners

The academically successful do not have sole rights to the learning methods they use. These can be employed in normal teaching and learning. The essence of teaching children how to learn is in recognising the individuality of each child, so as to find and strengthen each one's personal style. Because new learning depends so much on how prior knowledge has been stored, simply telling children what to learn is not always adequate. They need to relate the new to the old, in ways which are meaningful to them, from their own perspectives. It can be very straightforward such as teaching geometry in terms of football pitches and the movements of the football.

However, a high proportion of all the young people felt some lack of communication with their teachers. Improving that situation should be a priority in finding out about the children's learning styles. It is not as difficult as it might seem: when they are asked, most children are able to tell the teacher how they like to learn – though some may need a little help to think this through and find it out. Discussion of the different ways of learning and thinking, guided by teachers or parents, is a valuable method of helping children to reach understanding about themselves. Nor is the problem of organising a classroom to suit individual modes of learning insuperable. It is, after all, the same problem that all teachers face, with more or less success, every school day. The answer lies in a variety of lesson presentation. This helps children not only to pick up ideas in tune with their personal learning style, but also encourages them to adapt to different approaches to a subject.

To enhance learning strategies, younger children may be helped by talking through ideas or even acting out possible ways of approach to a new area. To do this, they must be really involved. In history, for example, basic information, such as the coming of the plague to a medieval village can be discussed or acted out, as to how it affected individuals and how they be likely to behave, than compare their present day thoughts with what really happened. Children can think up and try out different approaches to the subject area themselves. For example, they could take an aspect of technology, consider different ways in which it impinges on their lives, and then follow the trains of reasoning as far as they can in many directions. Once acquired, flexible learning and thinking strategies – on a sound knowledge base – can be transferred for use on other similar subjects with problems of increasingly greater complexity. Like the highly successful examinees, a positive outlook on learning, with a well practised and flexible mind, allows almost any child to apply and adapt a range of intellectual skills correctly in new situations.

Teachers and parents should also try to become aware of their own repertoires of teaching strategies. These might be, for example, a heavy reliance on the instruction of children to remember rather than interpret. Or adults might have a poor ability to cope with redundant noise, so that they demand constant silence from pupils. The strategies which adults teach children to learn by, may not in fact be the best ways for their recipients, which is another good reason for keeping things flexible.

Confidence

There is evidence that children who believe their abilities are fixed fail to aim as high as they could (Chapman and Lambourne 1990; Heller and Ziegler 1996). Enhancing children's sense of self-competence is possibly the most basic way of improving their potential for learning, as well as improving their learning strategies. Self-rating is the first step towards self-reflection and control. It helps any child (or indeed adult) towards a positive and realistic understanding of his or her own ways of thinking and learning. A very effective technique is to guide children in rating their own performances and products as they work through practice problems, instead of depending on others' assessments.

Challenge

Because the intellectually gifted have the potential to move into higher levels of intellectual thought, they, at least as much as any others, should be practised in the thinking strategies of analysis and evaluation. This would involve immersing them from the very start of school life in ideas which are complex, sophisticated and stimulating. To do this implies that they must be recognised as sufficiently able to tackle those tasks. It can come from the bright child, as nine-year-old gifted Chloe asked me: 'Why should I believe in history? All those things which people say tell us about long ago, perhaps they were false clues left for us to find. And God, why should I believe in God?', so we talked about assumptions, motivations, and faith.

A common example of unchallenging learning is in the teaching of reading. It still happens that very advanced early readers are kept at the same pace as the rest of the class. Twenty-three children in this sample were said by their parents to have read something by the age of three, and one mother spoke for many:

> 'When Anne went to school at five they wouldn't let her read. We were told she was too young to read. I went up to school and I said, "This is ridiculous, she's reading Black Beauty at home. Why can't she read at school?" The teacher said "Oh, I don't believe all this." So I said, 'Right. Pick any book off your bookshelf and fetch her and find out for yourself.' So he did. He sat her on her own, took a book off the book shelf, and she read it through, but it still didn't make any difference. They couldn't see that she was getting frustrated.'

Using a more challenging approach, the teacher would first have had to recognise the little girl's ability, then encourage her to have a stab at a higher level text. He would also have had to spend a little time with her, talking about what she was reading, getting her to elaborate on it – What happened next? – and relate it to other ideas she might have – Was this like the story you read before about the Prince?

All children need plentiful practice in sizing up tasks, analysing problems and assessing goals, as well as attempting solutions. These basic learning strategies, like looking for similarities and differences, are not difficult to do. They are readily found in the everyday commercial puzzle books for children. More specific techniques of improving ways of thinking and learning for older students can readily be found in self-help books.

Developing good thinking and learning strategies does not imply that a conscious decision should be taken every step of the way. It is usually more a matter of being able to draw on past experience so as to be aware of different possible ways of proceeding. For example, reading a science textbook calls for a more considered, stop-start approach, than the relaxed, flowing enjoyment of an easy story-book. Many youngsters do not know that the two types of text call for different approaches and processes. In describing their study methods, the poor examinees in my study often closeted themselves with their textbooks and notes and simply read them, many times, as though they were novels. They described how hard they found it to absorb the material. No one had ever helped them to learn how to use analysis and comparison of the information, and then how to fit the principles into an overall pattern – to learn strategically.

But even good learning techniques can be misused, like the very effective method of taking notes by writing down key words or 'outlining', which takes hours of practice to set up. If the system has not been well learned, the effort at remembering the technique can overload the working memory. For example, a student trying to use it inexpertly in a lecture, unless she is intellectually gifted, cannot pay attention to both the technique and the information at the same time, and may not only miss some of the information, but also become disheartened from using the method.

Since motivation for learning varies with the success and failure of endeavour, accurate feedback is vital. But even with good feedback, the first attempts may not be satisfactory, or the chosen course of action may begin to fail after a time, and sometimes it may seem that endless encouragement is called for. The insight gained into the ways in which most of the young gifted people in my study had used their minds, has shown that when they had the knowledge, the practice, and the confidence to act in their own way, they were extremely effective. And their methods are open to anyone.

Creative thinking

It is impossible to be creative about nothing because creativity is always context-bound and dependent on knowledge. The more one knows about something, the better one's chance of thinking creatively in that area. Educationally, then, attempts to increase creative thinking must emphasise content plus large doses of experience. Although creative thinking takes learning and analytic thinking to their highest levels, it is also a basic everyday activity involved in almost any decision – should you wear the red or the blue shirt with the green sweater? We can learn from those who do it well that creative thinking skills are improvable and teachable by using appropriate strategies and styles – with feeling.

But how does this tie up with the way most of us are taught, via critical thinking which pours doubt on everything it examines. Scientifically, one employs a critical analysis of an idea, using hypotheses against data to see how it fits into the known world. According to Thomas Kuhn, the philosopher and the inventor of the paradigm shift, scientific revolution occurs when a new paradigm emerges and becomes accepted by the scientific community. In fact, this seems to apply to creative thinking in all fields. Scientific thinking is not confined to scientists. The problem is how to reach the right balance to think critically as well as creatively.

The split brain

For centuries, great thinkers have written about the split between reason and emotion. But it was only in the early 1970s that the psychologist, Robert Ornstein, wrote his seminal book, *The Bicameral Brain*, in which he outlined different operating systems of its two halves (Ornstein 1972). The left hemisphere (opposite the right hand) works, he said, in a careful, ordered way, tackling problems analytically, while the right hemisphere (opposite the left hand) takes an all-over, more picture-like view. People who are dominated by the right half of their brain tend to see things as a whole. They are concerned with patterns, shapes and sizes, and are more imaginative and intuitive. Their ideas can seem vague and woolly to left-brain dominated people, who are often better at more logical and academic work such as mathematics and word skills. Whereas the right side will help you to hum a tune, write a poem or see a painting as a whole, the left side will help you to write grammatically, mend an engine, or admire the brush technique of the artist. For most people, the two halves work together in harmony for better effect.

Traditional teaching in schools is thought to have emphasised the more rigid left-brain activity, sometimes to the detriment of the right, so that conformity is usually more dominant by the time children leave school. Conformity and repression are the enemies of creative activity, but they're excellent for promoting high achievement in school exams, especially in science. Indeed, school and IQ tests seem designed more for left brain than right. Some psychologists believe that if certain right-brain activities are not exercised regularly, they will never develop properly. Since the greatest creative achievements require both halves of the brain, a heavily academic education can cut down creative potential. As Donald Purdey, at university studying science, told me:

> 'Sometimes I feel disadvantaged in that I crammed a lot of science and didn't develop myself culturally. I've never read novels or anything like that, and I've never bought a book in my life, even at university, though I intend to try and catch up on it one day. With having to do all that work, I was quite happy to be railroaded, and I didn't think a lot or question things. That's how I came to try LSD. I was just intrigued to know what it was like, because life is supposed to be about

the feelings you get out of doing something – pleasures and experiences. But it was hallucinogenic, horrible.'

Creativity in the classroom

The young people in this study had experienced some wonderfully creative teaching in which thinking was valued as much as memory, and they had felt themselves respected as individuals with 'permission' to experiment with ideas. They told me of the teachers they most appreciated who were creative facilitators – the agents of change – and not just authorities with the right answers. Their teaching was always held in high esteem by their bright pupils.

Alas, though, many of the lively-minded young people in the study were seen as nuisances when they attempted to think creatively in the classroom. So many described the non-creative classrooms they hated – authoritarian, rigid places, working by the bell. There, they had felt themselves to be disregarded as emotional people because the teacher was more preoccupied with discipline and the giving out of information, or when marking a piece of work was primarily concerned with superficial correctness and missed the deeper ideas. As one teenager said pointedly: 'Formalised learning stops your creativity'.

The evidence from the study shows up the need, especially among some ardent young scientists, to encourage high achievers to use their brains in a more balanced way. For some of them, when their emotional creative side was pushed aside, this not only impoverished their creative thinking, but also their feelings of self-worth. It made them feel like learning machines, grinding on for the glory of the school and maybe parental aspirations, rather than for their own fulfilment. If the gifted are to prosper in a balanced, creative way, they may need to ease up on the purely academic side and increase their social and leisure activities. But to do this they need the help and support of parents and teachers, in part to overcome their often own urges for hard learning. Especially for the highly able, this would not result in lower examination marks, but probably higher ones because of their wider experiences, greater maturity, and the depth they would bring to their answers. It would also be expected to bring them greater personal strength and happiness.

The value of play

There is some conflict between the two opposing tendencies – either to open up the world or to stay sheltered in what is familiar. The latter is sometimes difficult for the scholarly, conforming youngster, who is socially unsure of themselves. He or she can find the anxiety overwhelming and so may only accept learning from a safe source such as a teacher, and will question little. Individuals have to feel confident enough to take risks. Carl Gustav Jung (1964) described how people often erect psychological defences to protect themselves from 'the shock of facing something new', due to a 'deep and suspicious fear of novelty'. I suggest that the simplest way for children (and adults) to modify such anxiety about the new is through play which makes the unfamiliar familiar.

Every child's natural approach to a new experience is one of play – a wonderfully flexible and creative aspect of intellectual development. Children use it to comprehend social behaviour by re-playing what they have seen others do, as well in coping with their own fears and fantasies. Educators of young children use play as an assessment guide to development. When the quality of children's imaginative play is poor, it is a matter for real concern.

Play can be seen from either a cognitive or emotional perspective, though of course, there is overlap between the two. Jean Piaget saw it as vital to the developing intellect in the process of assimilating new information into the old. Emotionally, it is a social learning tool, and can also be a cathartic activity for young and old.

Shortage of play

It is a sad truth that parents and teachers who are ambitious for an intellectually highly able child can place too much emphasis on measurable achievement, and may regard play as a 'waste of time', prohibiting it until formal learning – the real business of the day – is finished. Even very young gifted children are often unconsciously perceived as quasi-adults with little need for play, so that the only approved and provided-for learning experiences they receive is relatively sophisticated and often 'bookish'. It cannot be assumed that all children play freely and imaginatively; cross-cultural studies indicate that in some cultures, as with culturally disadvantaged children, it hardly ever occurs. Even among children who have facilities and encouragement, there are very different levels of the frequency, amount, and quality of play.

The conditions for worthwhile play are the same as those for good learning: an educational atmosphere in which there is permission to experiment whatever the outcome, emotional support, the relevant learning materials, and a living cultural tradition from which to draw and build. Play at home or at school helps children to know something of the talents they possess, such as singing along with a recording or sense of visual perspective in setting up a model, and also to experience those talents, giving them greater control and productivity over them. It is also fun and makes learning more attractive.

Play in creativity

Examples of creative teaching techniques might include asking a child to play with alternatives to what appear to be unchanging situations, such as – What would happen if everyone worked at night and slept by day? Another might be working towards uses for apparently useless ideas, which a class could think up together, such as – What would happen if colours changed without warning? Encouraging creative thinking means giving children 'permission' to play with ideas, however odd, without criticism for a while, and giving time for them to ferment. It is that precarious balance between psychological safety and freedom which allows the child to feel both secure and free enough to take the chance of putting forward unusual ideas. The encouragement to tackle problems creatively is germane to all subjects in the curriculum, through the original thoughts and creative productions of the children themselves. For creative thinking, the emphasis has to be on the process, rather than on the end result. It starts with the knowledge and feeling, then the doing, and only then the product.

The very essence of gifted creativity is at risk through conformity to social desirability, when energy is devoted to being acceptable. For the creatively gifted especially, they are too often in the delicate position of being unappreciated. Not only are their potential contributions easily diminished or dismissed, but they may feel that there is something wrong with them for thinking differently from what is expected.

Talent in the arts

It is strange, in an age when all children are considered to be potentially creative, that so much artistic education is uninspiring – whether of stilted painting techniques or glued-together egg boxes. As a judge of a British national poetry competition to which there are about 35,000 entries a year, it was dispiriting to me to read so many poems on – The Daffodil, The Wind, The Fog, The Autumn, The Summer, etc., etc. So often too, one could see from a whole class's entries that the poems were half-written by teacher with a recognisable same wooden touch.

In this Follow-up study, the beginnings of future artistic talent often started as play. At seven, for example, Anna Markland thought the audition for the music school was great fun. However, as Thomas Edison is often quoted as saying, genius is 99 per cent perspiration and one per cent inspiration, and this was true for every one of these artistically talented young people. Their outstanding performances had inevitably meant hard, time-consuming work to acquire the artistic knowledge base and practise it. Their aims and their motivation were high. They had good support, though, from positive feedback from the performance itself as well as teachers and parents.

None of the sample made it to a high artistic level on their own; generous emotional support was essential all the way. Sometimes the whole family's energy became funnelled into support, at times to the detriment of other possible activities – and other children in the family. The parents of the most creative youngsters had always encouraged their children's curiosity and taken it seriously. They had read to their children, and taught them what they knew almost from birth, and as they grew up, often took to learning along with them. In 2001, when I spoke to many of these parents, they were (justifiably) extremely proud of their creative children.

Techniques to develop talent

When work needs inspiration, such as creating a book or a painting, one can help by trying to re-create environments which have encouraged inspiration before. This may involve arranging props to act as stimuli, such as working with a particular pen, or in a particular room or chair. Sometimes getting into the creative mood can involve an idiosyncratic ritual, like a preliminary walk in the park, a cup of coffee or sitting on a hard chair. Some people can only work creatively at certain times, such as the early hours of the morning. The important thing is that the environment for creativity must be free as possible from anxiety (there is more than enough in the creative act itself), which is why the surroundings should be familiar.

Another effective technique is quiet meditation, which can even be arranged in schools. It involves trying to empty the mind, thinking of nothing, but being aware of everything. When the mind can be free of conventional associations fresh ideas can emerge. The more successful creative young people told me how they were able to arrange their environments, keeping unwanted, distracting sensations at bay, controlling the level of redundant stimulation. A common example was by taking a break from the mental struggle, emptying the conscious mind by doing something completely different, then re-entering the growing web of associations with refreshed perspective and strength. Another method they used was to change from a higher to a lower level of thinking, such as moving from considering general concepts to concentrate on details, and then going back to concepts.

In creative thinking, it is necessary to keep in close touch with the elements of the problem, and yet be sensitive to one's own thoughts and feelings about it. Creative people do need both a global knowledge of their field to give consistency, as well as intuition. They need that information to work with, which can be frustrating for the gifted child who has not lived long enough to acquire it. But there are differences in subject area. Whereas creative scientists will make more use of the analytical control needed for verifying facts, creative artists make more use of intuition, because their need is not so much for consistency as emotional control. Possibly because of this heavy emotional load, creative artists have to have a higher tolerance of stress to keep their equanimity, because for them, unlike the scientist, there can be no retreat into impersonal data.

The gifted do have something special, something the world needs, and they also have as much right to fulfil their all-round potentials as anyone else. The unbalanced, uncreative force-feeding of many in this sample with examination fodder did not allow them to develop in a balanced way. And it caused real suffering. The answer to the question as to whether the gifted and talented need a change in their education is – yes, they do – urgently, and in the direction of creativity in their teaching and learning.

CHAPTER 11

Educating for gifts and talents

A genius is a talented person who does his homework.
Thomas Edison

Special educational needs are those which call for something different from what is normally provided. Gifted children are exceptional in their abilities and need special educational provision to reach their potential. The big problem in the classroom is that their needs may at times be at variance with those of the rest of the class. It is not easy for most schools to know how to cater for them, and too often their exceptionality is seen primarily as an ability to absorb lessons quickly and easily – achievement rules OK! But the evidence from this study has shown that there is much more to being gifted than having the potential for advancement and high grades.

Gifted style

Throughout the study, the young people of the highest IQ appeared to have a higher speed and often acuity of perception, as well as better memory and concentration than the others. Those who were emotionally well balanced were more likely to describe more efficient methods of thinking and learning, and to make the best use of their personal styles. The importance of personal study skills was thrown into relief when the supporting emotional structure was rattled, such as moving on from school to university. But even at school, when they used poor study strategies, most still managed to achieve high grades by relying on their excellent memories. Few teachers seemed to be concerned about improving their learning methods, and parents were often at a loss to know how to help.

Special training of teachers for teaching and guiding the learning of gifted children is still unusual in most of the world outside North America. The teacher, though, is in a position to enhance creative thought with an open, questioning and challenging style of teaching, providing a safe haven in which the gifted might try out their intellectual wings. The open approach asks that the teacher should give minimum directions to help children think about the subject, encouraging their ingenuity by asking the kind of questions which will enable them to go beyond the worksheet, the textbook, and the 'correct' answer. Problem-solving is also a diagnostic measure for the very bright – their intelligence will show up in their answers, as Robert Sternberg (1999) has pointed out.

Underachieving gifted children and why they did not fulfil their potential are featured throughout this book. It is particularly difficult for teachers to recognise children who are achieving above average and yet below their real potential. A major help in this is to look at how children handle language and knowledge, particularly in the area of their interest. There are gifted children, though, who keep a low profile in class and psychological tests via a specialist psychologist may be needed.

More than instruction

In general, teachers are concerned that their job is to instruct, rather than to deal with the psychological problems. Yet, adults are the child's main source of their good or bad feelings about themselves, and it was clear from my study that children want their teachers to care about them as whole people who have worries about exams or a dislike of sport, not to mention a divorce or a new baby in the family. Whatever their ability level, very few of the young people in the study received much psychological help from their teachers, and some were severely let down.

Praise seems to be in short supply in many schools, yet it has long been recognised that the carrot is more effective than the stick in producing better work. It was sad that so many of the gifted reported less praise than other children. It seems they missed out on congratulations when expectations of them were very high. Maybe it is part of the 'put down' syndrome that sarcasm often seemed to come more readily to their teachers' lips. False praise was not valued, but rather genuine approval and constructive comment on what they were attempting. Positive feedback helps all people to develop stronger feelings of proficiency in learning, which in turn makes them more likely to invest energy in it, enjoy it and do better.

The young people appreciated teachers who would work with them, rather than for them. They often described how their ideal teachers would be as concerned with the structure of their learning and their ability to cope as with the passing on of information. There was also evidence that with a teacher's enthusiastic help, sometimes unusual subjects could be studied in ordinary schools. Samantha Goldman's teacher, for instance, joined her in studying physical astronomy and they achieved A grades together.

It can be said that if educational provision were truly child-centred, there would be no reason for special concern for any exceptional group. Yet how can children be provided for appropriately, when their special nature goes unrecognised? Whatever their special talents, whether gymnastics, mathematics or reasoning power, those who are exceptionally good at learning will do it faster and at a greater depth and breadth.

- *Faster learning:* A wide variation in the learning speed of the class is difficult for teachers to manage; it interrupts the timing of lessons and classroom activity. The gifted also sometimes skip sequences in the learning process the teacher has prepared, particularly the mathematically able. A change of subject, such as art for the mathematicians, is often more beneficial than simply supplying more of the same kind of learning.
- *Depth and breadth:* Extending and enriching the subject area is essential for the gifted: going over it in finer detail and relating it to other areas.

School provision

Even in its simplest form, when just a few individuals are grouped together, they begin to form their own in-group, excluding others. It is true that when highly able children are grouped together for teaching, they do make better progress in their school work, and most of the young people in this sample said that selection for most teaching would be their preference, particularly those who were already at such schools. This did not seem to be a matter of intellectual snobbery, because they usually liked mixing socially with people of many kinds, and although they had not experienced it, they imagined that the slow pace of normal classroom learning would be irritating and hold them back. Yet some at comprehensives, like George Booth, went on to far greater life success than others in high-powered academic schools, such as Jeremy Kramer.

However, a few gifts do seem to call for full-time specialist education, including music and the performing arts, notably ballet. In Eastern Europe and the United States, there are also schools for other specialities such as technology and languages.

The key to educating special groups in a school is flexibility and organisation. Flexibility can be as simple, for example, as the trust which allows a child who has finished the lesson early to leave the classroom to work in the library, or an early reader to choose her own reading book.

The organisational methods most frequently used to help the gifted within a school, are acceleration, part-time withdrawal, and enrichment. Acceleration is based on the child's already recognised advancement, whereas enrichment can also promote hidden potential. Hence acceleration is reactive while enrichment is proactive. No direct comparisons appear to have been made in educational research, though, on how each procedure affects different types of learning styles in children.

Acceleration

The major problem with grade-skipping is that the child 'hurried' on in that way may be not be either physically or emotionally mature enough to fit in socially with the older children in the new class. Only two of the 17 accelerated youngsters in this sample thought it was a good idea at the time, but by 2001, even they decided it had not been good for them in the long run.

The conclusions from a wide survey were that 'A high IQ six- or seven-year-old is unlikely to have the necessary processing abilities to cope with many learning situations that would be straightforward for a much lower-IQ but same mental age ten-year-old' (Anderson 2001, p. 296). More specifically, certain subject areas, such as language, require the certain life experiences which come with age, and without them the necessary conceptual development may be lacking. Nor is a four-year-old as physically adept as a five-year-old, and particularly for grade-skipped boys, their apparently late physical development encourages the 'little professor' image as being hopeless at everything which is not school-learning (or music). Several accelerated children in this sample still in 2001 had the idea that they were physically small and inept at games, although they were normal.

Most research on acceleration has taken place in the United States where even ability or interest grouping within the class is prohibited in many states. Yet in a review of American research on emotional development of the accelerated gifted, Cornell *et al.* (1991), conclude that 'few authors have examined socio-emotional adjustment with adequate psychological measures' (p. 91), and few have looked at the long-term effects. Nor has any data emerged to indicate which students will fare well in early college entrance.

The success of acceleration is dependent on the context, such as the flexibility of the system, how many others in a school are accelerated, the child's level of maturation and emotional support. The age at which the acceleration starts could have different effects, a feature that has not been addressed in any research. Acceleration in the early years, for example, may seem to be successful, but problems may arise in adolescence, as they did for Robert Fraser. Educationally, it is often assumed that acceleration implies more complex content, but the child may merely be working along the same lines as before – simply shortening the number of years spent in school. There are times, though, when the general standard is simply too low and grade-skipping may be the only option, and when care is taken of the possible problems it has been found to be successful. There also has to be some continuity, as Stephen Kaye (now a medical doctor) explained:

> 'The primary school I went to was very good: it put a lot of our [gifted] people ahead. But when I got to secondary school I didn't learn any new maths for about eighteen months. There was no streaming at all, and maths is one of those subjects where some people can grasp it and others can't. We had no formal teaching as such in the first year in geography, history, English and R.E. [religious instruction] either. We did them all together and called it humanities. What a boring year!'

Most of the growing-up problems for all but one of the 17 youngsters who had been young for their class at school appeared to have been exacerbated by it. Having to make relationships every day with classmates who were emotionally more mature was confusing and also aggravated relationships at home. As one father said in sorrow: 'When he was sixteen, there were men of nineteen in the sixth form'. Nor did it even seem to benefit the young people academically, as other research has found; some had done less well in their examinations than had been expected, certainly with regard to their measured intelligence. Just four of those who had been advanced had managed to organise broader, non-academic educational experiences for themselves as leisure activities. Any child who is accelerated will need extra emotional support. It can only be concluded that unless a pupil is not only highly gifted but mature for his or her years, school acceleration is probably not the best option. The international research indicates these warnings:

Only accelerate when:

- There is no pressure to accelerate.
- The pupil is in the top two per cent of intelligence.
- The receiving teacher feels positive about it.
- The parents feel positive about it.
- The pupil is advanced in the subject area.
- The pupil is emotionally stable.
- The pupil understands what is involved.
- The pupil wants to be accelerated.

Part-time acceleration

The idea of taking children of below-average performance out of normal classes for remedial teaching is generally accepted. The teacher or a psychologist usually makes the decision and it is planned into the child's school curriculum. For the gifted in the United States, it is not unusual to find gifted children in 'pull-out' classes. But there, as in Britain, teachers fear that if some children are selected as brighter than the others it will detract from their relationships with their classmates, promoting jealousy and elitism. Deeper still, perhaps, is the implicit threat to the teacher's competence. Such feelings may be quite unconscious, but many teachers cannot help but feel slighted that somehow children are being withdrawn from their class for something 'better than they can provide'.

But American experience shows that it all depends on how this is done – on the outlook and practical approach of the school system. For example, if the gifted are taken somewhere exciting for a geography field trip, it is reasonable for the rest of the desk-bound class to feel envy – not least because they could all probably benefit from the trip. And yet it does happen that way. But withdrawing the gifted for specialist tuition in mathematics or a foreign language is less likely to be envied.

One added danger is that withdrawals of the intellectually gifted are often likely to be made during 'unimportant' lessons like physical education, which they need as much as any other child. It happened to the scientifically gifted in this sample, whose development of creativity in the arts was sometimes curtailed. Enhanced academic achievements in the gifted have been reported through such pull-out classes, as well as improved self-confidence and more positive attitudes towards school and school work. Handled sensitively, it does not seem to have the effect of upsetting the others in the class.

Enrichment

Enrichment is the butter between the bread of a standard school curriculum. But it is not a complementary diet; it should be a natural everyday part of the school day for all children. It can take the form of school outings, experts coming in to school to teach, laboratories left open at the weekend for keen physicists, time to spend trying novel ways of approaching a technical problem, and much more. It should never be confined to the most able. In a survey of 8,000 comparative studies of American education for the gifted, Walberg (1995) found that pupils in enriched education did better in school than equally able children without it. For the gifted, it is a particularly important aspect of their developing mental life. Enrichment is the vital stuff of a truly enhancing education for those who have the capacity to grasp the gist of the subject they are learning, relate it to other areas, and play with ideas in the processes of creativity.

The teacher's task in enriching education is to provide the groundwork, and to guide and encourage pupils to explore further. Giving children who are exceptionally able in any area the opportunity to work intensively at their own pace may mean that they need a higher (not a lower) degree of supervision. But that care need not always be by teachers, since parents and experts can step in with specialist knowledge. If there are just a few children who are similarly head and shoulders above their classmates, working groups of different ages can be made up within the school, as is already often done for a specific project.

A major problem with enrichment activities for the highly able is that they often lack clear goals. These should include the following (see Freeman (1998) for details and suggestions for teachers). Here are the three most important.

Enrichment goals

- Increase ability to analyse and solve problems.
- Develop profound, worthwhile interests.
- Stimulate originality, initiative and self-direction.

Vacation courses

Summer camps and weekend get-togethers can be very enjoyable for the gifted as they can be with others like themselves: they can relax and drop some energy-consuming psychological defences. For the duration of the course, the children can become enthusiastic with an energy which is daunting to the teachers, but discipline problems are rare and the overriding feeling is one of working together. However, comparisons between different programmes of special provision are extremely rare, if they exist at all. It is not unreasonable to assume that bright motivated youngsters, under intensive tutoring in an exciting atmosphere of learning, would indeed become more proficient learners, so that any course will have a positive effect. But the question still remains as to what kind of extra provision is the best way of helping them. Might not a climbing or canoeing holiday have the same effect? There is evidence that the most lasting benefit to already keen learners is social, in terms of improved relationships with other of their own age.

Mentoring

Mentoring is a fast developing form of enrichment. It is one of the oldest instructional models, in which a more informed and experienced adult (or even an age-peer) acts as an expert counsellor to a protégé, in the same way that Socrates was a mentor to Plato. It provides a highly specialist form of educational extension for youngsters whose needs cannot be met within the educational system (see Foreman 2001). This may be because they need a broader and more advanced approach than the school can provide, to identify unrealised gifted potential, maybe to realise creativity in high-achieving school learners, or to help able underachievers, perhaps for those who have been accelerated in their education, and also for the encouragement of the lifelong continuation of gifts. But there were no official mentors for any child within this study at any time.

Mentoring can take the form of observing and assisting an adult in their daily work, maybe a lawyer, a sculptor or an engineer. It is different from tutoring which is concerned with academic learning, usually in a classroom and takes place over a short period of a few weeks. Mentoring usually focuses on life-skills, often outside the classroom, involves a one-to-one relationship and can last for months or years. It is neither an apprenticeship based on instruction, nor does it indicate long-term commitment, but is a rather more diffuse relationship in which there must be respect on both sides for it to work. Because of that personal relationship, mentors have to be very carefully chosen to be trusted with youngsters and it is sometimes difficult to find female mentors.

However, only providing enrichment for some members of a class may mean that the disparity between them and the others is likely to grow. This can be handled well by outside-school enrichment meetings of such children with others who want to learn. These get-togethers need not be for selected children, but open to all who want to join in. Youngsters who find them too difficult or boring will normally drop out. Every neighbourhood, no matter how culturally deprived, has its share of interesting things for children to see and do, and interesting people to meet (see Freeman 1995a). This kind of enriched learning, which takes place in many settings, is difficult to measure in conventional academic terms, though improvement in school achievement usually follows. The wider advantages, such as improved relationships with other people, and the flow of ideas are usually easier to see.

Educational guidance

Helping individuals to get to know what they are good at, and helping them to do it, is a vital part of good education in school. Thinking about it cannot start too early. Although this is important for all children, it is especially so for the most able who may have the potential for many career routes. The best way is to integrate ideas into classroom teaching of all subjects. In fact, it is not unusual for lessons to be enriched by group discussions, debates and exploratory experiences for the pupils, and many already include careers concerns.

Making the right choice involves knowing what there is to choose from and one's own potential. Educational guidance is concerned with self-awareness, self-acceptance, competence, attitudes to work and how different kinds of work can be personally and socially significant. It involves exploring different lifestyles, including leisure activities and family roles. Doors should be kept open as long as possible. There is always the possibility of finding a way of breaking though cultural and economic boundaries to reach out for what the world has to offer.

There could be added experiences for the pupils, beginning perhaps with library research, then shadowing workers in areas in which they are interested and also work experience. There is considerable potential in the cooperation of schools with the world of commerce and industry. Already, work experience is helping gifted youngsters to see beyond traditional school and culture-bound choices of study. I believe that the most promising way of releasing potential is in this dynamic combination of in- and out-of-school education. This is especially true for children whose world is angled more to work than the classroom – however much we would prefer it otherwise. This route is known but barely charted; I hope that its exploration can gather momentum. The promise is exciting and the way is open.

The benefits of a school policy for the gifted

Even the richest country has a limit to the money it can spend on education. Every teacher and every administrator has to know what is available to mobilise resources most advantageously. But that is where another big barrier to gifted education arises. How can you have excellence for some and equality of opportunity for all? Whose needs are the most deserving, the slow-learners, the potentially gifted or the majority? It is every teacher's headache – how to cope with the basic learning of all children, allowing for differences in each individual's learning, as well as special groups such as the gifted. In normal, non-specialist schools, any special provision must be provided within the standard system, usually in mixed-ability classes. Yet pupils who learn differently from others – faster and in greater breadth and depth – have different needs. The key is differentiation in teaching. Easy to say and difficult to do.

A major challenge is to alter government and school outlooks. The installation of a specific policy for gifted and talented children in a school is a statement to that effect. The consequences would be of practical value for all the children because, as the British Schools' Inspectorate has found, provision for the gifted and talented can both improve their own achievement and motivate others' efforts in school (DES 1989).

A policy's primary aim would be to enable each individual to attain knowledge in a manner which is meaningful, and which can be used in a creative manner in different situations. However, one must recognise that it is not possible to regulate for excellence, to pass edicts that people should love learning, or to require teachers to be enthusiastic about their work and their pupils. A school policy, whether aimed at potential or demonstrated high-level achievement, would encourage and help those of high level potential to access high quality learning resources. But it cannot be effective without financial and administrative support. The pupils, too, need an accurate picture of what is provided and expected of them and the freedom to negotiate for what they feel is right for them.

Specific policy aims in the education of the gifted and talented

- Heightening awareness of the needs of the gifted and talented.
- Identifying and recognising high-level potential.
- Making provision for advanced learning and creative endeavour, both within and outside formal education.
- Using both evidence and feeling in decision-making for identification and action.

The most able have a need for *consistent* challenge through high-level teaching. This can be through specific courses, specialist advisors and focused events, or the last resort – grade-skipping.

A policy should include

- Counselling and vocational guidance with regard to their special needs.
- Out-of-school activities for highly able pupils from different backgrounds, such as weekend activities, competitions, or summer camps, where they can meet and relax with others like themselves.
- A system of mentoring: a carefully selected adult with particular expertise takes a special interest in one or two youngsters, who may, for example, do original research alongside a scientist in a laboratory. Mentoring often has additional positive emotional effects for at risk pupils.

Guidelines for the education of the gifted

The objectives summarised in the list below are the best that can be hoped for, though they are clearly not obtainable all the time by all educators, whether teachers or parents. They offer a focus for a practical style of education which has been drawn from the evidence of this research and that of many others from all over the world (Freeman 1998). They are perhaps an ideal, but one for which it is worth striving.

The specific educational needs of the gifted and talented

- A consistent challenge; there is a great variety of ways in which this can be provided by using the resources which already exist, such as those provided by local authorities in parks, libraries, etc.
- The opportunity to work at their own rate of learning, to pursue their own interests to a high level, and to practice their skills for the required length of time to produce expert performance.
- Help with vocational problems, especially when talents are many.
- Regular communication and interaction with others of like minds, e.g. through Internet clubs or out-of-school get-togethers.

Competence in teaching

- Teaching should be geared to the ability of the child.
- Particularly for the gifted, teaching must be intellectually sound and also challenging.
- The way pupils learn, their personal style, should be taken into consideration by providing a variety of approaches in the style of teaching.
- Learning material should be appropriate and adequate. Most schools in my study had enough basic resources, but some used them far more efficiently than others.

- Competence means a firm yet flexible hand on the reins, from both class and head teachers. The pupils need to know where they stand and what is expected of them in order to aim for agreed goals with a consequent higher chance of success.

Encouraging motivation in learning, thinking and creativity

- Doing things with children is much better than simply telling them what to learn.
- The pupils should be the focus of their own education; too many in my study felt like ciphers in the system.
- What is taught should be relevant to the pupil's values and interests, both to their present leisure activities and their future vocational possibilities.
- Schools, particularly those selecting the intellectually able, should be aware of the possible abuse of academic values which can result in sterile learning and inhibited emotional development. Teaching orientation can be changed from concern with the accumulation of information to its more creative use by a more questioning approach.
- Enthusiasm in teachers for their subject was very much appreciated, and had the effect of inspiring the listeners to greater efforts.
- Praise is very much more effective than punishment or sarcasm.

Adult involvement

- Concern for the all-round welfare of children always brings positive results.
- Accurate and regular feedback to children on what they attempt is vital for their guidance.
- Parental involvement includes helping school learning, as well as at home.
- Adults and children working together increases their mutual respect, including that for children of different abilities and backgrounds. The positive attitude it engenders improves learning.
- Adults who tried to hide their human side were less trusted by youngsters, who warmed to those who were relaxed and let their own failings show. A sense of humour in teachers is a great and very much appreciated gift.

The sports approach

In all cultures, excellence in some abilities is more acceptable than in others, and sport is universally loved. In the UK, for example, local education authorities normally encourage keen talented footballers to benefit from extra tuition outside school hours, provide them with equipment, arrange transport for them to meet and engage with others at roughly the same level as themselves – and pay for it all. Although there is some provision around for other subjects, notably music, and there are mathematics contests and extracurricular activities, such as art classes in museums, the idea of opening up the school labs for a Saturday morning practice in chemistry is rare, if it exists at all. It is not difficult or expensive to find out what interests and motivates pupils via questionnaires, interest tests – or simply by asking them. And the facilities are already largely in place to provide excellent support for a wide variety of abilities.

I propose that given the opportunity, and with some guidance, children should be able to work at any subject at a more advanced and broader level. I call this – The Sports Approach – because in the same way as those who are talented and motivated can select themselves for extra tuition and practice in sports, they could opt for extra foreign languages or physics. This would mean, of course, that such facilities must be available to all, as sport is, rather than only to those preselected by tests, experts, family provision or money to pay for extras. This is neither an expensive route, nor does it risk emotional distress to the children by removing them from the company of their friends. It makes use of research-based understanding of the very able, notably the benefit of focusing on a defined area of the pupil's interest, as well as providing each one with the facilities they need to learn with and make progress. Suggestions as to how this might be practised in schools are offered here.

The Sports Approach

- Identification of gifts should be process-based and continuous.
- Identification should be by multiple criteria, including provision for learning and outcome.
- Indicators should be validated for each course of action and provision.
- The pupil's abilities should be presented as a profile rather than a single figure.
- Increasingly sharper criteria should be employed at subsequent learning stages.
- Recognition should be given to attitudes possibly affected by outside influences such as culture and gender.
- The pupils must be involved in educational decision-making, notably in areas of their own interest.

Evidence shows that teachers would need specific training in differentiated teaching methods, in addition to a variety of techniques for bringing out high-level potential. For example, there would have to be some training in collecting information for a pupil's portfolio, or at least some unification of approaches within a school or authority, as well as recognition of the provision the pupils had access to. This could be done by a simple rating scale so that children who were excelling within their context would be seen to be doing so and not penalised because they had fewer opportunities than others. Emotional support is surely part of good teaching to help children learn and develop. Kindness and a helping hand to those who need it are essential in encouraging courage in children to step out of their expected ruts, whether gender or socially ordained.

Although The Sports Approach concept is easy, putting it into practice is, of course, less so. But on the basis of considerable research and evidence from such sources as the long study described here, I am sure is that the practice of finding and helping children of high potential in that way would bring about a manyfold increase in the number of children who we now regard as gifted.

APPENDIX 1

The British educational system

British education began to emerge as a force for national power from the mid-nineteenth century. But progress was slow. A century later the great majority of children received narrow, often irrelevant lessons in the elementary schools. Even the state secondary schools, picking up the outlook of expensive private schools, generally looked down on demonstrated intellect and on the sciences, which were associated with trade. Instead, they emphasised the humanities (especially dead languages) and 'character' building, for both girls and boys. Only one in a thousand reached university.

The Eleven-Plus

The Eleven-Plus examination was one of the grandest experiments in education the world has ever known. Beginning in the post-war thrust of 1945, every child was to be examined at eleven years old. Based on the results, its splendid aims were to educate children according to their 'age, ability and aptitude'. To refocus education to promote industry, a technical option was originally planned, but failed to survive. Around 25 per cent of all children were selected for academic study in the Grammar Schools, while the remaining 75 per cent received a more practical training (e.g. domestic science and woodwork) in Secondary Modern schools (Vernon 1957). The system still operates in pockets of the country in 2001.

Many good things came out of that child-sorting system, most notably the concern with ability rather than money, effectively slicing through some of the rigid social-class barriers of the time. It offered bright, working-class children the opportunity to attend the up-till-then largely middle-class Grammar Schools. In the 1930s, of the children of unskilled parents, only a third with IQs in the top one per cent had gone to the Grammar Schools, compared with 96 per cent of equally able children from professional homes. Once at the Grammar School, pupils had the chance of going on to university and to enter the professions. Indeed, several British Prime Ministers, including Harold Wilson, Margaret Thatcher and John Major found political fortune from a background of eleven-plus success in the Grammar Schools.

But the story was very different for about 75 per cent of the population of children who 'failed' their Eleven-Plus and were assigned to the Secondary Modern schools. They very often responded by lowering their self-esteem and their expectations. Parents rarely contested the Local Education Authority decision, and though some could send their children to private schools, most had no choice. The profound after-effects of that major life pronouncement of 'pass' or 'fail' at 11 years of age still influences the self-concepts of the many millions of adults who took it, and also their children.

There were many problems of incorrect placement of children, whose fate was usually decided on the basis of a single day's effort at the age of eleven. Nor were the local tests standardised. Whereas children in one area might be selected on an intelligence test, in another it was by achievement in English and mathematics; some authorities even ran officer training type activities to select children. In addition, the number of Grammar School places varied widely across the country: for example, in Gateshead it was 8 per cent, and in Merrioneth 60 per cent.

Nor did class bias and prejudice really die out as had been hoped. Middle-class parents were far more likely to seize the new opportunities, and working-class parents too often did not. One mother in the Follow-up spoke for several parents when she told me:

> 'My mother won a scholarship to the grammar school, but was too poor to take it up. It blighted her life with resentment, although she would never actually say it out loud. She was always very keen for all of her kids to do well. My father was almost illiterate – he still can't do joined-up writing – and his parents condoned him missing school to earn his living. But he was thrilled to bits when three of the four of us passed the eleven-plus. But once we got on well in the grammar schools, he bitterly resented that we appeared to be cleverer than him. He made sure none of us stayed on at school. My mother didn't fight about it; he was her life.'

Even during the heyday of selection, however, gifted children were not necessarily well catered for. Each type of school treated all its pupils as though they were of similar ability. The gifted mistakenly put into Secondary Modern schools were clearly in an untenable position, since neither suitable academic provision nor enrichment were available to them, and their expected performance was of a low level. But even at the Grammar Schools an enriched curriculum was unheard of, and provision for the top academic pupils there simply directed them to more, higher-level examinations.

It became clear in time that the Eleven-Plus system was too unfair and wasteful to be continued. Today, about 85 per cent of pupils in Britain go to all-comer, comprehensive schools, which began to replace the rigid divisions in the 1950s. In theory, they provide a social and intellectual mix, where pupils can move through different scholastic levels to suit their developing abilities. Indeed, proportionately, far more children are academically successful today than ever before. But still, comprehensives in middle-class areas are far more likely to provide capable staff, adequate facilities and an encouraging ethos, compared with those in working-class areas, which may suffer from limited opportunities and social problems. The present move is to make the comprehensives into specialist schools while retaining their all-comer provision. There are also other state-funded specialist schools for science and the arts.

About 7 per cent of the UK school population, about the same proportion as in the USA, is in private education. It is confusing in Britain, though, that the most expensive private schools – but not all the private schools – are called Public. It is a hangover from as early as the fifteenth century, when these schools did indeed provide free public education for poor, bright boys. The term Public School denotes special social status and is not available to all private schools who would like it.

Public examinations

At the time of the Follow-up study (1984–8), the major public examination in England, Wales and Northern Ireland, the General Certificate of Education (GCE), was taken in individual subjects by about half the population. There were two levels:

1. O-level (ordinary) was usually taken at about 16. It has now been replaced by the more course-work based General Certificate of School Education (GCSE).
2. A-level (advanced) examinations, still taken at around 18. They are of a highly specialised nature and very high standard, often referred to by teachers and politicians as the 'gold standard' and are sacrosanct. A minimum of two A-level passes is essential for university entrance, and taking more than three is unusual.

In Scotland, though, the O-level is being replaced by Standard Grade, and the school-leaving examinations at 18, which are a broader spectrum approach than A-levels, are called Highers. Scottish universities ask for between three and five of these for entrance.

In 1985 about 57 per cent of the population passed just one O-level and 28 per cent got five or more O-level passes (*Social Trends* 1987), so that only about 14 per cent of British youth was qualified to go on to full-time higher education.

The O-level exams were replaced (1988) by the new single General Certificate of School Education (GCSE), still taken in individual subjects and available to all ages. The new qualification, however, is the result of many kinds of assessment, most notably a concern with what pupils have accomplished over a two year period, rather than what they can do in a series of three-hour examinations. It appears to offer a fairer assessment of all children's progress, and it could be beneficial to the gifted, perhaps bringing back the joy of discovery to their lives.

But age is not the only determinant of these exams. There has been a steady flow of exceptionally advanced pupils in all areas of school work. In 1988 the Associated Examining Board, found that of 493,069 candidates there were 434 O-level entries from pupils under 15, including 30 from children between ages 9 to 12. Of 170 A-level candidates under 17, one was aged 11 and another nine. What is more, their results were as good or better than those of older candidates – at O-level, 35 per cent of entrants under 15 got a grade A, compared with 9 per cent generally, and 11 per cent of young A-level candidates came away with an A, as opposed to 6 per cent of sixth-formers. In their 1995 statistics, there were 43 candidates under 15 at A-level standard, but only seven at GCSE grade (no further breakdown was offered). Unfortunately, we know very little about what sort of schooling and home circumstances produce such results: these precocious examinees have never been investigated.

Provision for the gifted in 2001

There has been a shift away from only providing for advanced children towards the development of gifted potential. In this country of about 60 million, government policy aims to achieve excellence by positively changing perceptions towards special education for the gifted, along with providing access to realising it, often outside conventional educational frameworks. These changes have been as exhilarating as a fairground ride. The new government, in 1998, quickly set up a Gifted and Talented Advisory Group, and as a basis for future action I was invited to critically overview all the international research, and two copies of the resulting book were sent free to every Local Education Authority (Freeman 1998). The Gifted and Talented Programme is part of a £50 million initiative, *Excellence in Cities*, designed to raise the aspirations of children in the inner cities, and soon to be extended to rural children. There are also quite a number of non-governmental initiatives.

The practical programme
The major principles of gifted education – identification, acceleration and enrichment – have been accommodated in the programme. Identification is seen in the directive to distinguish 5–10 per cent of pupils in each age-group of secondary schools as gifted and talented, soon to be extended to primary schools. Acceleration is seen in the targets given to Local Education Authorities for early examination entries, encouraged by extensive out-of-school learning opportunities for selected children. The enrichment schemes emphasise networking facilities for study-support such as funded homework clubs and the use of educational partners such as museums, galleries, libraries, sports clubs, theatres, etc. The variety of schemes, each with a strict production plan, is outlined here.

- **Master classes** around the country are being extended. After piloted work in ten schools, 56 projects affecting more than 19,000 pupils have been approved.
- **Advanced Maths Centres** have been allocated £30,000 each this year. The 12 pilots are for primary school children who will take their national examinations early. Pupils selected for this fast-track tuition will continue with normal lessons, receiving their advanced work out of school hours. The centres are to be extended nationally.
- **University summer schools** are to be available for 5000 16-year-olds, particularly in the inner cities.
- **World-class tests**, starting with mathematics and problem-solving, are being developed, guided by internationally recognised high performance. Although designed for the top 20 per cent of 9, 13 and 18-year-olds, they can be taken years earlier. They will be largely taken via CD ROMS on computers – to be made available to every child – and are intended to elicit creativity and quality in higher-order thinking, to help select high quality students for university. However, there are still some loose ends to be tied up, such as what happens to the children who are successful on them. The tests have already been sold to other countries.
- **Advanced Extension Awards** are tests designed to challenge the most able 18-year-olds by requiring a greater depth of understanding and the ability to think critically.
- **Literacy and numeracy guidance** for small children to work at a high level is expected in January 2001.
- **Summer school programmes** have been piloted, and about 500 for 10 to 14-year-olds will be in place in the summer of 2001.
- **Learning mentors** are to be made available in all secondary schools in designated areas, with particular concern for developing high-level potential. There will be further training in this for coordinators and teachers.
- **A National Toolkit** for teaching the gifted is to be developed within the next three years, to be worked within the generic guidance for teaching the gifted at all stages of the National Curriculum in all statuary subjects.
- **Specialist schools** will increase to 800 and are eligible for community focus funding to be spent on study support activities for the gifted and talented. Music, ballet and drama scholarships are being increased to 2,200 by 2001. Gifted pupils may soon be allowed to drop some courses to specialise in their preferred areas, though they must still complete the compulsory timetable.
- **Beacon schools** are each to be awarded up to £50,000 per year to share best practice for teaching the most able. They will be part of a local network led by successful schools with a strong track record in providing for the gifted and talented, which can also include businesses and places of higher education.

- **Advanced skills teachers** are being designated to work in their own school or help in other schools. Best Practice Research Scholarships are available to teachers for action research in the classroom.
- **School inspections** are being pointed towards the teaching and learning of the gifted and talented, and reference must be made to this in reports. It is one of three identified areas for underachievement.

How it looks

One can never anticipate what will emerge from such profound changes. Personally, I hope it will ease out some of the self-styled 'experts' who (for a fee) offer questionable activities for gifted children and teacher training. This generous provision should also enable teachers and parents to redirect the energy they now spend in raising private funds for the gifted. It promises more uniform and easily available opportunities around the country for all children, and enables every teacher to take part. Above all, I believe that it can only be beneficial to provide the means to develop the unrecognised talents of children who until now had seemed to be invisible.

Questionnaires

The questionnaire for the young people

Education

- Views on own education, both academically and socially, and how they would like to change it. Preferences for mixed or pre-selected teaching, single or mixed sex, corporal punishment.
- Your teachers: rapport, academic feedback, how they saw you, preferred style of being taught, easy-going or firm teacher.
- Preferred style of studying: project work, working alone, talking about it.
- Vocational guidance, help in choosing, personal advice, problems at school.

Self

- Personal interests, boredom, creative activities outside school.
- Reading – newspapers, books for pleasure. Television: how much, temptations, preferences.
- Self concept: your attractive and unattractive points, awareness of others, attraction to others, same or different from others, ambition.
- Empathy: sensitivity; empathy; role playing; independence.
- Communication: talk a lot; life always fast enough.
- Emotion: anger, loneliness and depression, growing up experiences, relationships.
- Mental life – cognitive style.
- Memory: what kind and when it worked best.
- Concentration: revision patterns, style of remembering, length of concentration, attention to more than one thing at once, and mental processing.

Opinions of the world

- The present state: drugs, the bomb, violence, unemployment, politics, equal opportunities, homosexuality.
- Beliefs: religion, prayer, reasons for living.
- The future: how life on earth is likely to change, how you could help change it.
- What is best about living today, your personal pleasure.

The questionnaire for the family

About their child

- Health: allergies, coordination, sleep.
- Behaviour: liveliness, sensitivity, independence, obstinacy, talkativeness, perseverance, differentness, growing up.
- Educational progress: handwriting and spelling, relationships at school, progress at school.

Educational preferences

- Single or mixed sex.
- Attitudes to the arts and sciences.
- Style of teaching and discipline.
- Hopes for child's future.

Parents' educations

- School, age of leaving, satisfaction, career, recognised influences on child.
- Grandparents: their educational and social experiences, influences, politically or religiously active.

Own activities

- Interests: music – listening and playing; reading.

Home and neighbourhood

- Style of living; neighbourhood.

APPENDIX 3

The sample at school

Of the sample, 14.2 per cent had been to Grammar Schools, and about equal numbers of the others were divided between Comprehensives (40.2 per cent), private schools (39.6 per cent), and Secondary Modern schools (1.8 per cent). This disproportion from the general population was because they were a high ability sample, and were therefore more likely to go to selective schools – either to free state ones or to private ones on scholarships. Very few of their parents positively chose comprehensive education, though when they did, it was more for social than academic reasons. Looked at in another way, most (72 per cent) of the High-IQ group were at selective schools, proportionately fewer (45 per cent) of the Above-average-IQ group, and fewer again (36 per cent) of the Average-IQ group.

Level of examinations passed

Mean IQ	Level of examinations passed
151	Degree
142	A-levels
127	O-levels and CSE
113	CSE only

Numbers of examinations passed

Mean IQ	No. of O-levels	Mean IQ	No. of A-levels
150	10–12	147	4–6
140	6–9	142	1–3
130	1–5	121	None

Grades achieved

The High-IQ group achieved proportionally many more A grades in all school exams. This was especially significant at A-level, where 42 per cent obtained between 1–3 A grades, and 10 per cent 4–6 A grades.

IQ group	O-level grade A
High	71 per cent
Above-average	59 per cent
Average	27 per cent

Subjects taken at A-level

A-levels	Science only	Mixture	Arts only
High-IQ	41 per cent	49 per cent	10 per cent

Pupil's understanding of teacher assessment of their abilities

Does your teacher think you are bright?	Yes
High-IQ	76 per cent
Above-average-IQ	21 per cent
Average-IQ	7 per cent

Useful contacts/addresses

EUROPE

National Association for Gifted Children (NAGC)
540 Elder House
Milton Keynes MK9 1LR, UK
Tel: 01908 673 677
Fax: 01908 673 679
e-mail:
amazingchildren@nagcbritain.org.uk

Charity offering counselling and educational advice. Branches across the UK

National Association for Able Children in Education (NACE)
National Office
PO Box 242
Arnolds Way
Oxford
OX2 9FR, UK
Tel: 01865 861 879
Fax: 01865 861 880
e-mail: info@nace.co.uk

Teachers concerned with improving education for the most able in school. Produces teaching material and advice for teachers, runs teacher training and has a national network of schools and teachers concerned with providing good practice

European Council for High Ability (ECHA)
Bildung und Begabung
Kennedyallee 62–70
D-53175 Bonn
Germany
Tel: 00 49 228 959 1510
Fax: 00 49 228 959 1519
e-mail: bubev@compuserve.com

International Diploma on the Education of the Highly Able, international workshops, conferences, publications. Branches in 25 countries, some outside Europe. Contact point for European organisations

Children of High Intelligence (CHI)
Box 4222
London SE22 8XG, UK

Concerned with high IQ children, Saturday classes, once part of Mensa.

NRICH
University of Cambridge
School of Education
17 Trumpington St
Cambridge CB2 1QA, UK
www.iats.norfolk.gov.uk/enrichment

On-line maths club targeted at 11-14 year olds

The Children's University
Martineau Centre
Harborne
Birmingham B32 2EH, UK
Tel: 0121 464 2816
and 0121 303 8296
Fax: 0121 303 8295
e-mail: Wood.74@btinternet.org
www.childrensuniversity.org

British Association for Early Childhood Education
136 Cavell St
London E1 2JA, UK
Tel: 020 7539 5400
e-mail: office@early-education.org.uk
www.early-education.org.uk

Centre for Talented Youth (Ireland)
Dublin City University
Dublin 9
Ireland
Tel: 00 3531 700 5634
Fax: 00 3531 700 5693
e-mail: ctyi@dcu.ie
www.dcu.i.e/ctyi

Courses for children across Ireland and correspondence courses

National Association for Special Educational Needs (NASEN)
4/5 Amber Business Village
Amber Close
Armington
Tamworth B77 4RP, UK
Tel: 01827 311 500
Fax: 01827 313 005

Promotes the development of children and young people with special educational needs including the gifted. Supports teachers and offers practical provision and publications

The Able Child Centre
Calday Grange Grammar School
West Kirby
Wirral, UK
Tel: 0151 625 3726

Courses for teachers and children.

European Council of International Schools (ECIS)
21b Lavant St.
Petersfield
Hants GU32 3EL, UK
Tel: 01730 68244

Education Otherwise (UK)
PO Box 7420
London N9 9SG, UK
0870 730 0074
www.education-otherwise.org

For help with teaching your child at home

Local Educational psychology services can test your child's abilities, and offer advice, counselling and support to schools and parents. Contact directly or through schools. Tested evidence can be useful in getting the local authority to recognise special needs.

The Potential Trust
Kingston Stert
Chinnor
Oxfordshire OX9 49L, UK
Tel: 01844 51666

Runs summer schools and provides information

French National Association for Gifted Children
34 Rue Paul Deroulede
54520 Nice
France
Tel: 93 88 4016

Associação Nacional para o Estudo e Intervenção na Sobredotação (ANEIS)
R. José Maria Ottoni, no 56
4710 Braga
Portugal

Potential Entwicklung für Kinder un Jugendliche
Im Wingert 9
8048 Zurich
Switzerland
Tel: 00 41 1 341 32 30
Fax: 00 41 1 341 32 63
e-mail:
stedtnitz.switzerland@bluewin.ch
www.stedtnitz.ch

Centro Psyicológico de Diagnóstico y Terapia
Marvà, 30 - 1 - 2
46006 Valencia
Spain
Tel: 341 8614
Fax: 341 96 380 91 50

The Young Person's Institute for the Promotion of Art and Science
Tel Aviv University Dept. of Psychotherapy,
Technical College,
32 University Street
POB 17074
Tel Aviv 61170
Israel
Tel: 03 415 776

Prof. Dr. Pieter Span
Louis Bouwmeesterlaan 77
3584 GE Utrecht
The Netherlands

Prof. Joan Freeman
Middlesex University
21 Montagu Square
London W1H 2LF, UK
Direct fax: 00 44 20 7224 6153
www.joanfreeman.co.uk

NORTH AMERICA

Center for the Advancement of Academically Talented Youth (CTY)
N. Charles and 34th Street
Baltimore
Maryland 21218
USA
Tel: (301) 338 6340

The World Council for Gifted and Talented Children
18401 Hiawatha Street
Northridge
California 91326
USA
Tel: 001 (818) 368 7501

Fax: 001 (818) 368 2163
E-mail: worldgt@earthlink.net
www.WorldGifted.org

Arranges conferences and publications

American Association for Gifted Children

15, Gramercy Park
New York NY 10003
USA
Tel: (212) 473 4266

The Association for the Gifted (TAG)

Council for Exceptional Children
1920 Association Drive
Reston VA 22091
USA
Tel: (703) 620 3660

National Association for Gifted Children (USA)

5100 N. Edgewood
Drive
St. Paul MN 5512
USA
Tel: (612) 784 3475

President, Gifted Children's Association of BC

PO Box 35177 Station E
West 42cnd Ave
Vancouver BC
Canada
Tel: (604) 266 6624

Centre for Gifted Education

University of Calgary
Faculty of Education
2500 University

Drive NW
Calgary
Alberta
Canada T2N 1N4
Tel: (403) 220 6280

Duke University Talent Identification Program (TIP)

1121 West Main Street,
Suite 100
Durham, NC 27701
Tel: (919) 683-1400
Fax: (919) 683-1742
E-mail: vstocking@tip.duke.edu

ASIA

Gifted Child International Network

PO Box 639
Greenhills 3113
San Juan, METRO
MANILA
Philippines

AUSTRALIA

Australian Association for the Gifted

Darling Downs Institute
School of Education
PO Darling Heights
Toowoomba
Queensland 4350
Australia

SOUTH AFRICA

**Children with High Intellectual
Potential Foundation (CHIP)**
29 Ross Street
Toorak
Victoria
Australia
3242

Centre for Gifted Children
Private Bag X382
Pretoria 0001
South Africa

**Programs for the Gifted and
Talented**
2/F Ho Tim Building
Faculty of Education
The Chinese University of Hong Kong
Shatin, New Territories
Hong Kong
Tel: 2603 7463/2603 7485
Fax: 2603 7435
e-mail: hk/kmng@cuhk.edu.hk

References

Anderson, M. (2001) 'Annotation: conceptions of intelligence', *Child Psychology and Psychiatry* **42**, 287–98.

Bastick, T. (1982) *Intuition: How We Think and Act*. Chichester: John Wiley.

Battle, E. S. and Rotter, J. B. (1963) 'Children's feelings of personal control as related to social class and ethnic group', *Journal of Personality* **31**, 482–90.

Bloom, B. S. (1985) *Developing Talent in Young People*. Ballantine Books, New York.

Bryant, P. E. (1992), 'Arithmetic in the cradle', *Nature* **358**, 712–13.

Burton, H. (2001) *Menuhin: A life*. London: Faber and Faber.

Chapman, J.W. and Lambourne, R. (1990) 'Some antecedents of academic self-concept: a longitudinal study', *British Journal of Educational Psychology* **60**, 142–52.

Collins, W. A. and Gunnar, M. R. (1990) 'Social and personality development', *Annual Review of Psychology* **41**, 387–419.

Cornell, D. G., Callahan, C. M., Bassin, L. E. and Ramsay, S. G. (1991) 'Affective development in accelerated students', in Southern, W. T. and Jones, E. D. *The Academic Acceleration of Gifted Children*. New York: Teacher's College Press.

Csikszentmihalyi, M., Rathunde, K. and Whalen, S. (1993) *Talented Teenagers. The Roots of Success and Failure*. Cambridge: Cambridge University Press.

DES (Department of Education and Science) (1989) *Standards in Education 1988–1989, The Annual Report of HM Senior Chief Inspector of Schools*. London: HMSO.

Deslisle, J. R. (2000) *Once Upon a Mind: the Stories + Scholars of Gifted Child Education*. New York: Harcourt Brace.

Easton, C. (1989) *Jacqueline du Pré*. London: Hodder and Stoughton.

Edwards, T., Fitz, J. and Whitt, G. (1989) *The State and Private Education: an Evaluation of the Assisted Places Scheme*. Basingstoke: Falmer Press.

Freeman, J. (1979) *Gifted Children; their Identification and Development in a Social Context*. Lancaster: Medical Technical Press; Baltimore: University Park Press.

Freeman, J. (1983) 'Environment and high IQ – a consideration of fluid and crystallised intelligence', *Personality and Individual Differences* **4**, 307–13.

Freeman, J. (1991) *Gifted Children Growing Up*. London: Cassell; Portsmouth, NH: Heinemann Educational.

Freeman, J. (1995a) *How to Raise a Bright Child: Practical ways to encourage your child's talents from 0–5 years*. London: Vermilion.

Freeman, J. (1995b) 'Where talent begins', in Freeman, J., Span, P. and Wagner, H. (eds). *Actualizing Talent: a Lifelong Challenge*. London: Cassell.

Freeman, J. (1996) *Highly Able Girls and Boys*. London: Department for Education and Employment.

Freeman, J. (1997) 'The emotional development of the highly able', *European Journal of Psychology in Education* **XII**, 479–93.

Freeman, J. (1998) *The Education of the Very Able: Current International Research*. London: The Stationery Office.

Freeman, J. (2000a) 'Families, the essential context for gifts and talents', in Heller, K. A., Monks, F. J., Sternberg, R. and Subotnik, R. *International Handbook of Research and Development of Giftedness and Talent*, 573–85. Oxford: Pergamon Press.

Freeman, J. (2000b) 'Literacy, flexible thinking and underachievement', in Montgomery, D. (ed.) *Able Underachievers*, 26–40. London: Whurr Publishers.

Freeman, J. (2000c) 'Children's talent in fine art and music – England' *Roeper Review,* 22, 98–101.

Freeman, J. (2001) 'Mentoring gifted pupils', *Educating Able Children* 5, 6–12.

Gardner, H. (1983) *Frames of Mind: the Theory of Multiple Intelligences*. New York: Basic Books.

Goertzal, M. G., Goertzal, V. and Goertzal, T. G. (1978) *300 Eminent Personalities*. San Francisco: Jossey-Bass.

Gust-Brey, K. and Cross, T. (1999) 'An examination of the literature base on the suicidal behaviour of gifted students' *Roeper Review*, 22, 28–35.

Hallam, S. and Cowan, R. (1997) 'What do we know about homework: a literature review'. Occasional Paper, London Institute of Education.

Hany, E. A. (1993) 'How teachers identify gifted students: feature processing or concept based classification', *European Journal for High Ability* 4, 196–211.

Heller, K. A. and Ziegler, A. (1996) 'Gender differences in mathematics and natural sciences; can attributional retraining improve the performance of gifted females?', *Gifted Child Quarterly* 41, 200–10.

Herrnstein, R. J. and Murray, C. (1994) *The Bell Curve*. New York: Free Press.

HESA (Higher Education Statistics Agency, SFR 45) (2001) Qualifications obtained by and examination results of higher education students at higher education institutions in the United Kingdom for the academic year 1999/2000. Cheltenham.

Holahan, C. K. and Sears, R. R. (1995) *The Gifted Group in Later Maturity*. Stanford, Calif.: Stanford University Press.

Jackson, S., Mayocchi, L. and Dover, J. (1998) 'Life after winning gold; experiences of Australian Olympic gold medal winners', *The Sport Psychologist* 12, 119–36.

Jensen, A. R. (1969) 'How much can we boost IQ and scholastic attainment?', in *Environment, Heredity and Intelligence*. Cambridge, Mass.: Harvard Educational Review.

Jung C. G. (1964) 'Approaching the unconscious', in Jung, C. G. (ed.) *Man and his Symbols*. London: Aldus Books.

Kaufman, F. A. (1992) 'What educators can learn from gifted adults', in Monks, F. J. and Peters, W. (eds) *Talent for the Future*. Maastricht: Van Gorcum.

Lucey, H. and Walkerdine, V. (1996) 'Transitions to womanhood: constructions of success and failure for middle and working class young women'. Presentation at British Youth Research meeting: Glasgow University.

Mascie-Taylor, C. G. N. (1989) 'Biological and social aspects of development', in Entwistle, N. (ed.) *Handbook of Educational Ideas and Practices*, 992–7. London: Routledge.

Milstein, N. and Volkov, S. (1991) *From Russia to the West*. London: Barrie and Jenkins.

Ornstein, R. E. (1972) *The Psychology of Consciousness*. New York: Viking Press.

Perkins, D. (1995) *Outsmarting IQ*. New York: The Free Press.

Post, F. (1994) 'Creativity and psychopathology. A study of 291 world-famous men', *British Journal of Psychiatry* 165, 22–34.

Radford, J. (1990) *Child Prodigies and Early Achievers*. London: Harvester Wheatsheaf.

Rowe, K. J. (1991) 'The influence of reading activity at home on students' attitudes towards reading, classroom attentiveness and reading achievement: an application of structural equation modelling', *British Journal of Educational Psychology* 61, 19–35.

Schofield, J. and Ashman, A. F. (1987) 'The cognitive processing of gifted, high average, and low average ability students', *British Journal of Educational Psychology* 57, 9–20.

Selfe, L. (1983) *Normal and Anomalous Representational Drawing Ability in Children*. London: Academic Press.

Social Trends (1987) London: HMSO.

Sternberg, R. J. (1999) *Handbook of Creativity*. New York: Cambridge University Press.

Sternberg, R. J. and Davidson, J. E. (1986) *Conceptions of Giftedness*. Cambridge: Cambridge University Press.

Stipek, J. J. and Weisz, J. R. (1981) 'Perceived personal control and academic achievement', *Review of Educational Research* 51, 101–37.

Stott, D. H. (1976) *The Social Adjustment of Children*. London: Hodder & Stoughton.

TIMSS 1999 International Mathematics Report. Findings from the IEA's repeat of the third international mathematics and science study at the eighth grade. (Mullis, I. V. S., Martin, O., Gonzales, E. J., Gregory, K. D., Garden, R. A., O'Connor, K. M., Chrostowski, S. J. & Smoth, T. A.) (http://isc.bc.edu/tmss1999i/math_achievement_report.html).

Vernon, P. E. (1957) *Secondary School Selection*. London: Methuen.

Vygotsky, L. S. (1990) *Mind in Society: the Development of Higher Psychological Processes*. Harvard: Harvard University Press.

Walberg, H. J. (1995) 'Nurturing children for adult success', in Katzko, M. W. and Mönks, F. J. (eds) *Nurturing Talent; Individual Needs and Social Ability*. Assen, The Netherlands: Van Gorcum.

Wallace, A. (1986) *The Prodigy. A Biography of William James Sidis, the World's Greatest Child Prodigy*. London: Macmillan.

Waters, E., Wippman, J. and Stroufe, L.A. (1979) 'Attachment, positive effect and competence in the peer group: two studies in construct validation,' *Child Development* 50, 821–29.

Werner, E. and Smith, R. (1992) *Overcoming the Odds: High Risk Children from Birth to Adulthood*. Cornell: Cornell University Press.

Wiltshire, S. (1993) *American Dream*. London: Michael Joseph.

Index